D1550412

THE ENOCH FACTOR

Smyth & Helwys Publishing, Inc.
6316 Peake Road
Macon, Georgia 31210-3960
1-800-747-3016
©2010 by Smyth & Helwys Publishing
All rights reserved.
Printed in the United States of America.

The paper used in this publication meets the minimum requirements of
American National Standard for Information Sciences—
Permanence of Paper for Printed Library Materials.
ANSI Z39.48–1984. (alk. paper)

Library of Congress Cataloging-in-Publication Data

McSwain, Stephen B., 1955–

The Enoch factor : the sacred art of knowing god /
by Steve McSwain.
p. cm.
Includes bibliographical references.
ISBN 978-1-57312-556-7
(pbk. : alk. paper)
1. Spirituality.
I. Title.
BL624.M37 2010
204—dc22

2010009843

Disclaimer of Liability: With respect to statements of opinion or fact available in this work of nonfiction, Smyth & Helwys Publishing Inc. nor any of its employees, makes any warranty, express or implied, or assumes any legal liability or responsibility for the accuracy or completeness of any information disclosed, or represents that its use would not infringe privately-owned rights.

Praise for *The Enoch Factor*

The Enoch Factor is not just another book about God. It is an eloquently written masterpiece filled with deeply profound insights leading us to a more intimate relationship with God. Anyone seeking to fully embrace God and truly be at one with their Creator must read Steve McSwain's book. It contains the key to a Divine life. One of the most beautifully written books I've ever read!

—Janet Pfeiffer
Author of *The Secret Side of Anger*

A book you may want to argue with from start to finish, but one full of wisdom drawn from Scriptures, profound personal experience, and a cornucopia of sacred literature. Be warned: if you take this book in hand, you may learn as Enoch did what it means to walk with God.

—E. Glenn Hinson
Church historian and theologian

McSwain's anchor to a big and beautiful God gives him courage to explore the depth and breadth of religious topics that few dare to broach. More than a collection of disparate sayings and experiences, and far more than simply iconoclastic, McSwain's brave reflections bring more light to the mysteries and mercies of life. He makes me hopeful for the future of faith.

—Joseph Phelps
Pastor, Highland Baptist Church
Louisville, Kentucky

STEVE McSWAIN

The ENOCH FACTOR

THE SACRED ART OF KNOWING GOD

Also by Steve McSwain

The Giving Myths: Giving then Getting the Life You've Always Wanted

Basic Bible Sermons on Spiritual Living

For Pamela McSwain
On the occasion of our tenth wedding anniversary
You are my "inn within the wilderness" (Jeremiah 9:2).

Acknowledgments

I wish to acknowledge Enoch
whose spirit has guided this work.
Enoch was the son of Jared and father of Methuselah,
the two oldest persons on record within the human race.

Although the length of Enoch's life was shorter
than that of either his father or son,
the breadth of his life reached a dimension unknown to them
and only ever known by enlightened sentient beings.

"The measure of a life, after all, is not its duration, but its donation."
—Corrie ten Boom, Holocaust survivor (1892–1983)

Enoch's donation
to the world is that he
"WALKED WITH GOD."
If he did, so may we.

—Steve McSwain

Contents

Introduction

"There is no greater agony than bearing an untold story inside of you."

—Maya Angelou (b. 1928)

"The most important matter in life is your relationship to the Infinite."

—author unknown

You were born to walk with God, so why would you walk alone?

This book is about knowing God. It is not a defense for the existence of God, however. If that's the type of book you're looking for, then you'll need to go somewhere else. There are plenty of them around. Frankly, I find such books amusing. What's the point of arguing for God's existence when it is as impossible to prove he does exist as it is to prove he doesn't? It's like debating about whether there's intelligent life on other planets. Either there is or there isn't. But, until there's an indisputable encounter, it's one person's word against another and, too often, that turns into needless debate.

One thing is for certain: an encounter with a UFO will have to be more believable than some of the preposterous stories reported so far. For example, I recently saw a video—maybe it was on YouTube—that someone had taken of a UFO as it streaked like lightning across the Mojave sky. Have you ever noticed that none of these pictures are ever clear enough to be incontestable? An imaginary tale of temporary alien abduction that accompanied this video was equally indistinguishable and unbelievable.

As for the existence of God, my suspicion is that the real reason people write books that try to prove God exists is that they are secretly afraid he doesn't.

I have written this book presuming that God *is* and, more important, that God can be known, not in the sense of knowledge or information but in the sense of intimacy and inspiration. You can know about God, but not know God. That would describe most people today.

I used to think that I, and other Christians like me, had a monopoly on God. We held, as it were, a kind of title deed to ultimate Reality. What we knew about God was not only right, but what others knew was wrong or at best inferior to our knowledge of him.

> God does not die the day we cease to believe . . . but we die when our lives cease to be illumined by the steady radiance, renewed daily, of a wonder, the source of which is beyond all reason.
>
> —DAG HAMMARSKJÖLD

While I no longer feel this way, I realize many Christians still do, just as people in other religions believe their knowledge of God is superior to that of Christians. I have therefore come to the conclusion there may be a lot of knowledge *about* God in all religions, but there may be only a few people in any religion who ever actually *know God.*

As far as my life is concerned, I cannot remember a time when I have not had an interest in knowing God. Unfortunately, however, apart from the knowledge of the Divine I accumulated over the years, I cannot say with certainty that I knew God—at least not in a personal way. To be sure, there were passing occasions when I felt his nearness, but the feelings never lasted. Most of the time, I did not feel close to God at all. In fact, I felt distant, as if he were uninterested in me and maybe the rest of the world, too. The few times I felt connected to him were usually short-lived. Of course, whenever I did, the feeling was good. But it was always temporary and soon replaced with the feeling that God was displeased with how things were going with me and perhaps the rest of the world, too. Consequently, most of the time, my spiritual life was one big frustration, even a disappointment. I have the feeling it must be the same for many people.

Then, one day, something happened to me and everything changed. I instantly became aware of a transcendent and ineffable Presence. Was it God I suddenly became aware of? How would I know? In fact, since that experience, there are few things that I can say I'm sure about. The strange thing is that I'm okay with it. This is not something I would have been comfortable admitting a few years ago. Ambiguity, paradox, and contradiction used to annoy me.

Not anymore. Ever since this transformative encounter—whatever it was that happened to me—I enjoy the paradoxical. Eric Fromm said, "Creativity requires the courage to let go of certainties." I've let go of many certainties in the last few years. Now I enjoy instead the freedom of not feeling as if I have to explain everything. Life's mysteries are meaningful when not menaced by the mind.

> "Even belief in God is only a poor substitute for the living reality of God manifesting every moment of your life."
>
> —ECKHART TOLLE

If it was not God I experienced but, instead, a dream or something equally as strange, then I hope I never wake up. Since that day, I have been aware of a Sacred Presence almost continuously. Virtually everything about the way I think, what I believe, and the way I live has shifted for the better. The changes happen almost daily, too, or so it seems.

I'll note many of these changes throughout the book. The thoughts, feelings, and beliefs I used to have about my life, this world, and even death itself have morphed into something infinitely more meaningful to me than at any other time in my life. As a result, I've moved beyond the narrow, often negative, rigid, and rule-oriented perspective that distinguished my early adult life and the Christian tradition in which I was raised.

Make no mistake, however. I have not written this book to bash my religious heritage. As it is among all religions, the Christian religion is desperately ill. Even so, with all its faults, it has helped shape who I am and provided me and millions of others a path to follow in the human quest to know God.

I have written the book in three sections. The first chronicles my history, the things I grew up believing, and the strange day when everything changed in my life and I found true intimacy with God. In this section, I describe the human condition that interferes with

> "Life unfolds as a series of synchronous events that, though appearing coincidental, are actually conspiring together to bring you into union with God."

intimacy between God and humans and makes life problematic for almost everyone.

I also detail the story of the day when my father suffered a brain attack, a stroke that ended his life ten days later. It was the most traumatic life event I have experienced. Yet, it is amazing to me how this event conspired with other life events to create a portal through which my encounter with God materialized. I found the truth in what American author Louis L'Amour said, "There will come a time when you believe everything is finished; that will be the beginning."

In the second section, I introduce you to Enoch, pronounced *ē'-nik*. He is the human archetype of the sacred art of knowing God. History records the myths and legends of persons who lived at a level of God-consciousness never realized by the majority of their contemporaries. A few of them are Buddha, Abraham, Lao Tzu, Moses, Confucius, Mary the mother of Jesus, Saint Paul, Muhammad, St. Francis of Assisi, and, more recently, Mohandas Gandhi, Mother Teresa, and the Dalai Lama. There are many, many others, of course. Jesus lived at this level, too. In fact, most Christians believe Jesus embodied the Divine presence in his earthly life more completely than any other person who has ever lived.

Throughout history, the people who seemed to have arrived at an advanced level of spiritual awareness were known by specific names. Jews called them *tzadikim*, Hindus called them *avatars*, and Christians called them *saints*.

Labels are unimportant, however. What is more important is that they were rare souls indeed. Enoch was one of these rare souls, too, although not as widely known. Of him, it was said, "Enoch walked with God" (Gen 5:22). Only one other person in the sacred record of Jewish history was said to have reached this level of Divine consciousness. That was Noah (Gen 6:9). The words "walk with God" are an anthropomorphic way of describing closeness, awareness, knowing-ness, and intimacy. In this book, I use the words "walking with God" and "knowing God" interchangeably.

From the first day I met Enoch some thirty years ago, his mysterious life has fascinated me. A few times, I've actually sensed his spirit with me. That explains my acknowledgment at the front of this book. It's not like I've had conversations with Enoch or witnessed an apparition of him. I've simply been aware of his presence, much like being aware of another's presence in the room with you. You might not talk with the person, but you know he or she is there.

Maybe you've had an experience like this yourself—the kind of experience psychologist Abraham Maslow called a "peak experience."[1] Whenever I do, the sensations may not last long, but in the instant they occur, it's as if time momentarily freezes. If you know what I'm talking about, my guess is you've said little about it to anyone else. I understand, and you haven't lost your mind. The experience is real. I know, for things like this have happened to me on more than one occasion.

In the months after my father's death, for example, I had a couple of these encounters. While a psychologist might be inclined to suggest that I experienced a natural consequence of a grieving heart, I don't buy it. It is true I grieved my father's passing, but I cannot

> "It is quite possible to reach God. In fact, it is very easy."
>
> —FROM *A COURSE IN MIRACLES*

dismiss what happened to me as a mere trick of a mourning mind. I will always believe my father's spirit was present with me.

On one of those occasions, I drove down a busy street in the middle of a torrential downpour. It had been only a few months since we said our last goodbyes to Dad and buried his body at Cave Hill Cemetery. As I drove, I strained to see the road in spite of the fact that the windshield wipers were working overtime. All of a sudden, I sensed that my Dad occupied the passenger seat beside me. The aura of his presence was so pervasive that emotion overcame me. I had no choice but to steer the car to the shoulder of the road. When it stopped, I turned and looked, certain that I would see Dad sitting beside me. Of course, he was not. Almost as quickly as the sensation surfaced, it subsided.

Enoch has never spoken to me, although I would not be alarmed if he did. Mystical, inexplicable things like this no longer frighten me, nor do they seem odd or out of the ordinary. The unseen, spiritual world may be more real than the material world we see.

Over the years, I've come to regard Enoch like some people do guardian angels. I know he's there, not necessarily to provide guardianship, although he may be doing that, too, but certainly to serve as a companion as I wrote this book. Since it was his purpose in life to walk with God and leave a legacy for others to follow, I suspect he has been with me to provide inspiration and make sure I map out a path that will be an honest and helpful guide to others.

In this middle section of the book, you'll discover the unusual manner in which Enoch died. As with any folk hero, myths about his life have grown up around him. Perhaps none is more mythic, however, than the one people have believed for centuries—that is, that Enoch lived, but never actually died. Virtually everyone who has ever heard of Enoch believes he somehow escaped death.

I think this is a misreading of Scripture. Just as everyone dies, you can be certain Enoch died, too. What is true is that Enoch experienced death in a qualitatively different fashion than did his contemporaries and virtually everyone since him. In Enoch's life and death, we have a prototype for living and dying today. The remarkable way he lived and the equally remarkable way he died explains why his legacy has survived for thousands

> "As soon as a man is fully disposed to be alone with God, he is alone with God no matter where he may be; in the country, the monastery, the woods, or the city . . . At that moment he sees that though he seems to be in the middle of his journey, he has already arrived at the end."
>
> —FROM *CHOOSING TO LOVE THE WORLD* BY THOMAS MERTON

of years. It also explains why I chose to call this book *The Enoch Factor*. The *factor* is that which, if followed, will change how you both live your life and face death. Furthermore, you'll no longer simply know *about* God, but you will actually *know God*. There's an abundance of people in the former group; there may be only a few in the latter. One of the most remarkable, yet disturbing things Jesus ever said is that most people will live and die and never find Life—Life itself (Matt 7:14).

The third section of this book provides the tools that will guide you on this journey. To know God is to walk with God. It is to live your life in the awareness of an indescribable and eternal presence that is within you and all around you, beneath you but also beyond you. It is personal and yet mysterious, real but also surreal. You can know this presence but also not know it. You can experience God, but you will never explain God. When you live your life in union with God, you are at peace with yourself and with the world. You know joy, too, as well as security and a kind of fearlessness.

There's an inner sense that everything is as it's supposed to be. Anxiety, stress, discontent, and even boredom all but disappear from your life.

> **God is not difficult to find; God is impossible to avoid.**
>
> —DEEPAK CHOPRA

To know this kind of extraordinary life of intimacy with God does not happen by accident. It takes practice to live a God-realized life. If you are ready to take a further step into intimacy with your Creator, this book will show you a way. If you're not ready for what Brother Lawrence, the seventeenth-century Carmelite monk, called "practicing the presence of God," you may quickly lose interest.

There's a chasm of difference between intimacy and interaction. With the widespread phenomenon associated with text messaging, e-mail, and cell phones, a visitor from another planet might get the idea that, since humans are always connecting and interacting with each other, they must be friendly toward one another, even intimate and caring. It would not take him long however, to realize that his first impression was an illusion.

Although virtually everyone is endlessly talking and texting, the irony is that we may be the most disconnected, discontented, and dysfunctional generation on record. There is division in almost every family—yours, mine, and the families we know—as well as conflict in relationships both at school and at work. Furthermore, there is division between races, religions, cultures, and nations. People are more divided than perhaps at any other time in the history of the human race.

Conversation is no more communication than sex is intimacy. Communication and intimacy require presence and practice. They are learned skills. What is true of the horizontal relationships of life—humans toward other humans—is also true of the vertical relationship—the Divine/human connection. Those who know a God-realized life are those who practice the skills necessary for genuine communication and intimacy.

I love the way Rumi, the Persian poet of love, put it. He said, "You will know God the way you make love." Just as lovemaking is for many people a connection with little more than surface depth, so the world is full of people, many of whom are religious, whose intimacy with God is little more than skin deep.

I hope you'll consider the Enoch factor with me as we go through the following pages together. Jesus said, "You've been given insight into God's kingdom. Not everybody has this gift. . . . Whenever someone has a ready heart for this, the insights and understandings flow freely. But if there is no readiness, any trace of receptivity soon disappears . . . they can stare till doomsday and not see it, listen till they're blue in the face and not get it" (Matt 13:15). I pray that you find yourself with a heart ready to *know* God.

Note
1. Abraham Maslow, *Religion, Values, and Peak Experiences* (New York: Viking Press, 1970).

Part 1

The Sacred Art of Knowing God

"Everyone has a suitable path to follow. . . . You are here to realize your inner divinity and manifest your innate enlightenment."
—Morihei Ueshiba (1883–1969, founder of the Japanese martial art of Aikido)

I write this book because I am compelled to share what I am learning about the God who is both pervasive and present in everything seen and unseen. I am not writing, however, to promote a religious viewpoint or to debate the superiority of one religious belief over another, including my own.

It is true I am a Christian. I know the Christian church well. Frankly, I loathe some of the stuff I've come to know. At times, I've wondered if I should have explored some

> Beliefs are a cover-up for insecurity. You only believe in things you're not sure about. Faith, on the other hand, is the capacity to embrace the unknown; to step comfortably into uncertainty; to live in peace in the face of ambiguity.
>
> —Deepak Chopra

other career. Yet, I now realize it is part of my destiny to be right where I am, to know what I know, and to say what I say, especially through this book.

I am hardly qualified to speak regarding other religions, however. To be sure, I know some of them well, but I only know them from a distance. It would not surprise me to learn that many of my perspectives on Christianity are applicable to other religious traditions. In this regard, I trust the book will not only be instructive to Christians, but to devotees within all faith traditions.

I will refer to my faith, my perceptions about Jesus, and I will frequently quote the words ascribed to him throughout the Gospels of the New Testament. I will also quote The Buddha, Lao Tzu, and others, and refer to the religions of the world like Islam, Hinduism, and so forth. Even though I am a Christian or, as I prefer to put it, a follower of the Christ-way to know God, I will not try to convert you to Christianity.

> "The Way spoken of by the world's great teachers is not one single path, yet all paths lead to the same destination."
>
> —FROM *JESUS, BUDDHA, KRISHNA, LAO TZU: THE PARALLEL SAYINGS*, ED. RICHARD HOOPER

Make no mistake, however. The Christ-way is an enlightened spiritual pathway to God. Of course, I would be pleased to hear that you had chosen the Christ-way after reading this book. The path has guided me to an extraordinary place of self-discovery and God-realization.

It may not be the only way to God, but is the only path I have known. That is the most I can say. It is also the only pathway most of the people I've grown up with have ever known. And that's about all they can say, too, if they're honest. Unfortunately, honesty has not always been the most prized virtue among religious people. It would not surprise me to learn that parts of this book shock them, especially my acknowledgment that there may be other ways to know God. Even so, I can no longer pretend to know *the* one and true way with any certainty. I'm pretty sure nobody else knows, either. They may pretend they do, but there may be just as many ways to know God as there are stars in our galaxy. The last time I looked, one of the rare nights when you could actually glimpse the galaxy, there seemed to be as many stars in the heavens as there is sand on the shores of San Juan. I know one thing for certain: the more I learn about the spiritual path others have followed, or are following, the more I see the timeless, spiritual truth in all of them.

When I was young, my parents used to take my two brothers and me on the world tours they led every year for members of the Christian community. Dad was a Baptist minister and Mom a tour leader. It was a good combination, if you ask me. They made a good team. Since we didn't have much money, my industrious mother discovered an inexpensive way to take family vacations and enable her family to see the world at the same time. She organized her own touring agency. For every three or four persons she enlisted to go with her to an exotic, far-off place, one could go free. Naturally, the first two recipients of the free trip were always Mom and Dad, but Mom got good enough at this gig that she earned the reputation of being a fine tour planner and leader. The tour groups soon grew large enough that the whole family got to go on the trips without paying.

These trips to other worlds were more than enviable vacations. They were also eye-opening, life-enlarging events that have shaped my view of the world and the universal human quest to know this Intelligence I call God. Others call it Source, Being Itself, Higher Power, Consciousness. Frankly, I'm not too concerned with what people call it. I doubt it matters much to God, either. These trips influenced my perspectives on life, faith, and religion in ways I don't think my parents ever anticipated.

> **If the doors of perception were cleansed, everything would appear to man as it is, infinite.**
>
> **For man has closed himself up, till he sees all things through narrow chinks of his cavern.**
>
> —FROM *THE MARRIAGE OF HEAVEN AND HELL* BY WILLIAM BLAKE

> **It's a poor sort of memory that only works backwards!**
>
> —FROM *THROUGH THE LOOKING GLASS* BY LEWIS CARROLL

Chapter 1

Conspiracy of Coincidence: The Day I Met the Pope Himself

"There are no mistakes . . . all events are blessings given to us to learn from."
—Elisabeth Kübler-Ross (1926–2004)

The first world trip I remember taking was at age twelve. We traveled all over Europe and the Middle East. Almost every year after that, we visited some other place. By my sixteenth birthday, I had been to the Scandinavian countries twice, the Middle East three times, and the Far East twice, including Russia and China. The Far East trips always ended with a couple of days in Hawaii.

As you might imagine, I saw many things. It was a kind of education all its own. I also encountered many different religions on some of these trips. One of my first recollections, for example, was the time Dad successfully arranged an audience with the leader of the Roman Catholic Church—Pope Paul VI—while our tour group visited the Vatican in Rome. To a naive Southern Baptist boy from Kentucky, Roman Catholic was not only another religion, but it was also just as misunderstood and strange to me as Islam is to virtually every Christian I know.

On this three-week sweep of Europe and the Middle East, Dad thought it would be a good experience if we got up close and personal with the gentleman with the big tall hat, the head of the Catholic Church. Only my Roman Catholic friends, and I've made many of them over the years, can appreciate the ludicrousness of Dad's idea. But, as it is in most things, it's all in who you know.

I was thirteen at the time. We lived in Western Kentucky. As a member of the Kiwanis Club, Dad had become good friends with the Catholic Bishop of the Diocese of Western Kentucky. As these things go, the bishop shared a room while in seminary with another priest-in-training who was later appointed to handle the appointment schedule for Pope Paul himself. That's what I'd call a "conspiracy of coincidence"!

One day, Dad shared his hopes for our tour group with the bishop, who was more than happy to help us. He contacted the Vatican and his former roommate and, in a matter of days, Dad received a letter in the mail. It was an invitation, signed by the Pope himself and embossed with the Papal insignia, to enjoy a brief and private audience with the Pope. I have never told this story to a Catholic who didn't suspect I was stretching the truth, but this is exactly what transpired.

That is, until the day we arrived. It was mid-July 1968 when we arrived in Rome. That also happened to be the day that Pope Paul VI released his famous *Humanae Vitae*, Latin for "Of Human Life." It was a Papal Encyclical on social issues related to traditional marriage, abortion, contraception, and so forth. Though it mainly reaffirmed the Church's previous teaching on these matters, it sent shockwaves around the world, nonetheless. These were hot-topic social and ethical issues in the sixties. Some of them still are. The media converged on Rome like a pack of hungry wolves. A young Baptist boy like myself couldn't have cared less about the Pope's views on anything. I was just disappointed, as was everyone else in our group, that our chances of having an audience with the Pope looked bleak.

You just had to know my dad, however. Whenever he set his mind to doing something, I'm not sure God could have stopped him. As far as he was concerned, we had not come that far to let a little thing like a Papal Encyclical stop us. He immediately instructed us to board the bus, where he ordered the driver to make the 24-kilometer drive to Castel Gondolfo, the *Residenza Papale* or the Pope's summer residence, south of Rome. Off we went. Earlier that day, the news had reported the Pope would make a public appearance at his seventeenth-century residence—some kind of formal defense of the Church's views on human life.

Normally, the drive is no more than thirty minutes. It took us two hours. Thousands of Catholic devotees must have had the same idea and headed for a chance to see the Pope. Add the press corps, and it would have been easier to get through airport security during a bomb threat than to get anywhere near Castel Gondolfo. Our dream diminished more and more with each kilometer.

Eventually, however, our driver made a cautious approach to a heavily guarded entrance. Several uniformed men stood out front. They wore bright, colorful clothing, with thick, bold stripes. Later, I learned they were members of the elite Swiss Guard, the Pope's personal bodyguards.

When we slowed to a stop, a guard stepped aboard. Though I could not understand what he said, I could tell by his tone that he ordered our driver to turn back. No vehicles were permitted beyond the blockade. I watched as a flurry of people hurried around both sides of our tour bus toward the entrance. It looked like a mob rushing for front-row seats at a Jackson Browne concert.

Before he could finish barking out his orders, however, Dad presented the Swiss Guard with the official Papal letter. He did so with such confidence that I pictured Agent 86, Maxwell Smart, flashing his credentials to gain entrance to CONTROL. The guard's countenance changed almost immediately. He instructed us to disregard his previous directions and, instead, disembark and follow him. What happened next causes my priest friends to shake their heads in sheer disbelief.

Our little band of Baptist believers was escorted through the crowd of thousands, past the press corps and paparazzi, down the center aisle to the most popular seats in the assembly hall. We had front-row seats just behind the College of Cardinals who wore the traditional elaborate vestments, crowned with *mitra simplex*, hats made of white linen damask. To me, they looked liked a gathering of Dan Ackroyd's friends at a Conehead convention. Still, we were just a few feet from the ambo itself, the large pulpit area, behind which the Pope himself would stand.

As far back as I can remember, this was my first exposure of any kind to the traditions of Catholics. I will never forget the sense of awe I felt, even as a teenager. Though I understood little of what transpired, I knew this was a solemn moment of sacredness. It left me speechless, even as those around us were noisy with anticipation, especially when the Pope appeared.

He was carried into the hall on what is known as a *sedia gestatoria*, a kind of portable throne. He entered smiling, waving as the crowd shouted in unison, *"Viva la Pape,"* "Long Live the Pope." Devotees held their babies toward him in hopes of receiving a blessing. For those fortunate to be close enough, the blessing was accompanied by the touch of his hand. He even managed to kiss a few.

Before long, the Pope began his sermon, speech, and defense—maybe it was all three. As a teenager, I had little interest in most of what he said, but, because he delivered the homily in as many as eight different languages, I do remember being duly impressed. When he concluded, the applause went on for an eternity it seemed, even long after he was escorted from the stage. We applauded, too, shouted, but mostly we exchanged "high-fives" for the caper we had just pulled off. We didn't realize it, but our doggedness would yield a greater return than even this.

We gathered ourselves to make the push through the crowd and return to the bus. Before we could turn to leave, one of the Cardinals with the cone-shaped headgear approached our tour group.

"Is there a Thaburn Lawson McSwain in the group?" he asked in awkward English.

"I'm he," said my father.

"Would you be so kind as to follow me, sir?" he continued. "His Holiness will see you now."

Dad turned in our direction with a look on his face that complimented the astonishment on our own. He had no idea that an audience with the Pope meant "an audience with the Pope," an actual face-to-face conversation.

Later, as we made the return trip to Rome, Dad told us that the Cardinal led him down a narrow hallway to a small room with two oversized baroque chairs. In one sat Pope Paul VI. His chair was slightly larger, as you'd expect. The other chair was for Dad. With a degree of humility surprising only to those who did not know him, the Pope stood up as my Dad entered the room. A small-time, small-town Baptist minister from Western Kentucky had a personal and intimate conversation with the Pope himself.

For a half hour, they talked about many things, but mostly the Pope wanted to know about Dad, about our Kentucky Bluegrass—whether it's really blue—our race horses, the Kentucky Derby, and our world-renowned bourbon. They even exchanged a few jokes. As Dad shared their conversation, I could see that the experience affected him in ways too personal for anyone else to know.

I'm sure the experience affected me, too.

That was my first experience of a "different religion," as we thought of them and even of other denominational groups within Christianity. We thought those people were all strange and suspicious, but especially those who had icons all over the sanctuary and who, obviously, prayed to many idols. It would be much later before I learned that Catholics were around long before the Baptists, or any other Protestant or Evangelical group for that matter. It would also be much later before I realized that religions like Hinduism, which is actually the world's oldest organized religion, were around hundreds of years, perhaps more than a thousand years, before Christianity. Nevertheless, what I experienced that summer day in an Italian village outside Rome amplified my consciousness of the universal human quest for spiritual knowledge—the quest to know God.

Chapter 2

Silence, Solitude, and the Tibetan Monks of Kathmandu

"Silence is as deep as eternity; speech as shallow as time."

—*Thomas Carlyle (1795–1881)*

On one trip, we toured the world.

We visited the Far East and one of the most spectacular and beautiful places on earth—Kathmandu, the largest city in Nepal, nestled in a valley by the same name and surrounded by the stunning, snow-covered Himalayas.

One morning, we toured the *Swayambhunath Stupa*, also known as the Monkey Temple. This ancient religious site lies just west of the city. In some parts of the structure, monkeys actually live. They are considered sacred. As a teenager, I couldn't imagine anything stranger.

Stupa is a Sanskrit word meaning "heap." It refers to a holy site that somewhat resembles a mound of dirt like you

I think I'm going to Katmandu.
That's really, really where I'm going to.
If I ever get out of here,
That's what I'm gonna do.

—FROM "KATMANDU" BY BOB SEGER
AND THE SILVER BULLET BAND

might see at a construction site. It's a monument made of stone, and these monuments are as abundant in Nepal as drugstores are in the United States. These monuments are places where Buddhist relics are said to reside and, in some of them, we were told the remains of a Buddha or a saint were supposed to be buried.

As we strolled through the temple area, I watched as Tibetan monks sat like The Buddha himself is always pictured sitting—legs crossed, spine perpendicular, palms touching each other and pointing upward, and, of course, in utter silence. Others, however, spun Prayer Wheels, cylindrical devices made of wood, metal, or stone and fashioned in such a way that they would twirl on a spindle. For centuries, in the Buddhist traditions of Tibet, monks and other worshipers have used these Prayer Wheels as they offer petitions and recite mantras for wisdom. This spiritual practice is said to help them release and receive—to release all negativity and to receive good Karma.

In Eastern thought, karma refers to the law of cause and effect. The law of karma is similar to what Christians know as the law of sowing and reaping, to which Paul referred in his letter to the Galatians (Gal 6:7). But, it is not as automatic as Christians have interpreted Paul's words to mean. That is to say, karma does not mean that, when things are going well for you, it's because you're doing what's right. Nor does it mean that, when things are falling apart, you are being punished for past mistakes. Instead, the law of karma simply affirms that Life, or as I prefer, God, will give you whatever experience you need for the portal into the Eternal Presence to widen for you.[1]

I observed many new things, but the most curious to me was the way the monks sat motionless, silent, and still. Our guide told us that some of them had been silent for days, some for weeks. I could not imagine this. I watched them carefully, certain that at any second one of them would twitch or move or break the stillness in some way. They never did.

> All we are is the result of all we have thought. If a man speaks or acts with an evil thought, pain will follow him. If a man speaks or acts with a pure heart, happiness will follow him, like a shadow that never leaves him.
>
> —BUDDHA

I had never witnessed such discipline—indeed, devotion—anywhere, not even among the most devout Christian seekers at home. In fact, I knew no Christians who could go days without food or contact with others, much less sit motionless for hours in solitude and prayer.

I don't think I ever sat in silence, either. In fact, I would have found silence to be deafening. Most worship services I had attended were distinguished by their dissonance and noise—lots of activity, lots of information, and doctrines, beliefs, and dogmas. Usually, you left worship with little more than the minister's personal biases and opinions. And if you were a product of the sixties, many of the white preachers held prejudiced opinions about some segments of the population, so their sermons were punctuated with racial overtones.

Sunday worship was the Christian's "Hour of Power," an aggressive, one-hour spiritual workout session. If you were not exhausted when you came into church, which most people were, you were certain to leave that way. Since we were accustomed to living life at the pace of an Olympic marathoner, as most Westerners are even more so today, worship was conducted much the same way. I suppose those who planned worship were afraid that, if the hour was not a continuous cascade of activity, people might fall asleep. It never occurred to them that sleep was the one thing everyone needed.

While I watched the monks with amazement, a critic in our group made the following brazen remark: "Look at those poor souls, offering prayers to a God they do not know. Why, if only they knew Jesus, the real God, they'd be happy and wouldn't need all this preposterous spinning and spinning and spinning."

Even to a self-obsessed, self-centered teenager, as I was, these condescending words sounded offensive. The monks did not seem as unhappy as she presumed. They did not appear to be impoverished in spirit. Nor did they seem out of touch with God. As a matter of fact, they seemed enviably more in touch with God than any of us were.

Though I did not respond to her remark, I remember thinking, "Do you suppose they would say prayers for hours at a time, or sit in silence for days, or go without food or conversation because

> "Question everything.
> Learn something.
> Answer nothing!"
>
> —EURIPIDES

they have nothing better to do?" I reasoned, "If what they are doing, and have done for centuries, was not connecting them to Source, why would they keep doing it? If these practices were not working for them, why have they engaged in them for centuries? Are they thick and incapable of learning? Or could it be that they are the ones who really know God, and we are the ones living in delusion?"

Since I have been well endowed with what someone once described as the "Why Chromosome," it's not surprising to the people who know me that I question virtually everything. I especially question the assumptions of Christian people. In other words, to borrow from Tennyson, "The shell must break before the bird can fly."[2] There is nothing you can know, and no one you can know, without first asking questions—many of them.

Notes

1.For more on the law of karma, read Pema Chödrön's book, *Start Where You Are: A Guide to Compassionate Living* (Boston: Shambhala Publications, Inc., 2008).

2. Alfred, Lord Tennyson, "The Ancient Sage," in *Victorian Poetry and Poetics*, 2nd ed., Walter E. Houghton, G. Robert Stange, Gordon N. Ray, eds. (Boston: Houghton Mifflin Company, 1968) line 154.

Chapter 3

Through the Glass— Narrowly

"The intuitive mind is a sacred gift and the rational mind is a faithful servant. We have created a society that honors the servant and has forgotten the gift."
—Albert Einstein (1879–1955)

There's nothing amazing about the fact that I pursued a ministerial career similar to that of my father. What's considerably more amazing is how a minister who questions everything survived in the Baptist tradition as long as I did. I grew up believing that one of the most coveted distinctions of being Baptist was that you were encouraged to be a free thinker. The brand of Baptist bartered in many Baptist churches today is anything but what I remember . . . and, I suspect, anything but Baptist.

> **A man's either trying to live up to his father's expectations or make up for his father's mistakes.**
>
> —Barack H. Obama

My dad was not a perfect man, but in my youthful eyes, he came pretty close. He had a compelling personality, and the people who knew him loved him. He had a joke for every occasion, an anecdote for any situation. He mastered the skill of people pleasing, too. For most of my life, I lived in admiration of him.

The day I said I heard the Divine "call" to enter the professional ministry surprised no one. Nor did it surprise Dad. It was as if he expected it. He didn't push me into pursuing a ministerial career, but I'm sure he encouraged it when the opportunity presented itself. For most of my life, I tried to conform to his expectations, just as I did everyone else's. Had awards been given for the effort to please people, I would have earned an "A+." That's an exhausting way to live.

I believed, or tried to believe, just about everything I was supposed to believe. Because I organized my life around the beliefs and values shared by the people within my faith tradition, I made everyone happy. Like my father before me, I was driven by an inner need to please people. For the most part, I did please them.

At the same time, I waged an internal war with some of my beliefs. I questioned all of them, but I usually quarantined the questioning to my private thoughts. I seldom verbalized them in public for fear of being judged, reprimanded, or criticized. As you might suspect, therefore, I lived in a rather noisy head. I think many people do.

> "What is religious fundamentalism? It is mistaking faith for beliefs and then imposing those beliefs on believing and unbelieving people alike."

The "Beliefs" I Was Told to Believe

If you were raised in a Christian faith tradition similar to mine, you will readily recognize the following worldview. If you were not, this will at least give you an idea of what I was taught to believe and what many Baptists still believe. While I mention only a few below, these are some of the more important ones.

• The Christian religion is the correct religion. That is to say, all other religions are wrong, and the people who believe in them need to be converted to Christianity or face the dire consequences that await them in eternity (that is, they will go to hell).

• Jesus is the Savior of the world and the only way to God. All other ways may lead to something, but not to God. If you want to go to heaven, therefore, you'll have to believe in Jesus.

• God's word is the Bible. God's word is found only in the Bible. Be suspect of anything anyone else may call sacred scripture.

• The Bible is infallible (without error), at least in its "original manuscripts"—referring to the actual parchments on which the biblical writers wrote their words. (I must add, however, that no original manuscript has been found. Furthermore, the earliest ones we have date from the second century and are distinguished not only by their historical significance but by the innumerable discrepancies between them.)[1]

• The family God has ordained is made up of one man and one woman. A few other unions may be permitted, but they are hardly preferred.

• Homosexuality is a sin against nature and an abomination to God. God made them Adam and Eve, not Adam and Steve.

• Abortion is murder. No exception. No debate.

• If America wishes to remain strong, it had better side with Israel. Israel is God's chosen nation. Again, no exception and no debate.

• The Second Coming of Jesus could occur at any moment. (I must add that Jesus said it would occur only when people least expect it (Matt 24:43-44). Since some Baptists expect Jesus' return at any moment and even pray for his imminent return, I wonder if it has ever occurred to them that they might be responsible for his delay.)

• God is not finished with Israel. Thus, the nation of Israel will play a pivotal role in a pre- or post-tribulation rapture-of-the-church view of the end of human history. (Some Baptists and other Christians believe in what's known as the pre-millennial view of history, a few believe in what is known as the post-millennial view, and some believe in the a-millennial, meaning "no millennium," view of the end of the world. It isn't important to go into detail here about the meaning of these different views of history, but if you're familiar with the *Left Behind* series of fictional books released over the past fifteen years, you've met the most popular of these complicated apocryphal systems of thought. The novels themselves are based on the pre-millennial view of history, with its special devotion to the futuristic notion known as the "Rapture.")

• Christians go to heaven and everybody else goes to hell, which is a real place with fire where disbelievers burn for eternity.

• God is not a Republican, but any God-fearing soul knows there's no way she would ever be a Democrat.

• Oops, did I say "she"? A Freudian slip of the pen. Baptists know God is neither male nor female, but they are quick to remind women which of the two God created first.

There are many other beliefs, but these are among some of the more common ones. If you're guessing I've given up on most of these, you've guessed correctly.

What *do* I believe? I'll mention a few things soon, but I'm not sure I'd call any of them beliefs. They're more like perspectives, always expanding and frequently changing. Their importance is only related to the current stage of my spiritual journey.

> "Truth is at the bottom of the abyss, and the abyss is bottomless."
>
> —DEMOCRITUS

For too long, I have pretended to believe things I do not believe. For fear of not fitting in, or worse, fear of being judged, I ran with the pack. Fortunately, I am now beyond those fears as well as a host of others with which I lived for much of my young adult life. My feeling today is this: *what others think of me is none of my business.*

In case you're wondering, I have not abandoned my faith. Because I no longer accept some of the things I was raised to believe, some may conclude that I no longer follow Christ. I do. Admittedly, some of my perspectives today are outside the mainstream of conventional Christian thought, but conventional thinking and correct thinking are not synonymous. The fact is, my faith is more real to me today than at any other time in my life. The biggest difference is that I no longer need someone else's approval to feel okay about either my faith or me.

Some Christians mistakenly think doubt is disbelief, just as they think openness is compromise. I know this because I used to think this way. I've had doubts. I still have doubts. But then, I suspect every thinking person does. In fact, if you meet anyone who seems certain about everything, you can be sure he or she is certain of nothing.

I live with doubt, but I am not a disbeliever. I am simply open to truth—wherever I may find it—and I don't feel as if I'm compromising anything. Furthermore, if humanity is to survive, I think we must cease the insane labeling and judging that takes place between religions and between people within the same religion. There have always been and will always be many different ways of understanding Ultimate Truth, just as there will always be many different religions, even many subsets within every religion. To put it another way, there will never be only one way to know truth any more than there will be only one religion. Christians and Muslims alike, who often pretend their understanding of truth is the most complete, have not succeeded in avoiding the division and splintering among their own followers. Why, then, do they insist on living, for example, with the illusion of converting the world to Christianity or Islam? I think it's because they choose to live in a make-believe world instead where everything, as well as everyone, is fashioned in their respective images.

> "Thinking people welcome doubt. It serves them well as a valuable stepping stone to better knowledge."
>
> —CARL JUNG

Similarly, some say the world is rapidly moving toward a one-world government or one ruler. In my opinion, these people are just as delusional as Christians and Muslims who think they can convert the world to their faith. If the present divisions within any one religion have not made clear that humans are incapable of subscribing to the same beliefs, then there isn't much this book or any other book could teach you.

Throughout the history of humanity, religion has been the prime cause of most human division and destruction. In my own tradition, for example, Christianity has been either a divine blessing or a demonic curse. Though embarrassing to admit, it has been the latter far too often. If the human species is going to survive, it is imperative that we make room on this little planet for everyone, that we respect all religions as well as those who choose to have no religion.

> "Do not believe in anything simply because you heard it . . . because it is spoken or rumored by many . . . found written in your religious books . . . Do not believe in traditions just because they have been handed down . . . But, after observation and analysis, when you find anything that agrees with reason and is conducive to the good and benefit of one and all, then accept it and live up to it."
>
> —BUDDHA

Even as I say this, however, I realize that until a person experiences an awakening, this will likely be more than he or she can accept. Until people experience a shift in consciousness, making it possible for them to see everyone and everything through lenses clear of conditioned thinking, then they will resist virtually everything I've written so far. This is true whether they are a Christian, Muslim, atheist, or whatever. If I have learned anything over the years, it is that every religion, in its unique way, has something important to teach us about Ultimate Reality, or what I like to call the sacred art of knowing God. Even those who profess no religion may be able to teach the rest of us something about this Universal Intelligence or Divine Consciousness.

If you find my admissions that I have doubts and questions, that I do not have all the answers, and that there may be many ways to know God threatening and unacceptable, I understand your reaction. There was a time when I would have reacted the same way. Even so, I urge you to look within and find the child who wonders at this Mystery we call Life and who has lots of questions he or she would like to ask.

> All religions are subsets of a stained glass window through which the infinite light of the Divine shines in all its dazzling color and beauty.

There is nothing wrong with doubt; it is not a sign of weak faith. In fact, I've found that, until you question your faith, you don't have faith, no matter how clever the disguise. You might have beliefs and be a "religious" person, but, as you will see, there is a chasm of difference between faith and beliefs, between a religion *about* God and a relationship *with* God. In other words, until you doubt, you cannot believe.

As you read this book, consider releasing the need to cling to pronouncements, judgments, and ideas about yourself, too, even the beliefs you've been told are too sacred to question or too absolute to doubt. Open your mind to the inner impulse that covets the permission to question things. My own perspective is this: God delights in disbelief. Why? Because doubt is the divine portal into the depths of the human soul. Through this portal, Mystery meets you. When that happens, you will take delight in this Mystery and so enjoy Life in all its fullness.

Just try it and see what happens.

My Current Spiritual Perspectives

If you are open to the possibility of looking at life, yourself, and what you have believed in different ways, then many things in this book will be useful to you on your journey. Below I offer a few of my perspectives that I hold dear, at least for now.

I know that my perspectives are just that—my perspectives. If a perspective to you is a belief or a worldview, then call these my beliefs or my worldview. Beliefs are the assumptions one makes about life—the ideas, doctrines, or structures of thought that help one articulate one's human experience. Beliefs are not infallible, however. Nor are they superior to the beliefs of others. There has only ever been one spiritual truth, but it is experienced and interpreted in the crucible of one's cultural, racial, religious, and individual contexts.

• I call God *God.* I hesitate to say much more than this because anything I might say, no matter how correct it may be, seems only to diminish this Ineffable Reality. God is more than any name I give to her and infinitely more than anything I might say about her, or him, or whatever God is. Whenever I speak of knowing God, I refer to my inner sensation or feeling—my awareness that something infinitely grander than anything I could ever imagine has wrapped itself around me in love.

• I know that Jesus was a real person in whom and through whom God, Source, Intelligence (again, the name is not nearly as important as that Reality toward which the word points) manifested itself most fully. There was something unique about Jesus. He was like other avatars in that he, too, lived at a higher level of cosmic consciousness. But he was unlike them, too. Perhaps what made Jesus different is the degree of God consciousness with which he lived. He was so completely free of self, or the ego (see ch. 8), that it wasn't long before Christians began believing that God and Jesus were one and the same. This is why Saint John said, "In the beginning was the Word, and the Word was with God, and the Word was God" (John 1:1, KJV).

• Is Jesus the only way to God? His way is my way to God. There may be other ways, as I acknowledged above. Practitioners of the Baha'i faith, for example, speak of "One Light, but Many Lamps." God, as the Light of all, may be seen and known by the light of many different lamps. Whether it is light from the sun or light from a candle, it is the same flame, the same light. Throughout my life, I've met many people whose state of God consciousness is real. Yet, they do not share my Christian heritage. It would be nothing short of sheer arrogance either to dismiss the light of spiritual truth they have discovered or to pretend they are wrong and I am right.

• Furthermore, I think we Christians have misread for centuries the meaning of Jesus' words in John 14:6. I know I did. In this passage, Jesus affirms that he is "the way to God." For years, I interpreted that to mean Jesus was the "only" way to God. If you look closely, though, you'll see that this is not what Jesus said about himself. Admittedly, it is what Christian history has said about him. What Jesus said was this: "If you wish to know God, as I know God, follow my way." It is only as you follow the way of Jesus that you know the God of Jesus. I, for one, have believed in Jesus for most of my life, but, as noted, I cannot say I knew the God of Jesus. I knew *about* God, but I did not *know* God. There is a chasm of difference between the two.

• I am sometimes asked, "If there are many ways to God, how do you under-stand Jesus' instruction to 'Go and make disciples' (Matt 28:19-20)?" When Jesus said, "Go and train everyone . . . in this way of life" (Matt 28:19), he meant, as it is correctly paraphrased here in *The Message*, that we are to teach people his way of life, his way of thinking and living. Jesus did not say, as most Christians have mistakenly thought, "Go and train everyone to believe in me," or worse, "Go and train others to believe as you believe." Jesus said to spread around his "way of life." The world around you will never change until the world within you does. That's the message Christians know as the good news.

• Since I have grown up with the Bible and have spent the greater part of my life in its study, I suspect it will remain my primary source of spiritual insight and wisdom. However, I am also aware that other sacred writings, equally inspired, have guided others to know God. So, when it comes to the Bible, I no longer say things like, "The Bible is 'infallible,' 'inerrant,' or 'authorita-tive.'" In many ways, it's all of these things to me, anyway. Virtually every branch of the Christian church has at some time debated, battled, and even-tually divided over what they were going to "say" about the Bible. It seems to me that if what you "say" about the Bible is more important than what the Bible says to you, then you're living under a great delusion. The Bible is far more than anything I could say about it.

Once you label me, you negate me.

—SØREN KIERKEGAARD

I've come to embrace many other per-spectives on my spiritual path, and you will detect some of them as you read. Whether you agree or disagree, I hope you'll keep an open mind.

To Be Blind, but See

My favorite story from the Gospel of John is the one of the nameless and blind beggar. One day, he met Jesus and received his sight, or perhaps it was insight. Maybe it was both.

Imagine that this beggar is you. You're blind from birth. You've never seen the light of day, observed the petals of a flower in spring, or gazed upon a sycamore tree in bloom. Instead, you spend your days begging from people who'd rather make a case study of you or, worse, shun you altogether.

One day, however, and quite unexpectedly, you meet someone who neither studies you nor shuns you. On the contrary, he makes salve of spittle and soil and smears it over your eyes. Then, as if that were not strange enough, he sends you to the Pool of Siloam to wash. Although you go, or are led, you have no expectation that your life will be any different. But, to your amazement and everyone else's, a miracle of serendipity occurs. You are healed. You are given your sight.

Could you imagine anything more blissful? More exhilarating? You observe the world around you for the first time. What you had only known through the four other senses, you now know through the fifth sense. You see a human face, trees and flowers, plants and animals, and the amazing thing to you is this: nothing is as you imagined. Everything is different, and so is everyone, and both infinitely grander and more beautiful than you thought.

You expect everyone to share your joy, to be thrilled at the good fortune that has come your way, as well as the endless discoveries you are making. And, of course some are. But the sad fact is that most aren't. In fact, they're borderline offended. You are seeing things, as well as saying things about what you see, that they have neither seen nor said. Your words are foreign to them, even heretical, and consequently unacceptable. As self-appointed guardians of what others will see, as well as what others will say about what they see, they are disturbed and even outraged by you. Instead of inquiring what you know or who you know, they debate and defend what they do not know. Dragging you before the religious leaders in the court

> It is a terrible thing to see but have no vision.
>
> —HELEN KELLER

> I want to know God's thoughts; the rest are mere details.
>
> —ALBERT EINSTEIN

of sanctioned opinion, they demand that you tell them how you see and what you know.

It's hard to miss the Johannine satire, isn't it?

Here's a beggar who was blind, but now sees and knows.

Here are seers who think they see, but are actually blind and beg to know.

> "I consider myself a Hindu, Christian, Muslem, Jew, Buddhist, and Confucian."
>
> —MOHANDAS GANDHI

One of my favorite poets, Robert Frost, pointed to something of the same irony when he wrote, "We dance 'round in a ring and suppose, / But the secret sits in the middle and knows."[2]

Who are the blind beggars of this world?

Aren't they the people who think they see? Rather than reclining at the table of abundant Presence, they settle for scraps of knowledge about Presence—beliefs, doctrines, their religious opinions and viewpoints, all mere substitutes for Source and hardly satisfying to the deepest hungers of the human soul.

It is noteworthy, too, that the beggar gave no explanation to his critics who demanded to know about his transformative experience. If he had one, which I doubt, he was aware that they wouldn't accept what he said, anyway.

Why? It would not have fit into their narrow perspectives. They remind me of the time in my life when, in sheer arrogance, my attitude was, "My mind is made up; don't confuse me with facts!"

As for my own spiritual transformation, I have no explanation for it. Even if I did, I'm not sure I'd tell anyone about it for the simple reason that I don't think I'd have the words to describe it. Anything I could say about what has happened to me seems a poor substitute to the mystery and beauty of it. How do you explain the inexplicable or express the inexpressible?

This much I know: those who only know *about* God usually have a lot to say. Those who genuinely *know* God have little to say.

"I was blind . . . I now see," was all the blind man had to say (John 9:25).

That's enough for those who see.

It's never enough for those who don't.

Notes

1. For the most honest treatment of this subject I've seen in recent years, read Bart D. Ehrman's book, *Misquoting Jesus: The Story Behind Who Changed the Bible and Why* (New York: HarperCollins Publishers, 2005).

2. Robert Frost, "The Secret Sits," in *The Road Not Taken: A Selection of Robert Frost's Poems*, introduction and commentary by Louis Untermeyer (New York: Henry Holt & Company, 1971) 214.

Chapter 4

Knowing about God, Knowing God, and the Law of Attraction

"The destiny of the soul is to see as God sees, to know as God knows, to feel as God feels, to be as God is."
—Meister Eckhart (1260–1328)

In every religion, indeed in every subset within every religion, lies a structure of beliefs, a depository of doctrines and dogmas about God. How could any of these be an adequate substitute for knowing God? They're simply a collection of words, beliefs, and concepts. Meaningful? Maybe. Conveyors of spiritual truth? Sometimes. Helpful? Not often. No word, concept, belief, or doctrine could ever capture the mystery that is God, much less take the place of personal intimacy with the Creator.

God has no religion.

—MOHANDAS GANDHI

Knowing God's name is no substitute for knowing God. Besides, what *is* God's name? Nobody knows. Even if we did, God would be more than a name. A name is only a talking point. It provides a context or a frame of reference for identification. Just as we are infinitely more than our names, so is God.

God has many names or, in my perspective, aliases or disguises. In Hinduism, for example, God is Bhagavan, Brahma, Krishna, and many others. In fact, the *Sahasranama*, Hindus' sacred scripture, offers more than a thousand names for God. Two words comprise the name of the scripture itself: *namas* meaning "name" and *sahasra* meaning "thousand." Hence, God is the God of a thousand names.

In monotheistic religions—Islam, Judaism, Christianity—where followers believe not in many gods but in one God, they still call their God many different names. To Muslims, for example, God is Allah, but he also known by ninety-nine other names. In Judaism, God is Elohim, Yahweh, Adonai, El-Shaddai, and so on. To Christians, God goes by the names familiar to Jews, but he's also Lord, Christ, Father, Logos, Spirit, and so forth.

> All the different religions are only so many religious dialects.
>
> —G. C. LICHTENBERG

Persons with no specific religious association sometimes refer to God with such words as Intelligence, Source, Higher Power, Being, or Consciousness Itself.

So what is God's name?

I suspect God bears them all, but who knows? Frankly, what difference does it make? Knowing God's name does not mean we know God. Almost everyone knows, for example, the name "Michael Jackson." But, as has become abundantly clear since his death, practically no one truly knew who he was. At best, the person we knew was a fictitious fabrication of our minds, shaped largely by his public persona, the media and paparazzi, pop culture, hearsay, and our opinions.

I'm inclined to believe it's a good thing that God has many names. Otherwise, we might make the following assumptions:

> No one can make me angry unless I carry the seeds of rage within me.
>
> —BUDDHA

1. Because we know God's name, we know God. Most people today make this basic error.

2. Since we know God's name, we have superior knowledge. We may become disdainful toward those whom we perceive to have inferior knowledge of God. Maybe we believe that, because we know God's name, we have control over God.

Assumptions like these come from the ego, a human condition that is the culprit in virtually all inner turmoil and conflict. I will go into all of this in greater detail in chapter 8.

The "Law of Attraction"

"The antecedent to every action is a thought." —*Ralph Waldo Emerson (1803–1882)*

Similarly, a naiveté about how the universe works is quite popular today. Just as the ego in some religious people enjoys the illusion of controlling God by knowing God's name, other religious and pseudo-religious people believe they can harness the divine laws of the universe for their personal wishes and self-aggrandizement.

These individuals practice the Law of Attraction. This spiritual and universal law is hardly as abstruse as the popular book *The Secret* by Rhonda Byrne would suggest. It's been around for a long time, although we know it by different names. The Law of Attraction is known in the New Testament as the Law of Believing, or the Law of Asking and Receiving. Virtually every culture and religion proposes some form of this law.

The Law of Attraction has roots in quantum physics. Simply put, it states that our thoughts dictate our reality. The theory suggests that thoughts are made of energy waves that attract like energies in return. Positive thoughts, for example, operate at higher energy or vibrational frequencies. Thus, when we think positive thoughts, we both broadcast and receive, or attract, positive results. Conversely, negative thoughts vibrate at lower energy frequencies. When our thoughts are charged with negativity, we get negative results.

Essentially, Saint Paul pointed to the same spiritual law in his letter to the Philippians. Although he knew nothing of either quantum physics or the Law of Attraction per se, he wrote, "I'd say you'll do best by filling your minds and meditating on things true, noble, reputable, authentic, compelling, gracious—the best, not the worst; the beautiful, not the ugly; things to praise, not things to curse" (Phil 4:8-9). In other words, today's thoughts manifest tomorrow's reali-

> "By three methods we may learn wisdom: First, by reflection, which is the noblest; Second, by imitation, which is the easiest; Third, by experience, which is the bitterest."
>
> —CONFUCIUS

ties. The Buddha himself said, "All that we are is the result of all that we have thought."

The Law of Attraction operates with as much reliability as the Law of Gravity. The former is a spiritual law, the latter a physical. While neither is visible with the naked eye, we can witness their somewhat predictable effects. For example, the Law of Gravity makes it possible to predict with uncanny certainty what will happen if you leap from the fifty-fourth floor of a high-rise in Manhattan. The Law of Attraction makes it possible to predict the kind of life you will live by the kinds of thoughts you think. If you think angry thoughts, for example, you may frequently find yourself in volatile, even hostile situations, such as those involving road rage, which occurs when angry motorists trigger dangerous responses in each other. As another example, if you consider your life with pessimism, believing nothing will ever work out for you, there is a good chance you'll be right. You experience what you expect. When you realize life works this way, you may get cautious about the kinds of thoughts you think. As Wayne Dyer once wrote, "You'll get what you think about whether you want it or not."

The Woman with Breast Cancer

I once heard gynecologist Christiane Northrup, who authored the bestselling *Women's Bodies, Women's Wisdom*, tell of a patient who came to her worried that she had breast cancer. After performing a mammogram on the woman, Northrup reported the good news: "You do not have breast cancer."

The good news was not enough to assail the patient's fears. In the months that followed the examination, she continued to worry. "What if the test was wrong? What if they got my report mixed up with someone else's?" Eventually, the worry got the best of her, so she made an appointment for another mammogram. Again, the results came back negative. She was in good health.

Several more months passed, but the anxious thoughts prevailed. She scheduled yet another mammogram. This time, however, the report came back positive. Northrup said to the worried woman, "I'm sorry to have to tell you this, but we've found cancer in one of your breasts."

"What a relief!" cried the patient. "Finally, I can stop thinking I have it!"

Sickness is the wage your body pays when you spend your mind on fear.

Remember the Old Testament saint whose name was Job? He lost his wealth, his family, his fortune, and finally his own health. When his world collapsed around him, he confessed, "The worst of my fears has come true, what I've dreaded most has happened" (Job 3:25). Again, "you get what you think about whether you want it or not." This is the Law of Attraction.

The Collapse of the Financial Markets

Many will remember 2009 as one of the darkest times in America's recent financial history. The stock market collapsed. To almost everyone's surprise and out of everyone's control, the economy spiraled downward. Even as I write these words, the markets struggle to rebound, and some predict it may take several years before they do . . . if they ever do.

The markets have behaved like a seesaw—up one day, down the next. The thoughts and feelings of most people have taken a similar ride. From Wall Street to Main Street, negativity fills the air like a dense fog. If you regularly watch or listen to the news, for example, you might be victimized by the reports that fill the airwaves with distrust and fear, skepticism and cynicism. It's everywhere.

Do you suppose it is possible that our thoughts about the financial markets attract a lingering negative effect? If we changed our thoughts about the markets and our cynicism toward the future, might the markets begin reflecting our optimism? In my opinion, the markets reflect our minds.

What's "Unattractive" about the Law of Attraction?

The Law of Gravity makes life possible on this planet, but it's also the law that brings down a malfunctioning plane. There's an equally unattractive side to the Law of Attraction, at least where the ego is involved. Some practitioners of this law, for example, mistakenly believe it guarantees that they will get whatever they want, especially if they give what they want their undivided attention. They believe that if they think resolutely about what they want and have no doubt that they will get it, then it will eventually come to them.

Just as no Christian can use Jesus' name to get anything he or she wants, we cannot use the Law of Attraction to land a career, the house of our dreams, the coveted career position, the income we desire, and so on. While there's nothing wrong with wanting to improve our lives or our life situations, whenever ego drives ambition, then our desires usually become self-serving, self-centered, and self-obsessed. Neither God nor God's laws can be so manipulated.

In chapter 8, I describe the ego in detail and explore its insidious nature. For now, remember that the ego is a monster that resides within the psyche of every person. It is problematic and dysfunctional—problematic because it is the principal cause of human unhappiness and discontent, and dysfunctional because it is only interested in itself. In its more extreme forms, ego manifests as insanity.

Until recently, religious people labeled those with highly dysfunctional egos as insane or even demon-possessed. Since they had no other way of explaining strange and aberrant behavior, they assumed these people were under the control of an evil power they called Satan, or the Devil. My opinion is that Satan is actually a kind of alter ego or the dark side of one's personality.

This alter ego, or the Devil, also bears many other names. In Islam, for example, it is called Iblis. In Buddhism, it was *Mara* over whom Siddhârtha Gautama finally prevailed at his spiritual awakening under the Bodhi Tree. Because he successfully triumphed over his own alter ego, The Buddha, which means *Enlightened One*, is a source of spiritual inspiration to millions of people. Many believing people in my religious tradition don't realize that they, too, have an alter ego, a dysfunctional and sometimes insane little demon inside each of them. The difference is only in the degree of insanity.

Whether it's something we "wish to attract" as a pseudo-religious person or "pray to receive" as a person of faith,

> "Imagine there's no countries
> It isn't hard to do
> Nothing to kill or die for
> And no religion too
> Imagine all the people
> Living life in peace . . ."
>
> —FROM "IMAGINE" BY JOHN LENNON

whenever our ego takes precedence, the Law of Attraction is interrupted. It is corrupted and ceases to operate as we might desire. The same happens to the efficacy of prayer when those who pray do so in an attempt to manipulate reality.

James, author of a New Testament book that bears his name, understood this. While he did not use our labels of "ego" or "Law of Attraction," he was well acquainted with the realities beneath and beyond those terms. He wrote, "When you ask, you do not receive, because you ask with wrong motives" (Jas 4:3, NIV). He might have put it this way: "When you want something and believe you'll get it, either through prayer or focused thinking, but you do not receive it, there's a simple reason: *it is because your wanting and craving is only for yourself.*"

Chapter 5

The Supreme Purpose in All Religions (and Their Shared Failure)

"All religions serve the purpose of reuniting the soul with God."
          —*Paramahansa Yogananda (1893–1952)*

I once read of a rabbi who corrected a student named Jacob who loved to make fun of Christians. The student regarded Christians as ignorant and ill informed and Christianity as an absurd religion.

One day, the rabbi took Jacob aside and said, "Jacob, why do you suppose Christians make it a habit to tap the side of the saltshaker while Jews always tap the bottom?"

> **We were led to believe a lie, When we see not thro' the eye.**
>
> —FROM "AUGURIES OF INNOCENCE" BY WILLIAM BLAKE

Certain the rabbi was going to join him in ridiculing Christians, Jacob was more than ready to play along. "No, Rabbi, I don't know. Why do Jews tap the bottom of the saltshaker while Christians tap the side?"

"To get the salt out!" answered the rabbi.

There are many ways to tap the shaker, but the purpose is the same—to dispense salt.

Ask the followers of almost any religion what is the purpose of their religion and they will say it is to guide them to know God. They may use different words or ideas to say this, but it is essentially the same purpose.

Even in religions like Buddhism, where there is no belief in a Higher Power per se, they still speak of the "Universal Mind." What is that, if it is not the same Reality toward which the words and names that others use point, too?

Similarly, a spiritual seeker in Christianity is really no different than a spiritual seeker in Islam, Taoism, or Hinduism. All want to know God or the higher self or to reach what Hindus call *Samadhi*, which is "bliss consciousness," what Christians may call "salvation," or "God-realization." In other words, everyone wants to be complete, to be happy, and to alleviate human suffering, which The Buddha showed us is mostly self-induced anyway. In other words, we all seek the same thing. We just know it in different ways based on our cultural, social, ethnic, and religious conditioning. Since everyone is seeking God-consciousness, which is sometimes confused with "happiness," then it stands to reason that every religion has evolved to help facilitate this purpose.

> **God talks to everybody.**
>
> —FROM *CONVERSATIONS WITH GOD* BY
> NEALE DONALD WALSCH

In Christianity, the purpose is called by as many different names as there are names for God. Sometimes it's called "salvation." At other times it's called "redemption," "justification," and "conversion." In some repressive cultures where Christian missionaries have carried the Christian message, the promise of "liberation" has great meaning to the indigenous but oppressed peoples. This is known among Christians as "liberation theology."

In Buddhism, it is *nirvana* or freedom from *dukkha*, which is "suffering." In Hinduism, the purpose is called *moksha* and the goal is to escape earthly suffering and cyclical existence—and ultimately to arrive at *nirvana*. In Islam, a follower is known as a *Muslim*, which, by definition, means "one who submits to God."

Those without a specific faith orientation are also part of the shared human quest for self-realization or self-fulfillment. It is expressed, however, with terms like "inner transformation," "awakening," "unity consciousness," and so forth. Again, the terminology may differ, but the purpose in each search is to know unity with the Self and live with a sense of connectedness to the universe or Intelligence.

Even those who do not believe in God share in the same human longing for wholeness. Just like everyone else, they instinctively seek fulfillment. "Spiritual atheism" may seem paradoxical to some, but I know devout atheists who've had some kind of spiritual awakening. Even Albert Einstein referred to himself as "a deeply religious nonbeliever." Whatever happened to them, they found it deeply satisfying and life-transforming. It rewarded them with a sense of the Sacred that gives them peace, joy, gratitude, and contentment in ways many religious people I know have never experienced.

How do religious people explain this experience? Some dismiss it as a trick of Satan himself. They argue that the atheists are deceived—that they merely think they're happy, satisfied, contented, and at peace. I'm not so sure. The ones I know seem quite content, happy, and at peace. As a matter of fact, some of them think more like Christ and live in more Christ-like ways than many Christians I know.

Since I have always believed in God, it is hard for me to understand what some describe as "atheist spirituality." However, I will not deny that anything is possible. Besides, after reading some of the writings of Andre Comte-Sponville, a contemporary French philosopher and a self-professed atheist, I can't disagree that he has had some kind of transcendent and transformational life experience. He does

> **I am a deeply religious non-believer.**
>
> —ALBERT EINSTEIN

not call this experience "God," but it has left him with the satisfying sense of belonging to something much grander than he. Moreover, it is shaping him into a more ethical and felicitous human being.

In *The Little Book of Atheist Spirituality*, Comte-Sponville writes,

> I personally have no trouble at all living without religion. . . . Not only was I raised a Christian, but I believed in God. My faith, if occasionally laced with doubts, was powerful until around age eighteen. Then I lost it, and it felt like liberation—everything suddenly seemed simpler, lighter, stronger and more open. . . . Such freedom! Such responsibility! Such joy! Yes, I am convinced that my life has been better . . . since I became an atheist.[1]

The Failure of Religion

While all religions share the same essential purpose, all of them are failing miserably. They start out well but end up obsessed with matters of lesser importance and become, in some instances, pure insanity. Consider the following points:

• Instead of a bridge to God, religion is often a barrier to God.

• Instead of freeing people from their burdens, religion itself is the burden.

• Instead of knowing God, religion is obsessed with knowing *about* God.

• Instead of divine acceptance, religion is preoccupied with guilt and failure and the depiction of God as a deity displeased about both.

• Instead of bringing unity to humanity, religion is the principle cause of most disunity.

• Instead of peace and tranquility, religion is a circus of endless activity, beliefs, dogmas, and doctrines that are more divisive than unifying.

Since I know other religions only as an outsider, I'll reserve my observations to what I know best as an insider to Christianity. I have served as a spiritual leader within the Christian church for decades. I have also had the added experience of providing consultation within almost every part of the Christian church. For example, not only was I a former Baptist minister for twenty-plus years, but for more than a decade I have been a professional consultant to Roman Catholic, Evangelical, and Protestant churches all across the United States—from theologically conservative churches to liberal ones, from mid-sized congregations to those accustomed to more than 10,000 worshipers every weekend. I've consulted with churches vehemently opposed to anyone but males in positions of authority, and with those served by female clergypersons; with those who openly welcome gays and lesbians, and with those who insist that they return to the proverbial closet.

> No one knows enough to say with confidence that his religion is superior to any other.
>
> —ARNOLD J. TOYNBEE

I feel more strongly today than ever that the future of humanity is at stake. Unless there are profound changes in human consciousness—that is, changes in how we look at each other and how we treat each other, there is little hope for humanity's survival. Some Christians intuitively know this already, which is why they are anxious for the "return" of Jesus, as they call it. Madness has reached an unimaginable and unsustainable level. Unfortunately, however, the one place where you would expect to find sanity—in your religious tradition—is where you often find the opposite.

To begin with, the literal meaning of the word *religion* is, ironically, "to return to bondage." The word comes from two words, the prefix *re* meaning "to return," and the root *legare* meaning "to bind." Since everyone wants freedom, and many turn to religion to find it, the regrettable consequence is that often they get greater enslavement. This is the dysfunction found in every religion, and Christianity and Islam may be two of the most dysfunctional religions in the world today. Again, however, I offer perspectives on the faith I know best.

The Failure of Christianity

In my experience, instead of helping people know God, many Christian churches and their leaders are obsessed with achieving the status of being the biggest church with the largest crowds and the most elaborate campuses. They measure spiritual progress in terms of the number of attendees, the size of their annual incomes, and the square footage of their facilities. Furthermore, virtually every Christian leadership conference showcases the largest of these churches, as well as their leaders, as if they were role models for all other churches. Over the years, a celebrity-like cult has developed around some of these churches and their leaders. It is not so different from the cult following associated with celebrities in Hollywood.

Instead of showing people how to live a Christ-conscious life, most likely because they do not know how themselves, some church leaders saddle their followers with a catalogue of "do's" and "don'ts" as onerous as the proverbial Sears catalogue. Believers are told what to think, how to believe, and the way to live. Furthermore, most of these leaders disregard the fact that their founder repudiated the religious leaders in his day for doing this to the followers of Judaism. "Instead of giving you God's law," Jesus observed, "as food and drink by which you can banquet on God, they package it in bundles of rules, loading you down like pack animals" (Matt 23:4).

This madness has become so commonplace that many people think it is normal. Has it occurred to you that the one time Jesus became angry enough to lose his temper was the day he entered the temple? I have sometimes wondered how Jesus would react if he entered almost any church in America today. In the last ten years, for example, it is estimated that Christian

> A dog starv'd at his master's gate, Predicts the ruin of the state.
>
> —FROM "AUGURIES OF INNOCENCE" BY WILLIAM BLAKE

churches have spent more than $100 billion on buildings and facilities. In that same time, more than 400,000,000 people have died of hunger on this planet. Something is wrong with this picture, especially when the man, Jesus himself, confessed that he had nowhere to lay his head at night (Luke 9:58).

And what of the circus of endless activity? In some churches, were it not for the cross resting on top of the building, you might suppose you had stepped into a Barnum & Bailey circus. There may be little to connect you to God, but there's plenty to keep you occupied. In some churches, for example, it's not only a Ferris wheel of perpetual activity; it's also a Piccadilly buffet line from which to select any number of diversions from God.

> An infinite God . . . does not distribute himself that each may have a part, but to each one he gives all of himself as fully as if there were no others.
>
> —A. W. TOZER

When religion moves away from its shared purpose with other religions, it gives secondary matters a place of superior importance. This is precisely what's happening in many churches today, and it has been going on for decades, even centuries. Although countless people have advocated for internal change throughout the history of Christianity, almost no one seems to listen anymore.

For a large number of people, religious belief has supplanted a relationship with God. How to know God has been relegated to a place of secondary importance. To put it another way, knowing about God is frequently regarded as equal in importance to knowing God. It's as if religious leaders believe what people need is more beliefs, doctrines, dogmas, moral judgments, and expositions. But if beliefs and doctrines were what people needed, why are they leaving the church in greater numbers today than ever before in Christian history?[2]

No specific belief will automatically mean you know God. If that were the case, the belief itself would be God. There is nothing you need to know in order to know God. You know God already. You have just forgotten that you do. Or you've been misled and confused, thinking there's something missing or that you must believe something before you can know this Something or Someone we call God. In either case, you are spiritually unconscious, asleep to the indwelling presence of God—a presence within you already. If you were awake, you would see God in yourself, in others around you, and in the world. You would know this Presence, too, in an intimate and transformational way.

To know God is the supreme purpose of every human life. The fact that so many people are unaware of God's presence explains why there is widespread discontent among Christians in almost every church and division between virtually every religion. It also explains why many of them often swap churches. They are looking for God and for themselves, but they enter a church only to discover that the church is more lost, confused, and dysfunctional than they are.

> "Share our similarities; celebrate our differences."
>
> —M. SCOTT PECK

Replacing the members they are losing, as well as the equally difficult task of keeping the ones they have, are some of the most important priorities among ministers today. Instead of helping people know the indwelling Christ—a Presence no awakened person would ever leave—most church leaders spend an inordinate amount of time teaching doctrines about God and looking for the latest gimmick to attract a few more people. If they succeed in getting them to come, they spend the rest of their time trying to be pleasing enough, as well as entertaining enough, to get them to stay.

Many churches and church leaders are preoccupied with peripheral matters of faith. Beliefs, dogmas, positions, what they believe—which, by implication means, "What we believe is right; what others believe is wrong!"—lead to debates, disagreements, and even division within the Christian church. How else do we explain the multiplicity of denominations? The Baptists, for example, with whom I was raised, regularly boast about how many churches they start each year—typically more than any other mainline Christian denomination. Any honest observer knows, however, that most of these new church starts are born of disagreement and division.

> "They don't know who they are, because if they did, there wouldn't be wars. Like the little girl who says to a little boy, "Are you a Presbyterian?" And he says, "No, we belong to another abomination!""
>
> —FROM *AWARENESS* BY ANTHONY DE MELLO

In most instances, people divide over beliefs, positions, power, and so forth. In extreme forms, the madness goes far beyond mere disagreement and division. It leads to the defamation of character, and, on many embarrassing occasions in the history of Christianity, it has resulted in the killing of those who did not convert or conform to the beliefs of the church. For example, the Medieval Crusades alone should cause every Christian to look with compassion, instead of abhorrence and judgment, on the more extreme and sometimes violent religious groups within Islam. The history of violence in both religions is far more similar than it is different.

Furthermore, whenever the purpose of religion is obscured, people within the same religion eventually display disdainful behavior toward each other. In what is still the *locus classicus* on the religions of the world, noted scholar and historian Huston Smith sketches this revealing conclusion:

> . . . it is well to remind ourselves again of the human element in the religious equation. There are people who want to have their own followers. They would prefer to head their own flock, however small, than be second-in-command in the largest congregation. This suggests that if we were to find ourselves with a single religion tomorrow, it is likely that there would be two the day after.[3]

Why are there so many branches or traditions within Christianity itself? There are, for example, the Eastern tradition (Christianity in Eastern Europe and beyond) and the Western tradition (Christianity in Western Europe, including most of the United States).

In Western Christianity alone, there are Catholics, Anglicans, Lutherans, Methodists, Presbyterians, and so forth. Even in my own Baptist tradition, there are as many different kinds of Baptists as there are flavors of Baskin-Robbins ice cream—each with a slightly different taste from the other and, of course, each a little more "right" in its understanding of truth than all the others.

There are American Baptists, Southern Baptists, National Baptists, and even Bible Baptists. There are Regular Baptists, General Baptists, Primitive Baptists, and Free-Will Baptists. There are Covenant Baptists, Fellowship Baptists, and Seventh-

> You have your way. I have my way. As for the right way, the correct way, or the only way, it does not exist.
>
> —FRIEDRICH NIETZSCHE

Day Adventist Baptists. There are Bible-Believing Baptists and We-Believe-More-of-the-Bible-than-You-Believe Baptists. There are Independent, Conservative, Moderate, and Fundamentalist Baptists. And, while more common among Pentecostals in the Appalachian regions of Kentucky where I live, there are even Snake-Handling Baptists and Holy Ghost Baptists.

There are as many different kinds of Catholics, Lutherans, Presbyterians, and Pentecostals, too. If this were not puzzling enough, some Evangelical churches in Christianity have repudiated identification with any denomination whatsoever. To them, a denominational affiliation is something akin to the Evil Empire. They represent themselves as non-denominational churches, and this distinction does appeal to people who may feel there is something spiritual about such independence.

When I first encountered this phenomenon, I was providing consultation to one these self-proclaimed independent and non-denominational Christian churches. One afternoon, I asked a leader, "Now, let me make sure I got this straight. You are a non-denominational church."

"That's correct."

"So what does that *really* mean?" I asked. "Since the word 'denomination' means 'to name,' are you suggesting, instead of being, let's say 'The Vine Street Methodist Church,' you are 'The Non-Denomination Church'?"

He just looked at me.

"Let me put it another way," I said. "By being a non-denominational church, you are saying that you are a denomination of one—a denomination unto yourself?"

"Well," he responded, "I can see where you might think that, but we are really not a denomination at all. In order to be a bonafide denomination, you have to be in cooperation with other churches."

"So then," I pressed, "instead of cooperating with other churches, you are competing with them?"

"Well," he said, "that's probably true that we are, in one sense, although to hear you say it makes it sound bad."

I thought, *Of course it's bad!* So I asked, "Why would you, a Christian non-denominational church, be in competition with other Christian churches, no matter what they may call themselves?"

He paused, perhaps considering the lack of logic in his analysis.

I picked up the conversation. "I think I'm getting the picture. What you really mean by a non-denominational church is that you are an independent church that has no official connection to or control by other churches."

"Well, you have it partly right, I think," he acknowledged. "We aren't controlled by any other church or hierarchy, but we do associate with other churches from time to time. It's just that we're not affiliated with any of them."

"Why is that?" I asked.

"Because," he explained, "we don't want anybody telling us what to believe. We know what we believe already, and what we believe is different from what others believe."

I pressed on. "Could you give me an example of a belief you believe that would be different from the beliefs that others believe?"

He whispered, "We believe in the baptism of the Holy Ghost."

At this point, I returned to my task as a consultant. He seemed relieved that I did so.

Our religious differences always become problematic when, instead of mutually respecting and affirming the one and only thing all traditions share —their desire to know God—we become more interested in what distinguishes, even divides, us. Had I not changed the conversation, I would have bordered on violating my own perspective—that we should magnify the one thing around which we can agree, instead of the many things about which we disagree.

The doctrines, distinctions, differences, and divisions within Christianity are nothing short of exasperating. Yet, this too is not a phenomenon unique to Christianity. I'm told I would find this same madness in other religions. Hinduism, for example, has a denominational complexity that would make what I've described look sophomoric by comparison.

Why are there so many distinctions within Hinduism? There are probably many explanations, but the primary one is that Hinduism has been around longer than any other religion. Given time, the same destiny awaits all of them, including Christianity. Instead of becoming more unified, all religions are destined to become more diverse. In other words, there will never be just one religion. As long as people come from different places, cultures, and backgrounds, their experience of the world and of God will be dissimilar, even though their purpose may remain the same.

Religion and it leaders, especially within Christianity and Islam—religions that believe strongly in world evangelization and domination—must abandon the illusion that their way of knowing God is the only way. If not, the future holds more of the same—disagreement, division, and, eventually, violence and destructive behavior. As the Dalai Lama says, "Until there is

peace among the religions of the world, there will be no peace in the world."
If history has not taught us this already, there is nothing history *can* teach us.

Mark Twain wrote,

> When I, a thoughtful and unblessed Presbyterian, examine the Koran, I
> know that beyond any question every Mohammedan is insane; not in all
> things, but in religious matters. When a thoughtful and unblessed
> Mohammedan examines the Westminster Catechism, he knows that
> beyond any question I am spiritually insane. I cannot prove to him that he
> is insane, because you never can prove anything to a lunatic—for that is a
> part of his insanity and the evidence of it. He cannot prove to me that I am
> insane, for my mind has the same defect that afflicts his . . . . When I look
> around me, I am often troubled to see how many people are mad.[4]

The Crisis within Christianity in America

Mark Twain also wrote, "If Christ were here now, there is one thing he
would not be—*a Christian.*" With few notable exceptions, the church across
denominational lines is fundamentally out of touch with the teachings of its
founder and the purpose of his ministry on earth. Jesus said he came "to seek
and to save that which was lost" (Luke 19:10, KJV). Look at almost any
church today, however, and what you'll see is an institution that is substantially more interested in saving itself.

The Christian church today needs a
radical transformation. If it does not return
to the God it pretends to know, the church
will continue its present downward spiral
and eventually be marginalized altogether.
Many churches have achieved this status
already. To borrow Macbeth's words, they
are "full of sound and fury . . . signifying
nothing."

Admittedly, there is plenty of "sound
and fury" coming from churches that make
a lot of noise, especially in the political and
cultural worlds. The problem is this: *nobody
is listening to them anymore*, a fact only a scant few church leaders seem to
realize. Most religious leaders think the growing secularization of our culture
is the root cause of the lack of interest in church and the church's consequen-
tial decline. What they do not know, however, is that the real causes of

> "Spirituality is far
> too important a
> matter to be left to
> fundamentalists."
>
> —FROM *THE LITTLE BOOK
> OF ATHEIST SPIRITUALITY*
> BY ANDRÉ COMTE-
> SPONVILLE

decline have more to do with dysfunction, delusions, and division people find in most churches today. The American church was once a powerful voice in a cultural wilderness. Today, it is little more than paltry whimper in an urban forest.

Across denominational lines, church people have become narrower in their thinking. They are often judgmental of virtually anyone who disagrees with their beliefs and values and seek to use whatever means necessary, including the legislative branch of the U.S. government, to impose their moral and social agendas on others. Furthermore, the church has become isolated from the real world and has created a make-believe world with little or no connection to life on this planet.

In my home state of Kentucky, for example, we have become hosts to the $27 million, high-tech, special effects Creation Museum. It's our Disney World, so to speak, and equally as unreal. Conceived first by Creationists themselves, the museum has supporters who believe it provides people with the "correct" explanation on the origins of the universe.

In spite of the fact that virtually every reputable scientist believes the universe is billions of years old, Creationists contend it is only about 6,000 years old. According to Creationists, the Genesis story of creation must be regarded as a scientific description of the origins of the universe. What they do not tell you, however, perhaps because they do not know, is that many devout Scripture scholars do not believe this is the purpose of the book of Genesis at all. Instead, they suggest that the Genesis story of creation is a sacred but mythical story, portions of which may have been a poetic hymn sung in worship. Its purpose was to affirm that God, or Universal Intelligence, created everything that is. Period.

> **Science is not only compatible with spirituality; it is a profound source of spirituality.**
>
> —CARL SAGAN

This explanation does not suffice for Creationists, however, who believe Genesis teaches that the earth was fashioned in six twenty-four hour days, even though the word translated "day" in our English Bibles could mean "a vast expanse of time." While this would be more consistent with what science has taught us about the actual age of the universe, Creationists insist that the word "day" must be taken literally—that is, as a twenty-four-hour period.

Further, creationists believe dinosaurs and humans coexisted. Whatever caused the extinction of dinosaurs, Creationists explain the mysterious presence of fossils, many of which carbon dating traces to a time millions of years ago, by maintaining that God placed the fossils in the earth with the mere "appearance of age."

Appearance of age? Since when did God take up the art of deception, an art humans themselves perfected long ago? Why would God deceive people into thinking the earth is much older than it is? Who is God trying to fool, and why? Or is this whole thing a cosmic joke to which I have missed the punch line? Why would God, whom Creationists agree is a God who wishes to be known, make it all the more complicated to know him?

> The reformer is always right about what is wrong, but generally wrong about what is right.
>
> —G. K. CHESTERTON

Furthermore, I have never understood why Creationists insist the universe is younger than science tells us it is. Why do they wage war with science? For years, I thought a lot about questions like this. When I experienced a spiritual transformation, however, I suddenly realized that, while Creationists provide many explanations, beneath and behind all of them, they're afraid. They are frightened by the thought that, if the creation story is not taken literally, then the rest of the Bible might not be taken literally, either. And, if the Bible is not taken literally—or so their reasoning goes—then the authority of the Bible is up for grabs. Moreover, if the Bible holds no authority over people's lives, the end result is moral collapse, social chaos, and, ultimately, the end of the world—which is, ironically, the thing for which many of them are praying. It is a convoluted and insane belief system . . . and one to which I once subscribed myself.

Clearly, fear motivates Creationists. They wage a religious and cultural war with science because they're scared. They do everything in their power to defend their understanding of truth. What they do not know, however, is that spiritual truth never needs defending. Only a weak, unexamined faith needs defending.

Why do many people have a weak and uncertain faith? Precisely because they haven't examined it or questioned it. That is, they survive on what might be called a "borrowed" faith, a belief system someone passed on to them with the fallacious promise that if they simply believed the beliefs, they would be "saved." Rather than questioning the beliefs and searching for the truth themselves, they mistakenly think it would be wrong to question or disagree with any of the beliefs. Consequently, they exist by clustering in groups of likeminded believers where they can reinforce their untested assumptions and inherited beliefs. As a consequence, they live a sub-par existence in an environment divorced from the real world.

My experience has taught me that, until you question your faith, looking closely at its suppositions and assumptions, your faith will always feel under attack by something or someone. You may attempt to disguise a weak faith with religious pronouncements and actions that appear to others as if you are full of certainty about everything. But you can be sure that beneath the pretense hides a frightened and threatened person.

As I noted at the beginning, those who argue for God's existence do so not because they know he does but because they're afraid he doesn't. Thomas Jefferson purportedly said, "Question with boldness even the existence of a God; because, if there be one, he must more approve of the homage of reason, than that of blind-folded fear."

Interestingly, the battles Creationists wage against what they see as challenges to their worldview will never give them the victory they seek. They may win a few skirmishes here and there, but in the end, they will lose the war. Waging war with anyone makes losers of everyone, which is, ironically, what our spiritual master said: "All who use swords are destroyed by swords" (Matt 26:52). A contemporary spiritual teacher, Eckhart Tolle, said the same essential thing, although in different words: "Whatever you fight, you strengthen. What you resist, persists."[5]

It is not my intention to be critical of Creationists. There was a time when I subscribed to many of the same assumptions and arguments they make. But, with my spiritual awakening, I discovered a new freedom to stop warring with imaginary enemies. I mistakenly had thought it was things like Darwin's theory of evolution that caused the secularization of our society and the loss of any sense of the Divine presence. So, with other Creationists, I joined the battle religion has waged against imaginary enemies—Creation being just one of these—completely unaware that what Pogo said was right, "We have met the enemy, and he is us." I was my own greatest enemy. Like most people in pews today, I did not feel close to God. But, it was not because I believed the wrong things. No, the irony is, it was my beliefs which had become one of many substitutes for God. In short, my beliefs *were* God.

This is the main error made by many Creationists, indeed by many Christians. Jesus said something similar to the religious people of his day: "Knowing the correct password—saying, 'Master, Master,' for instance—isn't going to get you anywhere with me. . . . 'Master, we preached the Message, we bashed the demons, our God-sponsored projects had everyone talking.' And do you know what I'm going to say? 'You missed the boat . . .'" (Matt 7:21-23, The Message).

The Christian Church: Out of Touch with Its Founder

The church has missed the boat. It is fundamentally out of touch with the spirit of Jesus, not only in this matter of Creation, but in other ways, too. Below, you will find familiar statements attributed to Jesus by Christian history, followed by an italicized, imaginary, response by the church or followers within the church. How do the two statements compare with your experience of the church today?

• "Love your enemies" (Matt 5:44). *Unless, of course, your enemy is of a certain nationality or ethnic background.*
• "'Eye for eye, tooth for tooth' . . . but I say: Don't hit back at all" (Matt 5:38-42). *This word of Jesus applies to every situation except those like the terrorist attacks on September 11, 2001.*
• "Don't hoard treasure. . . . You can't worship God and Money both" (Matt 6:19-24). *Don't let a minor statement like this keep you from trying.*
• "Love . . . yourself" (Luke 10:27). *Easy for Jesus to say.*
• "Love your neighbor" (Luke 10:27). *Easy for Jesus to do.*
• "Judge not" (Matt 7:1). *Except in the case of those who don't believe as we believe.*
• "Do not worry" (Matt 6:33). *Jesus has no clue what the financial collapse did to my 401k. How could I not worry about the future?*

Do any of the italicized responses sound familiar? Despite the unequivocal teachings of Jesus, Christians who think they are his followers consistently ignore or explain away what he taught as the Way to knowing the heart of God. Why should it be surprising, therefore, when religious people say they no longer feel the Divine presence in their lives?

The church is more homogeneous, too, in a time when the world has become more heterogeneous. In many of today's churches, for example, people look alike, think alike, talk alike, and believe alike. A few years ago, church growth enthusiasts encouraged homogeneity as a means of rescuing the church from its rapid decline. Since some ministers were more interested in numerical growth masquerading as spiritual growth, this became the *modus operandi* in various churches. Instead of helping the church to grow, however, it only succeeded in escalating its division and decline.

> **Every day people are straying away from the church and going back to God.**
>
> —LENNY BRUCE

The few churches in the United States that show numerical growth are often deceived by this growth. Admittedly, compared to the majority of other churches that are losing members faster than they are replacing them, these churches appear to be gaining headway. As it turns out, though, this is an illusion. Compared to the larger numbers people who do not attend church at all, or are leaving the church altogether, they fail woefully. Furthermore, much of the growth they report is simply transfer growth that occurs when disappointed or disgruntled members leave one church and transfer membership to another church down the street or across town.

If the current decline in church attendance were the medical case history of a hospital patient, the diagnosis would read, "Chronically ill; resistant to change; on life support; likely terminal." The church itself is the one institution most in need of the thing it proclaims to the world—salvation. It boasts of knowing God, but by the sheer numbers who have given up on the church, it is right for us to question whether the church knows God at all.

Notes

1. Andre Comte-Sponville, *The Little Book of Atheist Spirituality*, trans. Nancy Huston (New York: Penguin Books, 2007) 5–6.

2. A recent study reported, "More than one-quarter of American adults (28%) have left the faith in which they were raised in favor of another religion—or no religion at all." From the Pew Forum on Religion and Public Life, "U.S. Religious Landscape Survey" (19 March 2010) http://religions.pewforum.org/reports.

2. Huston Smith, *The World's Religions* (HarperCollins: San Francisco, 1991) 385–86.

3. Mark Twain, *Christian Science* (New York: Harper & Brothers, 1907) bk. 1, ch. 5.

4. Eckhart Tolle, *A New Earth: Awakening to Your Life's Purpose* (New York: Plume: 2005) 75.

Chapter 6

The "Half-lived" Life

*"The things that make you weep contain something
you need to know about."*

—*Christiane Northrup*

As I stated earlier, the purpose of Christianity is *to make God known.* The fact that the church has all but replaced that purpose with matters of lesser importance is the church's greatest failure.

Please understand that I do not make these observations about the church with detachment. I am concerned about the failure of the Christian church because, in many ways, I have lived much of my life making the same fundamental mistake. For example, I tried for years to figure out why I showed up. I did not realize that I am here, just as you are, for one purpose: "to know God and to enjoy him forever," as John Calvin put it. The irony is that Calvin obscured his simple but sublimely stated purpose of humanity when he wrote the sixty or more volumes of doctrines and dogmas that became known as *Institutes of the Christian Religion.* For all the seminal insight and understanding his brilliant, legal mind provided to the articulation of a systematic theology, one could also point to the equal or greater degree of dissent and division that has resulted from it.

Jesus said, "And this is the real and eternal life: that they know you, the one and only true God" (John 17:3). Period.

> "When I let go of what I am, I become what I might be."
>
> —LAO TZU AND THE *TAO TE CHING*

No explanation. No interpretation. No qualification. No *Institutes.* Just "that they know you." Yet, because I did not know this, I confused my primary purpose with secondary ones. Most believers do, too.

My religious upbringing, for example, conditioned me to think that the way to happiness was to believe the "right" beliefs—which meant what Baptists believed and, more precisely, what Southern Baptists believed. I also had to please God in everything I did, which basically meant I had to go to church every Sunday, read my Bible, show respect for the flag and civil authorities, and leave my neighbor's wife alone. And if I *really* wanted to please God, I had to attend the mid-week prayer service at church and tithe my weekly income. I did most of this stuff, but none of my rigid and diligent efforts made me joyful. In fact, much of it made me miserable, just as it does most Christians.

I was taught that the words of Jesus, "Be ye therefore perfect . . ." (Matt 5:47, KJV), meant it was my Christian duty to achieve moral and spiritual perfection, or get as close as possible to that ideal. If ever I had a lustful thought, which of course I did, or if I ever felt as much as a twinge of attraction to a person of the opposite sex, then that proved I was a sinner deserving of hell and a miserable disappointment to

> The most important thing is to find out what is the most important thing.
>
> —ZEN MASTER SUZUKI ROSHI

God. We sang about our misery in a common and popular song. In my opinion, this song is anything but Christian in terms of its lyrics: "Amazing grace, how sweet the sound that saved a wretch like me." God's grace is amazing, but no one is a wretch. I don't care how many dirty thoughts you've had. This is Puritanical poppycock.

When I look back from the perspective of a spiritually awake person, I am not surprised that I felt the way I did. Instead of bringing me closer to God and making my life happier, my Christian experience only succeeded in making me feel guilty, broken, and distant from God.

Happiness Substitutes

Happiness is the fundamental human desire everyone longs to feel. Instead of looking for happiness in the only place we can find it, in knowing God, people look for it, just as I did, in what might be called "happiness substitutes." There are hundreds of them, and none can do more than provide a temporary feeling of happiness or a transitory feeling of fulfillment.

Religion is only one substitute wherein people look for such happiness. It's where I looked because I was raised in that type of social environment, but there are others. One is career. Many people mistakenly think that if they choose the right career, they'll be happy. Furthermore, if they select a high-paying career, they'll have the added benefit of being financially secure. In no way would I diminish the importance of pursuing the career of your dreams or, as some Christians like to put it, the calling on your life. To be sure, too many people find themselves in jobs that match neither their passions nor their gifts.

But one can never find real happiness in a career or a calling. Both can enrich our lives, but neither is the purpose for our lives. We can pursue a great career, for example, and receive a hefty income, but the day will come when whatever we achieve does not reward us with what we

> **You never get enough of what you don't need.**
> —AUTHOR UNKNOWN

hoped. Why? Once the exhilaration of a career, job promotion, pay raise, or a few "Salesperson of the Year" awards wears off, and such exhilaration always does, boredom and discontent set in. Our calling, contrary to much of what's been written over the years, is *not* our purpose for being here.

When the job or calling doesn't give you what you want, what do you do? Many blame the job for their feelings of discontent and begin looking for another job that will bring more recognition, fulfillment, or greater financial security—more happiness. It does not occur to these people, however, that no job, no calling, could ever reward them with that for which they truly long—intimacy with the Creator. This is your purpose in life, and nothing substitutes for it. Until you realize this, you will keep looking for yourself in the wrong places. If you look long enough, you will most likely find something that brings you more of what you are looking for. At long last, though, it too will become the "old" job, and the cycle of insanity will return.

If you look for yourself, for your feeling of oneness and unity with the Divine, in any place other than where it actually exists, you will meet disappointment. Sometimes a major disappointment in life is all it takes to awaken us out of this delusion and insanity. It did for me, but only after I experienced many disappointments and squandered more than half my life.

Many other people will go to their graves never figuring out the point of human existence. In this respect, they'll end up like the Preacher, as he is called, in Ecclesiastes, who expressed his confusion and cynicism about virtually everything—pleasure, possessions, profession, you name it.

> What do I think of the fun-filled life? Insane! Insane! My verdict on the pursuit of happiness? Who needs it? . . . I tried my level best to penetrate

the absurdity of life. I wanted to get a handle on anything useful we mor-
tals might do during the years we spend on this earth.

Oh, I did great things: built houses . . . designed gardens . . . made
pools . . . had children . . . acquired large herds and flocks . . . piled up
silver and gold . . . voluptuous maidens for my bed.

Oh, how I prospered . . . . Everything I wanted I took—I never said
no to myself. I gave in to every impulse, held nothing back. I sucked the
marrow of pleasure out of every task—my reward to myself for a hard day's
work!

Then I took a good look at everything I'd done. . . . There was nothing to any of it. Nothing . . . . One fate for all—and that's it. (Eccl 2:1-14)

Perhaps you can see why I like the Preacher so much. Although confused,
he's at least an honest preacher.

We find satisfaction of the universal, human longing for happiness in
one way: *by being in the presence of Being itself.* That is to say, we will not
know God in beliefs, however correct they may be, or by being good people,
as important as that may be, or in some rigid religious duty, as significant as
that may be. At best, we could only ever *meet* God through such things, but
we could never *know* God through them.

My Roman Catholic friends believe in what is known as the "Doctrine
of Transubstantiation." This English transliteration of the Latin word
transsubstantiatio is derived from a Greek word, *metousiosis,* meaning "to
change." Catholics are taught that whenever they celebrate the Eucharist, the
bread and wine mutate into the actual body and blood of Christ. Most
Protestant and Evangelical Christians are
not taught this. Instead, they are taught
to believe that the bread and wine (or
grape juice) are symbols of the body and
blood of Christ.

I'm inclined to ask all of them—
Catholics, Evangelicals, and Protestants
alike—this question: "Regardless of what
you've been taught to believe, isn't it true
that all we can expect through this sacred
observance is to meet the Eternal Christ,
and isn't there infinitely more to knowing Christ than simply meeting him?"

> "Christianity has not
> been tried and found
> wanting; it has been
> found difficult and
> left untried."
>
> —G. K. CHESTERTON

In my religious experience, I went to church every weekend. Yet, more
often than not, whenever I left worship, even services that left me vigorously

inspired, it wasn't long before I returned to the same patterns of living and thinking from which I desperately wanted to escape. In other words, my spiritual life was a roller coaster, and nothing of consequence ever seemed to change. I could never escape, for example, the feelings of failure. Nor could I transcend the struggles of my daily life that weighed on me almost continuously. While I felt close to God on occasion, these feelings never lasted. Since I was led to believe this was my fault, that I did not have *enough* faith or the right kind of faith, I lived with an inner feeling that something was wrong with me.

Most people, even devout people, are as confused as I was for much of my life. They live a schizophrenic spiritual existence. They meet God on Sunday, but soon after they leave church, they lose any sense of God's nearness as their day or week unfolds. Knowing the Eternal Christ as a moment-by-moment transformative Presence is unimaginable to them. It has never occurred to them that it is possible to know God as a conscious, intimate, and indwelling Reality and, as a consequence, experience a radical transmutation in the way they think, feel, and live. While Jesus said, "And this is the real and eternal life: that they know . . . God" (John 17:3), to these Christians, eternal life is not knowing God in the present moment; instead, it is some far-off, future fantasy with no reality in their lives today.

Although Jesus emphatically said, "Judge not" (Matt 7:1, KJV) and "Love your enemies" (Matt 5:44, KJV), it would never occur to these Christians that they could be free of self-criticism, self-hatred, and guilt (which are the seeds of criticism and hatred toward others); or that they could live without the incessant stream of mental judging, fault-finding, complaining, confronting, debating, and battling that takes place as a result. Why? For most of these people, drama is their life. Since the church has perfected the art of drama, or conflict, over the centuries, how could churchgoers know anything different in their personal lives?

> "What you do to yourself, you do to others; what you do to others, you do to yourself."
>
> —PEMA CHÖDRÖN

Further, while Jesus said, "Take no thought for your life" (Matt 6:25, KJV), these people can't fathom their lives free of worry, anxiety, and fear. They worry about virtually everything—life, their children, careers, retirement, illness, what they eat, what they don't eat, how they dress, the way they look, and what others think of them. They worry about their past, the future, when they'll die, how they'll die. The notion of living in a virtual state of uninterrupted peace and tranquility is not only inconceivable to them, but equally unbelievable.

Only by living in a state of Christ-realization—or, as I like to put it, by learning to walk with God—will we ever know joy that is greater than pleasure, fulfillment that is deeper than accomplishment, and an inner sense of security

> **God cannot be found in a book of religion; God can only be found in the present moment.**
>
> —DEEPAK CHOPRA

that does not fluctuate with the stock market. Though God is unseen, knowing God is more real than anything we could ever see with the naked eye. Everything else—our bodies, our minds, the world—is but an illusion, and an illusion can only mirror what's real.

When you look at yourself in a mirror, for example, what do you suppose is more real? The image you see in the mirror? Or the *you* who observes? Careers, accomplishments, six-figure incomes, and so on may offer a temporary feeling of satisfaction and security, but they could never do more than mirror the real satisfaction and security we can know in unity with Being itself. This, then, is our superior purpose—the real reason we're here. It's not complicated. There's nothing to discover, no career assessment we must undergo. As the Westminster Shorter Catechism puts it, we are here simply to "enjoy God forever."

Why, then, does it take most of us half our lives to figure this out?

On the Meaning of Lostness

We have a hard time with realizing our true purpose because we are all lost. However, being "lost" doesn't mean, as I was taught, that we are bound for hell or deserving of it, and therefore need saving from it. As Walt Whitman wrote,

> I have heard what the talkers were talking, the talk of the beginning and the end.
> But, I do not talk of the beginning or the end.
>
> There was never any more inception than there is now,
> Nor any more youth or age than there is now,
> And will never be any more perfection than there is now,

Nor any more heaven or hell than there is now.[1]

In my religious tradition, we learned that everyone is going to spend eternity in hell if they do not get "saved."

As Jesus described it, being lost is being confused and misguided. It is not knowing or being aware of our infinite connectedness to the ineffable Presence we call God. Consequently, we can believe in Jesus and in God but still be lost; attend church regularly but be misguided and feel confused; memorize the Bible, attend church every Sunday, and still not know who we are; do everything right and still be clueless as to why we're here. I've come to understand an important truth: you don't have to wait for hell to be in it already any more than you must wait to enter heaven to enjoy the bliss of it now.

Here are the four different ways Jesus described how people are lost.

> For as this appalling ocean surrounds the verdant land, so in the soul of man lies one insular Tahiti, full of peace and joy, but encompassed by all the horrors of the half-lived life.
>
> —FROM *MOBY DICK* BY HERMAN MELVILLE

(1) Some are lost like a sheep from its shepherd. That is, they meander through life unaware of who they are and never seem to figure out what they're looking for. They wander restlessly. They go here, then there, and nothing satisfies them for long, so they're always on the move. They're oblivious to danger. They seem disconnected from everything around them. Were it not for a benevolent shepherd who willingly leaves the many to find the one lost sheep, this person might remain lost, continue to meander through life, and never figure out what it's all about. (Luke 15:4-7)

(2) Some are lost through no fault of their own. They're like a coin someone inadvertently drops from his hand. They're misplaced, perhaps misled, and maybe misdirected. Left to themselves, they would be helpless to find their way back, which is precisely why God goes looking for them. He uses whatever means to find them, too. Sometimes he uses other people, or he arranges the circumstances of life, situations, conversations—the list is endless, but each is a portal God provides and through which his hand reaches out to them.

In the parable as Jesus told it, the owner of the lost coin is a woman distinguished by her determination to find the coin. She will be neither deterred nor discouraged. Whatever it takes, she will find it. No one will be lost, not forever. This is one of the most precious spiritual truths expressed in these stories. (Luke 15:1-8) The lost will be found—all of them, if the coin is truly representative of everyone. If it isn't, who do you suppose Jesus meant to leave out of the equation?

(3) Some are lost because they choose to be. Of the four ways Jesus described that people could be lost, perhaps the most familiar is that of the Prodigal Son (Luke 15:11-24). Even people who know nothing else about the Christian faith know this story of the young man who rebelled against his father, demanding both his independence and his inheritance.

People in virtually every culture and religion are familiar with this story because every family, indeed every culture, has such people within it and a religious story similar to it. The prodigals of this world often experience great drama and sadness, sometimes with far-reaching implications. In our modern world, for example, this kind of "lost" is frequently reported in tabloids, especially when high-profile persons and celebrities act in dysfunctional and self-destructive ways. But there are prodigals in every family. You have likely known a father or mother, brother or sister, son or daughter, or someone else who is just as lost as those you read about at the grocery store magazine rack.

> **Without knowing what I am and why I'm here, life is impossible.**
>
> —LEO TOLSTOY

(4) Some are lost and do not know it. While any of the previous three ways of being lost, or disconnected from oneself and one's Source—are worthy of contemplation and exploration, religious people seldom discuss this fourth kind of being "lost." Yet it may be as common, if not more common, than all the others combined. It is the kind of "lost" experienced by religious people. The story, as Jesus told it, is that of the Elder Brother, or the Prodigal Son's older brother (Luke 15:25-32).

I think of him like this: Unlike his younger, wayward brother, this son stayed home, played by all the rules, and sought to please his father as well as everyone else. He mistakenly thought that his purpose in life was to conform to prescribed social and religious mores. He was taught that if he met everyone's expectations, he would find happiness and know success in all his endeavors. He dreamed of the happiness others said he would experience, but, unfortunately, it never happened for him. In terms of distance, he could not have been closer to his father. In terms of closeness, he could not have been more distant.

It started out as disappointment, but then it became frustration mixed with sadness. Sarcasm helped him keep from crying, but then cynicism set in. In time, he became disillusioned and embittered about his situation. He had measured both his worth and his wealth through insidious comparison, and he usually came up on the short end. Whenever he succeeded at something, the exhilaration never lasted. No matter how high a summit he reached, another higher peak appeared, and standing on top of it was someone else—his competitor who had managed to go a little higher and achieve a little more than he had.

Though unconscious of it, he quietly resented people who were more successful. He was suspicious of virtually everyone. This explains why he had few friends. It also explains why he was infuriated when his father held a party for his younger brother—the fool. Unlike his foolhardy brother who not only screwed up his life but also broke all the rules, he had played by the rules, but no party was held for him.

His younger brother made the headlines, albeit the sleazy tabloids. He, on the other hand, had been on the cover of such reputable magazines as *Time, Fortune, Newsweek,* and the like. He had proven himself worthy of the family's good name. He was the one son his father could trust. He alone, therefore, deserved the family business as well as the family fortune.

> To get into the core of God at his greatest, one must first get into the core of himself at his least, for no one can know God who has not first known himself.
>
> —MEISTER ECKHART

Instead of being able to celebrate his success and his status within the family and community, he suffered inside. He felt incomplete, unappreciated, unhappy, and unfulfilled. He was neither satisfied with his life nor content with it. Beneath the surface of his skin, a cauldron of disappointment bubbled like a witch's brew.

The promise of peace in the performance of his duties proved to be phony, too. He had not found peace. He did not even know who he was.

Though he had mastered the art of hiding his feelings from others, his inner thoughts were mostly cynical. When he spoke up, people thought his sarcasm was funny, perhaps because they were too shallow themselves to know the difference. Like others wear an overcoat, he wore his sarcasm to hide his cold, embittered soul.

Life had not turned out as he had planned. Sure, his father occasionally slapped him across the back and said, "My oldest and wisest son, I'm proud of you." But the recognition was never enough. What's worse, whenever he received such praise, instead of feeling good about it, he felt undeserving of it. In many ways, he couldn't win for losing. Maybe that's why, whenever he lay down at night and stared at the dark ceiling above him, he wondered how he had managed to live half his life without knowing his purpose for living.

Does the story of the older son sound familiar to you?

I Was Lost

I have just described my life and probably the lives of many other believing people. I was this Elder Brother. For years, I tried to fulfill everyone's expectations for my life. For example, I never made most of my career decisions. Obsessed with making and keeping everyone happy, and afraid of failing, I let others make those decisions for me.

I often asked my father, friends, and others what they thought I should do. Their advice dictated my choices. In other words, I danced to everyone else's tune.

Was I trying to please everyone? Did I fear making a mistake? Failing? Being judged by someone? Was I hoping that if I did everything I was "supposed" to do, I would come out on top? That I would be happy? Most likely, it was all of these things.

I called myself a Christian and, for half my adult life, a Christian minister. However, I had neither a clear sense of self nor any clue as to what my life was about. I looked for myself and for my

> "Your children are not your children.
> They are the sons and daughters of Life's longing for itself.
> They come through you but not from you, and though they are with you yet they belong not to you."
>
> —KAHLIL GIBRAN

purpose in the places where I thought I could find it. I did exactly as I was supposed to do. Apart from a few mischievous antics as a preteen and teenager, I was a good "preacher's kid." Sons and daughters of military personnel are known as "army brats." Daughters and sons of Protestant ministers are called "preacher's kids." A minister's children were expected to be the worst behaved children in the church. Most of us made it our ambition not to fall short of that expectation. Yet, for the most part, I wasn't such a bad kid, not nearly as misbehaving as my older brother. (I'm sure he'll enjoy reading his younger brother's assessment of his behavior.)

As all Baptist children were supposed to do, and as everyone prayed they would do, I eventually found myself standing before the congregation and saying I believed in Jesus and wanted to be baptized. This was known as making my "profession of faith" or getting "saved." To most Baptists and other Evangelicals, this is life's most important decision. One is never considered too old to make this decision, but the younger, the better. If a person grew up in the church, as I did, and did not make this eternal, destiny-determining decision by the time he or she reached puberty, others regarded that person as a reprobate and sometimes hopelessly damned. Fortunately, I was seven years old when I made a profession of faith, so I escaped this judgment.

Exactly what can a seven-year-old understand about the nature of the human condition, the significance of Christian baptism, the point and purpose of Jesus' life, or what it means to pursue the path of Christ as a way to know God? About as much, I suppose, as an infant baptized into the Roman Catholic Church can understand: nothing. Yet Evangelical Christians regarded my decision at age seven as the most important decision I would ever make in life. From my perspective, this is insane.

Why is this my perspective? Many Christians believe that once a child reaches the age of "understanding" or "accountability"—the age when the child knows the difference between right and wrong—then the child must be saved from sin. If pressed to explain what "wrong" a child could do or understand at age seven, advocates of early salvation define "wrong" as disobeying one's parents, not sharing a roll of Sweet Tarts with one's brother, or telling a white lie. None of these trivial matters get at the heart of the human condition, however. At best, they're symptoms of a condition, but they are by no means what the New Testament means by *sin*. Nevertheless, this obsession with guilt is taught to children in most Baptist churches.

Confessing to the severity of my own depravity, and feeling duly remorseful for it, I asked Jesus to forgive my horrible, hell-deserving misdeeds, to come into my heart, and to save me from the flames in the pit. Because I did, I was spared eternal damnation.

Following my public profession and salvation, I was baptized. This gave me the needed passport to permanent bliss in the afterlife we called heaven. Because I had resolved the single most important issue of my life, I deserved to miss "the bad place," as we called it—hell. We didn't say the word "hell" because it qualified as a curse word, and using a curse word made us guilty

> "We are each our own devil, and we make this world our hell."
>
> —FROM *THE DUCHESS OF PADUA* BY OSCAR WILDE

of another sort of sin. We grew up in a religious culture preoccupied by strange, shallow, and, frankly, silly beliefs regarding sin.

For example, I remember questioning the idea of hell when I was young. While I knew I was not perfect, I could not imagine that the things I did were so awful that I deserved to burn in hell forever. I could think of a few things some of my best friends did that deserved a week's worth of writhing in flames of torment, but not me. Torment and fire forever? It doesn't make sense, does it?

Recently, my son, Jonathan, who is in his twenties, and I discussed the subject of hell. He said, "Dad, you know this belief in hell as a place of fire is a pretty unbelievable belief, isn't it?"

"What do you mean?" I asked.

I could not have agreed more with the implied answer in his question. Even so, I taught my children to think for themselves. While I'm ready to impart the wisdom I've learned through the years, I don't tell them what they must believe or even how they should live. They're God gifts to me, which means they're not my children at all. They are God's children, and my experience of God has taught me that God makes a good parent. Since God has temporarily gifted me with the opportunity of sharing parental privileges, I did the best I could to love, guide, discipline when necessary, and enjoy these children for a few brief years.

But they're grown now and must choose and follow their own paths. God will find them, just as God found me, and God will guide them to their intended destinies, just as God is guiding me. Of this much I am sure.

Jonathan explained, "I'm talking about the burning in hell forever and ever stuff."

"What about it?"

"Well, don't you think, after so much burning, so much suffering, for an eternity, that you'd finally just give in to the suffering?"

"I suppose, but where are you going with this?"

With insight beyond his years, he said, "When you finally surrender to something, even to pain, your suffering ceases, doesn't it? You know what you always say, 'You only suffer when you resist what is'?"

He paused.

"Keep going," I said.

"Wouldn't your torments in hell become tolerable with time?"

"Continue."

"I just think, eventually, suffering would transmute into acceptance. What would be the point of hell then? Hell would become heaven!"

Wow, I thought, *maybe he should write this book.*

Beyond my profession of faith, not much else seemed to matter about being a Christian. As long as you were a good American, did not fudge on your taxes, kept your wedding vows, went to church regularly, and paid your tithes, you were certain to go to heaven. After all these years, not much has changed in the church where I was raised.

To Baptists, and I suspect this is also true in other Christian communions, it was important to know what you believed. As young Baptists, we attended what was known as Training Union, then Church Training, and later Discipleship Training. The name went through many changes, but the content was basically the same —indoctrination in what Baptists believed. This was important to Baptists. Otherwise, you might get confused about which Christian beliefs were right and end up marrying a Methodist or a Presbyterian or, God forbid, a Roman Catholic. If you ended up marrying a Catholic, you were told to expect chaos and confusion to reign in your household. Furthermore, your children would be

> The greatest tragedy in life is to spend your whole life fishing only to discover that it was not fish you were after.
>
> —OFTEN ATTRIBUTED TO HENRY DAVID THOREAU

disobedient, perhaps even godless. Your household would be divided, and no one would know either the church to attend or the right beliefs to believe.

Purity along racial lines was next to godliness. Godlessness was mixing the races, but it was equally important to Baptists to keep denominational lines pure. Imagine the chagrin felt by believers when you defected from the Baptist faith, dated a person who attended another church, or worse, no church at all. If the date happened to have a different skin color, then such actions might not send you to hell, but you would smell like the place! You would also be the subject of everyone's conversation and, most likely, your name would be added to the church's prayer list.

Speaking of the church's prayer list . . . a prayer list was often the only way the church could sanction gossip without feeling guilty. This was especially true during what Baptists called the Midweek Prayer Service, a small gathering of the devoted followers of God, the church's spiritual elite. If you attended midweek services, you were regarded as among the most devout of Christians. At these services, gossip dressed up as prayer requests was publicly paraded for everyone to hear and savor.

As teenagers, we were constantly drilled on the proper behavior of Christian youth. In no uncertain terms, we were told, "Do not dance, drink, cuss, or chew, and do not run with girls who do." Of course, that is exactly what we did. I always suspected that those who warned us against physical contact with the opposite sex did so because they didn't want us doing what they did as teenagers. The more they exhorted us not to drink, smoke pot, or have sex before marriage, the more intent we became in finding out why. Forbidden fruit is almost always the most desirable and, in this regard, some things will never change.

> Why would you stay in prison, when the door is so wide open?
>
> —RUMI

In terms of career, many sons or daughters of ministers have heard the "Divine call" and followed, as I did, the same career path as their minister parent. In our family, I was the son who got the "call," and quite early, too. I was a teenager at the time, perhaps fourteen or so, and I received this high calling while attending an Arthur Blessitt Crusade in Kentucky's biggest city.

Youth came from everywhere to hear this evangelist named Blessitt. He was an odd but compelling hippie-like preacher who drew considerable media attention by pulling a ten-foot, makeshift cross around the country.

I'm not sure how he did it, but he managed to rig a couple of wheels to a ten-foot crucifix. He then raised it up, laid it across his back, and pulled it along the shoulder of the highways and interstates. I learned later that, in the last three or so decades since, he has not only pulled his cross across the continental United States, but across practically all other continents of the world as well.

Sometimes people ask what it's like to get the "call" to pursue a ministerial career. You can be certain it isn't an audible voice from heaven. For me, my call was the feeling that I was supposed to give my life in service to God. Though it was not the first time I felt this way, the impulse was unmistakable on the night Blessitt spoke.

> When wisdom awakens you, you will see truth wherever you look. Truth is all you'll see.
>
> —AJAHN CHAH

When the service concluded, I rode home with Dad. I reported the experience to him, and my father's response shocked me. He said he knew I had gotten the call in the Blessitt service. Even though we sat in two different places during the emotional performance, when the inner impulse to pursue a sacred career came over me, it came over him, too. I've always thought he told me this so that, if I ever doubted the validity of my call, the fact that he also felt my call would drape it with an aura of authenticity.

It did, but especially when he told me the story of his own call. When he was a teenager, he went with his church to a summer camp for Baptist youth. One evening, he hiked up a mountain, and when he reached the summit he felt the impulse to pursue a ministerial career. When he returned to the cabin later that evening and called home to tell his parents, his mother said she knew about his call already. I've never known what to make of this, but the fact that Dad knew about my call and that his mother knew about his worked its magic in me. I have never doubted that I pursued the right career path for my life.

What I did not know for many years, however, is that our real purpose for showing up on planet earth has little to do with career or calling. Our reason for being here is infinitely more significant than any career choice we might make. As I stated earlier, we are here for one purpose: to know God and walk in the joy of his Presence. When we know this, then it doesn't matter what we do. Our feeling of significance isn't found through service, however noble, but in God-realization. This is not to diminish the importance of our service in the world, but to heighten the importance of our relationship to Source.

> **It's not what we don't know that gets us into trouble, but what we are sure we know.**
>
> —MARK TWAIN

The night Blessitt spoke was one of the rare moments in my life when I actually felt God's presence, but for much of my life, I rarely felt close to God. Most of the time, I felt I couldn't quite make it with him. Something was always missing. The few times I felt close were short lived. The good feeling that accompanied the closeness quickly morphed into a feeling that I was not deserving of God. As a result, I lived with the feeling that something was not quite right about my spiritual life. I seldom felt complete, or whole, or even myself. For the most part, my religious life was a frustration, even a struggle. I think it must be this way for many people of faith, but particularly those who have spent, as I did, the greater part of their lives involved in church. Had it not been for my rare feelings of connectedness to God, I might have given up on my faith entirely.

This went on for many years. But then, one unsuspecting Sunday afternoon a few years ago, everything changed. I cannot explain what happened to me, except by use of metaphor and simile. Easterners would describe my experience as a *satori*—a sudden flash of insight, awareness, or understanding. The late James E. Loder, who

> **Where you are at this moment in your life is precisely the place where you're supposed to be. How could it be otherwise? This is where you are. Only when you resist do you become restless. When you accept what is, there is peace.**
>
> —AUTHOR UNKNOWN

was professor of philosophy and education at Princeton for nearly forty years, would likely have dubbed my experience "a transforming moment." Personally, I have found no word, likeness, or comparison that captures the wonder, mystery, and, in some respects, the absurd manner in which this spiritual encounter took place.

It was as if a door opened and, without any planning or preparation on my part, I stepped through it. As a consequence, I experienced a transformation in my thinking, feeling, and living. I suddenly became acutely aware of who I am and why I'm here. Most importantly, I became conscious of a sacred Presence. Joy and tranquility wrapped around me like a warm blanket on a frigid winter night. The spiritual transformation, or *awakening* as I now describe it, has been a continuous source of comfort ever since. Since that day, nothing about my life has been the same.

It was a Sunday afternoon, and I had not gone to church that day. In fact, I had not gone to church with any consistency for quite some time.

Note

1. Walt Whitman, lines 31–36 from "Song of Myself," first published in *Leaves of Grass* (http://www.bartleby.com/142/14.html).

Chapter 7

Afternoon of My Discontent . . . and then Discovery

"The hour I have long wished for has now come."
—Saint Teresa of Avila (1515–1582)

I reclined on the living room couch, picked up the remote, and began surfing the plethora of television programs, most of which are repetitive and useless. I paused from channel surfing long enough to listen to the opening remarks of a popular psychologist on a PBS special. His name? Wayne W. Dyer. Though I knew of him only vaguely, I remembered he was the author of several bestselling books and one in particular that propelled him to a level of notoriety few authors ever attain. You might recall the book was *Your Erroneous Zones.*[1]

I can remember when it was first released in the late seventies. Though it garnered a lot of press then, I refused to read it. As a young theologian doing graduate work at what was once a highly regarded seminary, I judged Dyer's book, as did many others, as a sleazy book on sex. The title was a dead giveaway. Not until several years later did I realize I misjudged the book entirely. It was not a book about sex at all.

> Life's "Aha!" experiences are flashes of insight that come to us in an instant, without effort . . . what Zen Buddhists would refer to as a sudden insight–a "satori" —what Christians would call a "revelation."
>
> —FROM *JESUS, BUDDHA, KRISHNA AND LAO TZU*, EDITED BY RICHARD HOOPER

The first time I saw the book up close, my family and I were having lunch after church one Sunday in the home of a prominent church member. On her living room coffee table was a copy of Dyer's book. I thought, *Why would our luncheon host read a book about sex? Surely she's more spiritual than that.* The irony is that the actual subject matter of the book is how to overcome some of our more common hang-ups in life—like that of judging people and situations too quickly before knowing all the facts.

On the Sunday afternoon PBS special, Dyer's subject matter seemed benign enough. I decided to give him half a chance. I listened intently for several minutes. Many of the things he said seemed sensible, even applicable to one's life, but that's about all I can say. The funny part is this: now, I can't recall a single thing he said. That's not a critique of his subject matter, but an indication of my readiness for what transpired next. As they say in the east, "When the student's ready, the teacher will appear."

Sometime during the special, an intense peace invaded my consciousness. An unfathomable and profound calmness swept over me like nothing I had felt before. The living room itself took on a kind of surreal sense, too. It was as if I were in the room but not in the room at the same time. What's more, this peace invaded my consciousness. It was sudden, unanticipated, and outright surprising. I had not prayed for peace. I had not searched for some assurance that my life mattered. In fact, I think I had resigned to living with a cynical view of my life as well as the world in general. Instantly, though, the awareness of peace and

O night, that guided me!
O night, sweeter than sunrise!
O night, that joined lover
with Beloved!
Lover transformed in
Beloved!

I lost myself. Forgot myself.
I lay my face against the
Beloved's face.
Everything fell away and I
left myself behind,
Abandoning my cares
Among the lilies, forgotten.

—FROM "SONGS OF THE SOUL" BY SAINT JOHN OF THE CROSS, TRANSLATED BY MIRABAI STARR purpose filled my consciousness. Nothing seemed negative, accidental, or wrong with either me or the world.

I have said I felt joy most profoundly, but maybe I felt gratitude or a blend of the two. It's hard to explain. I know it was not the laughter kind of joy, the kind you have after somebody tells you a funny joke or after drinking too much. It was simply extreme joy and appreciation, not for anything in particular but for everything in general. I don't know how else to express it.

With the joy and peace came an inexplicable awareness of Life itself. This part is most difficult to explain. Whatever I say only seems to diminish the profundity of the experience. The few times I have tried to describe to others what happened to me, I get the feeling people are looking at me as if I'm Rod Sterling on a return trip from *The Twilight Zone.*

But here goes, anyway.

It lasted only a minute or two, perhaps a little longer. No matter how long it lasted, however, it was as if I entered a no-time zone, a kind of time warp or something. I became immediately aware of two dimensions of reality, the world I could see and the world I could not see. I was aware of the room around me and the objects in the room, but I was also aware of another dimension, a kind of emptiness. I became aware of nothing. There were no objects in this awareness, but it felt to me just as real, maybe more so, than the material dimension or the room around me with walls and furniture and so forth.

Call it a glimpse of the spiritual world, if you will, but I honestly don't know what to call it. I simply became aware, not only of the objects I could see around me, but of the emptiness out of which those objects appeared. In that awareness, I felt what I've already described—intense joy, peace, love, security. Even more significant, I felt Presence in this emptiness.

Have you ever looked into the heavens on a clear night and tried counting the stars or identifying the constellations? It is one of my favorite pastimes. Ever since my transformation, I have found myself more attracted, even connected, to the nothingness that is our heavens. That infinite vastness of space without which no objects would appear. For years, for example, I often looked into the heavens, but all I ever saw was the stuff scattered throughout the heavens—the stars, the planets, the constellations. Certainly, it was an amazing sight. As awesome as it was and still is, though, it pales in comparison to what I now see. Since my transformation, whenever I look into the heavens, I see an infinity of Emptiness, Nothingness, or, as one

could call it, Stillness. It's as if, on that Sunday afternoon, I received the gift of seeing *everything in nothing*.

The psalmist said, "The heavens declare the glory of God" (Ps 19:1). With all due respect to the psalmist, I think the heavens declare very little about God. You cannot look into the heavens and see God; otherwise, every disbeliever in Divine Intelligence would change his or her views. In fact, the opposite is often the case. Those who seriously study the universe often become atheists or agnostics. A recent report of the Pew Research Center for the People and the Press, in collaboration with the American Association for the Advancement of Science, showed that only a third of today's scientists believe in God.[2]

> "It no longer matters to me what others think about me; but it matters a great deal what I think about me."
>
> (ADAPTED FROM THEODORE ROOSEVELT)

Furthermore, if the heavens actually declared God's glory, then everyone who believes in God would actually know God and be conscious of the Divine Presence. However, as it was with me, most believing people who say they believe in God rarely feel connected or close to God. On this day, I made a remarkable discovery: only when I could see seeing Nothing did Everything seem to emerge.

This is why I find it bizarre whenever a person attempts to prove, or disprove, God exists. For a Christian apologist to argue for God's existence is to mask a secret fear that God does not. For an atheist to argue against God's existence is to mask a secret fear that God might. In either case, they argue for or against what neither knows. The apologist defends what he does not know; the atheist decries what he refuses to know.

Here is the real truth: only after looking into the heavens and seeing Nothing (or No-Thing) was I able to see Everything (who is God). It is only after looking into the eyes of somebody whom the world says is a nobody that you see and know the Everybody in all living things. It is only after sitting in a room surrounded by walls and furniture, carpet and curtains—objects in awareness—and simultaneously being aware of the space around them that the empty space itself becomes the Eternal Source to you.

Buddhists would call my experience a *satori*. If that's what this was, then maybe I haven't lost my mind. Even if I have, I'll take this insanity any day over the kind I lived with for nearly three decades. This has been, and continues to be, infinitely more wonderful than anything I knew before. I woke up to Life and have remained awake ever since. This is why the word *awakening* comes closer than any other in capturing the essence of what happened to me. It was a sacred experience, an unexpected instant of profound insight and awareness, and more hallowed than any moment I knew in church.

Yet, the whole thing is a bit comical, too. Right after it happened, for example, the first thought I had was, *How will I tell anybody about this?* I wanted to tell someone. It was too splendid to keep to myself. Yet, it was also too ordinary in the way it transpired. *Why couldn't it have been more spectacular?* I thought.

> "The word enlightenment conjures up the idea of some superhuman accomplishment . . . but it is simply your natural state of felt oneness with Being."
>
> —ECKHART TOLLE

Most of the great religious leaders, divine avatars, spiritual masters, and teachers had their *satori* in the midst of a great crisis of suffering or during some horrific tragedy or drama. Take Saint Paul, for example. His *satori* came with blinding lights and strange voices on his way to Damascus, where he had planned to make more trouble for early followers of Christ (Acts 9:3ff.).

During the Hindu-Muslim conflict in Calcutta, India, in 1946, which brought unprecedented bloodshed, starvation, and death, Mother Teresa had her "call within the call," as she later described it. That moment of intense suffering transformed not only her life but its direction and its focus. The rest of her story is a remarkable history of unprecedented compassion.

In his quest to find the meaning of life and freedom from suffering, The Buddha himself left his royal life and became a mendicant. For years, he lived on the edge of society, nearly starving on several occasions as he fed off the scraps of kindness people tossed his way. Only after six rigorous years as an ascetic did he finally attain Enlightenment.

And who doesn't know the story of Jesus' own wilderness struggles for forty days and forty nights (Matt 4:1-11)?

Against this backdrop of dramatic spiritual awakenings, I sat on a living room couch, holding a remote in one hand and a drink in the other, and fell half asleep during a PBS special on television. It was hardly a hallowed setting for a holy *satori*! I saw no bright lights. The earth beneath me did not shake. I heard no strange or loud voices. Instead, a quiet stillness slipped into the room. As I noticed it, I woke up. In an instant, I was more aware of my surroundings than ever before. The space or emptiness within the room grew just as alive to me as the objects in it. Out of that space of awareness, I sensed a Presence nearer than the air itself. In fact, it was as if, when I breathed, I absorbed the very Emptiness that surrounded me.

I admit it was strange, but it's even stranger to try to explain it to someone else. In that moment, I knew that, no matter what happened in this world or what happened to me, everything would be okay. My life, my family, and indeed everything in this world were as they were supposed to be. Nothing was missing, and everything would be provided at the right time. Since then, this knowledge has fluctuated with intensity, but it has remained with me.

This was a new way of thinking because, for much of my life, I had felt as if nothing was right in the world and that nothing was right about my life. I had not only made many mistakes, but sometimes I felt as if I *was* the mistake. As far as the world goes, I thought it was capricious and unfair and that there was little anybody could do to change it.

Whatever happened to me, I knew life from that day onward would be wonderful to me. I sensed a shift in my mind, and I knew I would no longer look at or think about anything in the same way as before. That is perhaps the most remarkable long-term change I've noticed.

The cynicism left me, too. I was done with negativity. I had no idea how I would stop being that way, but even that didn't concern me. I knew the changes would come naturally and at the right time. It was, indeed, a profound spiritual awakening. The consequences have been bewildering but beautiful.

In one sense, the changes were instantaneous. In another way, the awakening initiated a process of change that continues to this day. Maybe what I experienced was the thing I had told others about for decades but only vaguely understood myself. I don't know, and, frankly, I don't care. Whatever it was, it must be what Saint Paul described as "the renewal of the mind" (Rom 12:1-12). Like scores of other people, maybe you, too, I had been a Christian, a believer, for years. Apart from churchgoing and trying to be a decent person and, later, a good church leader, I cannot say my thinking or living was any more fulfilling or any different from that of unbelieving people.

As my thinking about everything began changing, however, I started to notice a shift in my feelings, too. Almost all the time now, I am at peace. I feel contentment, self-acceptance, and self-assurance. Joy and happiness supplement these feelings. I knew these qualities of the human experience before, but only briefly. Now, however, joy is my normal state of consciousness.

I realize how remarkable, perhaps even unbelievable, this sounds. It *is*. But it does not mean my world has become an enchanted fairytale. Nor does it mean I have achieved a level of spiritual awareness that puts me in the ranks of other spiritual avatars in history. I use words like "awakening," "enlightenment," "redemption," and so on, but only because they offer a way to describe some little aspect of

> " I have lived on the lip of insanity, wanting to know reasons, knocking on a door. It opens.
> I've been knocking from the inside! "
>
> —RUMI

my otherworldly experience. For me, it's not unlike a gemologist attempting to describe to a blind person the clarity, cut, colors, hues, and tones she might see while observing a multi-faceted diamond. No one word can say it all, but they all express something of the inexpressible Mystery.

Reflections on the Spiritual Awakening

After reflecting on my transformation, I came to several conclusions.

First, whoever you are and whatever the circumstances of your life, nothing about your life is a mistake. You were not born into the wrong family or raised in the wrong religious tradition. Nor are you the screw-up you may sometimes think you are. Instead, you are exactly who you're supposed to be and where you're supposed to be. What sometimes seems as a random, disconnected amalgamation of life experiences is actually the mysterious manifestation of your destiny. No matter how you're inclined to label some of the things that happen—good, bad, benign, toxic—all of them work in concert with each other to create the symphony that is your life. Each experience interacts in some inexplicable fashion to bring you to a place of God-realization—to your own awakened state of grace.

You don't have to be religious to know God or believe as Catholics or Protestants believe or even become a Tibetan lama. An old Hasidic saying goes, "God has no synagogue but the soul." No religion holds title deed to God. Some religions may be a bit more advanced in their understanding of this Transcendent Reality, but knowing this Reality is not predicated upon subscribing to the "correct" belief system. The moment any religion assumes it alone knows God, you can be sure that religion knows nothing of God.

Furthermore, no religious belief magically unlocks the door to God. I advise that we remember this: *the impulse we feel to know God* is *God.* Having said that, I would advise that we not get too attached even to the impulse because God is even more

> "Grace comes to those who stop struggling. When it really sinks in that there's nothing you can do to find God, he suddenly appears. That's the deepest mystery."
>
> —FROM *WHY IS GOD LAUGHING?* BY DEEPAK CHOPRA

than any impulse we feel. I realize it sounds like I speak from both sides of the mouth, and I suppose I do. It's a great paradox, but I know of no other way to put it.

Start with the impulse because that's closer to the truth of who God is than anything else. When you give attention to your impulse, it will grow and expand. There is nothing more you need to do in order to know God. The Eternal is not a reward you get for completing a course of religious instruction. If you follow your inner longing to know the living God, you *will* become conscious of God. Try it and see what happens.

Albert Einstein is often quoted as having said, "I want to know God's thoughts; the rest are mere details." I often wonder whether Einstein recognized the significance of his words. The desire to know the mind of God is the desire to know God. There is no need to make a problem of this, yet most religions do. God wants to be known. Why would he make it difficult? Religion often complicates knowing God, saddling it with beliefs and steps and requirements. The prophet Jeremiah put it this way: "I [God] will put my law within them—write it on their hearts . . . they'll know me firsthand" (Jer 31:33-34). It doesn't get much simpler than that.

Everything else, no matter how significant it may be to your religious leaders or your religious tradition, is little more than detail. Further, no detail about God could ever substitute for knowing God. Even those who cling to their details, doctrines, and beliefs eventually may come to the point when they need more; indeed, they want more than this.

The prophet Isaiah said, "Seek the Lord while he may be found . . ." (Isa 55:6, KJV). On the surface, that sounds like good advice to give a spiritual seeker. Upon closer examination, though, it's not such wise counsel. Seeking God implies effort, even struggle, and neither is necessary in God's kingdom.

It is true that Jesus said, "Ask, and it shall be given you; seek, and ye shall find; knock, and it shall be opened unto you" (Matt 7:7, KJV). Christians have greatly misunderstood these words. Even devoted followers of the Christian path assume Jesus meant we are to ask, seek, and knock, and continue doing so, as if there's a Divine resistance that only our persistence can overcome.

To the contrary, however, God desires that you know him, which is precisely why you feel the inner impulse to pursue him. Again, start with the inner impulse. You have found the mystery of Grace already. St. Francis of Assisi put this most profoundly when he said, "What you are looking *for* is what *is* looking!" Jesus provides his own clarification, too:

> Don't bargain with God. Be direct. . . . This isn't a cat-and-mouse, hide-and-seek game we're in. If your child asks for bread, do you trick him with sawdust? If he asks for fish, do you scare him with a live snake on his plate? . . . You wouldn't think of such a thing. You're at least decent to your own children. So don't you think that God who conceived you in love will be even better? (Matt 7:7-11)

A line in *A Course in Miracles* goes, "When we are ready, God will take the final step in our return to him."[3] When you ask, seek, and knock, it is not to overcome God's resistance. You ask to know God, and keep asking, and you seek to know God, and keep seeking only because, as you do, the result is an ever-expanding awareness of this Presence you know already. That is to say, the asking, seeking, and knocking are the spiritual practices necessary for the God-realized life.

You can make knowing God a struggle. Most religions, including Christianity, have succeeded in doing this, but it actually takes no effort to know God. Yet, if you ask almost any religious person about his or her Christian experience, they will say things like, "I'm trying to be a good

Christian." This is role-playing. It is unnecessary. There is no checklist of actions that, if you do them, define you as "Christian" or reward you with a sense of God's presence.

Being Christian is simply recognizing and responding to the inclination you feel to know God. Everything else is inconsequential. If you step toward what you feel, you will discover that what you feel is the God you wish to know. Add anything else, and it becomes a religion and not a relationship. Responding to the inclination brings you face to face with Inspiration. To be inspired is to be "in-Spirit," a word made up of two others, the prefix *in* and the root word *spirare* meaning "to breathe." Hence, to know God is as simple, indeed as natural, as "breathing in." Whether you are conscious of it or not, with every inhalation, you literally breathe in the presence of God. Know this and celebrate.

This is the Mystery that is God and the miracle of God's grace: *the desire you feel to know God can only mean a spiritual awakening has occurred in you already*! I love the simple but stunning way Lama Surya Das puts it. Perhaps the most highly skilled Western lama in the Tibetan tradition of Buddhism, he says, "The finding of God is inseparable from the longing for God."[4] Saint Paul put it like this: "Saving is all his idea, and all his work. All we do is trust him enough to let him do it. It's God's gift from start to finish! We don't play a major role. If we did, we'd probably go around bragging that we'd done the whole thing! No, we neither make nor save ourselves. God does both the making and the saving" (Eph 2:8-10).

Recently, I drove by one of the many churches near our home in Louisville. I pay regular attention to church marquees and the messages of faith churches and parishes share with the community. On this day, the marquee carried a message about the minister's upcoming Sunday sermon, titled "How to Find God."

My first thought was, "Is God lost?" Before my awakening, I felt far enough from God that he might just as well have been lost. Consequently, I did what virtually every other seeker of a spiritual life does. I looked for God. I looked for God at church, in my identity as a "Christian," and even in my professional role as a minister. I can remember thinking, if I pursue a ministerial career, I will not only please everyone, but I will find and feel close to God.

I did not realize that no profession I could enter, no role I could assume would ever reward me with the feeling of God's presence. The desire to find God *is* God; the looking for him *is* the seeing of him. God is the inexplicable reality that can only be recognized and celebrated, but never analyzed and explained. Although it took me half a life, I finally got it. When I woke up, I understood for the first time what Catholic mystic Meister Eckhart meant when he said, "The eye through which I see God is the same eye through which God sees me."

How could something so remarkable be an effort or a struggle? To know God is as natural as breathing, as simple as opening your eyes at dawn. This is what it means to awaken to Presence.

Hidden Treasure and the Meaning of Grace

Jesus likened the awakened state of Presence to a man who accidentally discovers a hidden treasure in a field. He said, "God's kingdom is like a treasure hidden in a field for years and then accidentally found by a trespasser. The finder is ecstatic—what a find!—and proceeds to sell everything he owns to raise money and buy that field" (Matt 13:44).

Notice that this man *stumbled* upon the treasure. That is to say, he was not looking for it. Instead, he was apparently simply walking across an available piece of real estate, not because he was interested in buying it, but because it served as a shortcut to some other destination. He was clearly looking for something other than what he found. But he was willing to give up everything else to keep what he found. In this respect, he is symbolic of every human being who suddenly and unexpectedly wakes up to the reality of God, the ineffable and invaluable Treasure.

What happened to this representative person is what can happen to you, if it has not happened already. God awakens within you, or, to put it more accurately, you wake up to the abiding presence of God. In that instant, you realize you have made a discovery of infinite worth. As you make it, an awareness comes with it that, though you did nothing to get it, you have everything to gain from it. In the New Testament, this treasure is understood as grace. As such, it is both a gift and a treasure—a gift you did nothing to get and a treasure you'll give everything to keep.

> Grace shines like a sliver of light. It penetrates the universe . . . At any moment someone may be touched by its mysterious power.
>
> —FROM *WHY IS GOD LAUGHING?* BY DEEPAK CHOPRA

Recently, I was paying for a tank of gas when the attendant advised me, "You should buy a lottery ticket!"

"Oh yeah?" I responded. "Why should I?"

"Prize is worth $270 million!" he said, though he never looked up from the cash register.

A few seconds of silence passed as he counted out my change. Then, he offered additional unsolicited advice. "Fella, nobody ever won the lottery without buying a ticket!"

"You're right," I said. But then I thought, *You're also wrong.*

As far as state lotteries go, he was right that you must buy a ticket to win. But when it comes to God's grace, it's an entirely different transaction.

Had Jesus been in line behind me and overheard our brief exchange, he might have said to the attendant, "Sir, what if someone tossed a lottery ticket into your trash bin beside Pump #5? Later in the day, you observe a homeless, hungry man rummaging through the bin looking for something to eat when, suddenly, he discovers the discarded ticket. You think little of it until he enters the store and asks you to scan the ticket to see if he holds the winning numbers. You feel inclined to tell him to go away, since you've got paying customers to see and no time to waste on a losing and discarded ticket, but, being the kind attendant you are, you take it from him and scan it anyway. Can you imagine your chagrin and the homeless man's ecstasy when the two of you discover the crumpled and discarded ticket bears the winning numbers to a $270 million prize?"

> **"Those who dwell . . . among the beauties and mysteries of the earth are never alone or weary of life."**
>
> —FROM *THE SENSE OF WONDER* BY RACHEL CARSON

That's grace. It occurs when you least expect it and, sometimes, even to those you've judged as least deserving.

There's something else. Imagine Jesus adding another detail to his story: "There's more, Mr. Attendant. After getting over your initial shock, you prepare to speak up and object to the homeless man's unimaginable discovery—because, after all, you know he really didn't buy the ticket. He found it in the garbage heap—*your* garbage heap at that. So you're thinking it really belongs to you. Just as you're about to voice your opinion, the homeless man looks at you and says, "You know, there's such a thing as 'Finders Keepers,' but, I was just thinking, since I found this ticket in your trash bin and didn't really buy it, what would you think if I shared half the winnings with you personally?"

Surprise! Grace again.

Finding God's kingdom, as Jesus called it here, and elsewhere the kingdom of heaven, is like stumbling upon a buried treasure. God appears sometimes even to those who are unaware they've looked for him. In other words, when you make this discovery, it's like waking up in a new world. It's as if, until that moment, your life has been only a dream, even a nightmare at times. Then you wake up and realize you're in the kingdom of heaven already. From that moment on, the world around you is alive with God's presence. Sometimes that Presence is in the foreground of your consciousness; at other times it lies in the background. But never again do you feel detached from God, or that God is disinterested or displeased with you. No longer is God the good but fading feeling you knew him to be throughout most of your life.

Remember the following two points: First, until the spiritual awakening occurs in you, there isn't much you can do to awaken yourself. You can only prepare yourself, as a gardener might prepare soil for spring planting. In part 3 of this book, I describe the spiritual practice that may help you wake up. Even so, I do not mean to imply that Divine grace awaits human preparation. Spiritual preparation is helpful, but God's grace is like a hydroponic plant. It needs no soil whatsoever in which to germinate, take root, and flower into Life.

> "I tell many lies but am always believed
> If the worst happens, I'll be greatly pleased
> On the day you were born I poisoned your heart
> I'll still be there on the day you depart.
> Who am I? FEAR"
>
> —FROM *WHY IS GOD LAUGHING?* BY DEEPAK CHOPRA

Second, a spiritual awakening may occur anywhere, anytime. You don't have to be in a church, temple, or mosque. Although it may occur in a sacred space, once you awaken, every place will become sacred to you. Since God is everywhere and in everyone, where could you be that God is not? Whom could you meet who is not the embodiment of God? Hafiz, the Sufi poet, put it this way: "Everyone is God speaking, so be polite and listen to him!" I would add, "Every-*thing* is God speaking, so be still and observe him!"

I have long suspected that the real reason people go to a church, synagogue, temple, and so forth is not because they are looking for God, although this is what church leaders often mistakenly think. Instead, many go to church precisely because they have found God already. They simply don't know they have. Others think there's something they must believe or do first in order to know the nearness of God in their lives.

None of this is necessary. Rumi once described spiritual seekers as persons who "look for the sun while holding a candle." It is a mistake to believe that the Eternal Flame burns somewhere other than within you. Jesus said, "You are the light of the world" (Matt 5:14). He did not say, "One day you'll become the light of the world," or, "After you've been initiated, walked the church aisle, been baptized or confirmed, and so forth, you'll finally become light in a dark world." Various religions have added these requirements, and as important as they are to each religious tradition, none of them is necessary for knowing God. Saint Paul said, "You are the temple of God, and God himself is present in you" (1 Cor 3:16). What more should we add to this? Equally important, why would you continue to look for the One who has found you already?

> "What if you slept? And what if, in your sleep, you dreamed? And what if, in your dream, you went to heaven and there plucked a strange and beautiful flower? And what if, when you awoke, you held the flower in your hand?"
>
> —AUTHOR UNKNOWN

Life: Less than Satisfying for Most

While I do not know what it is like in other religions—although I suspect it's not so different from my own—I know that in Christianity, many people rarely live with a consciousness of God's presence in their daily lives apart from an occasional feeling of spiritual inspiration.

If they knew their honesty would not invoke the shock and disapproval of others, many would confess that their religious lives are anything but satisfying. Although some of them regularly attend worship and try to do what they're told will please God, they seldom feel as if God is pleased. Furthermore, their spiritual lives are little more than a collection of beliefs they're told to accept without debate and believe without questioning. Instead of living a joyful life, however, they feel incarcerated, as if they were suffocating spiritually.

They know little peace or serenity. Virtually everything frightens them—their enemies, terrorists, the economy, their jobs (or lack of jobs), their health, their aging bodies and diminishing minds, even dying and death. These realities are too terrifying for them to think about. As for "thinking," their minds never cease to bombard them with thoughts about a past they wish they could forget or a future they cannot fathom. Further, they live burdened by guilt and shame for what they've done or failed to do.

> "We are not human beings having a spiritual experience. We are spiritual beings having a human experience."
>
> —PIERRE TEILHARD DE CHARDIN

When they try to picture the future, they become preoccupied with it—what might happen or how history will come to a close. They do not realize that their preoccupation with future arises from a fundamental fear of it. Their obsession with prophecies only serves to mask this fear. With elaborate charts of future events and God-talk about the culmination of human history, they sound full of great faith. Truthfully, they're only full of great fear.

Were these people aware of God's presence, they would have no fear of the future. Neither would they live with guilt and regret over the past. In fact, they would have little interest in either the past or the future. The past is done and the future does not exist. Jesus said, "Give your entire attention to what God is doing *right now*, and don't get worked up about what may or may not happen tomorrow" (Matt 6:34). Words do not get much clearer than this.

These people have no clue as to the point of their human existence. Were it not for their network of social connections at church, an occasional religious high, and the good opinion of their friends, they would give up on the church altogether. Many have already. Others are following. What they get from their religion is often problematic instead of helpful.

As for me, I was regarded as a devout and religious individual, a professional minister. However, I cannot say my life was much different from people who have no religious affiliation. In fact, at times I wondered whether people with no faith were freer and happier, as well as

> "Wherever I climb I am followed by a dog named "Ego."
>
> —FRIEDRICH NIETZSCHE

emotionally and spiritually healthier than I was. When I looked more closely, I discovered to my chagrin that many of them were.

My awakening brought this insanity to an end. The storms of doubt, confusion, and loneliness calmed. My life became precious to me and has remained so ever since. The fact that this radical transformation occurred outside a house of worship and without the benefit of a sermon or a "Sinner's Prayer" is likely more than many religious leaders can accept. This is due largely to their misguided belief that we can know God in only one way, which is always, of course, *their* way. What has happened to me, however, is too amazing to ignore and too wonderful to deny. I liken it to a homeless man rummaging through a trash bin in search of scraps to eat when, suddenly, his eyes are opened. He looks around with astonishment and finds a banquet table spread before him, filled with every delicious delight imaginable. Best of all, his host and dinner companion is none other than God.

Notes

1. Wayne W. Dyer, *Your Erroneous Zones* (New York: Funk & Wagnalls, 1976).

2. *Scientific Achievements Less Prominent than Decade Ago: Public Praises Science; Scientists Fault Public/Media*, survey, Pew Research Center for the People and the Pew in collaboration with the American Association for the Advancement of Science, commentary by Dr. Alan I. Leshner, CEO. For more information or a copy of the report, contact Andrew Kohut, Director, and Scott Keeter, Director of Survey Research, at 202-419-4350, or visit http:///www.people-press.org/reports/pdf/528.pdf.

3. Helen Schucman and William Thetford, *A Course in Miracles* (Mill Valley CA: Foundation for Inner Peace, 2007) xiii.

4. Lama Surya Das, *The Big Questions: How to Find Your Own Answers to Life's Essential Questions* (New York: Rodale, 2007) 84.

Chapter 8

Ego: The Culprit in Human Unhappiness

"Why is everyone unhappy?"
—Jean Jacques Rousseau (1712–1778)

Why are so many religious people discontent with life, often dysfunctional, and disconnected from Source itself? Why are people asleep to the presence of God in them, in others, and in the world? Or, to borrow the simple but searching question of Jean Jacques Rousseau, whose writings influenced the French Revolution, "Why is everyone so unhappy?"

> Ego, our "precious little selves."
>
> —IMMANUEL KANT

The answer to any of these questions is a three-letter word: *ego*.

Ego is the culprit of human unhappiness. It is the part of the human self that went south with Adam's sin in the Garden of Eden. The human condition—that is, the ego—is the one thing everyone shares in common. However, many people do not seem to know that ego causes the discontent they feel and the dysfunctional way they treat themselves, others, and the planet. Furthermore, the ego interferes with what would otherwise be a natural intimacy with God.

What Is the Ego, Anyway?

Ego is your make-believe self—your "social self," as Martha Beck calls it.[1] It is the cover you wear that you often confuse for your real self. Your real self is the inner person behind your social mask. It took me half a lifetime to figure out this simple and understandable truth. A phrase I once read may help: "I see you seeing me; I see the me I think you see." The "me" you think others see is your social mask, the mental image of the self you portray to the world.

Much like someone might carry in a wallet, this is the snapshot of yourself you carry around in your head.

This snapshot of you, this ego, attaches itself to many things. One is your physical body, which partly explains the preoccupation with the body and the anxiety virtually everyone feels about his or her appearance. But the physical "you," just like the social "you," is really not who you are, either. You are not your body. You are infinitely more than this. You are the person behind both your face and your form or your mask and your material frame. Of all the things I've learned through life, this may rank as one of the most important. I imagine it will be so for you, too.

Your ego can also be an idea you fashion in your mind about yourself— a function or role you perform. It is the fictitious, mind-made, "little me," as Eckhart Tolle caricatured it.[2] Ego is any identity you pick up that gives definition as to who you are or, more accurately, who you *think* you are. But no role is you, any more than the character an actor assumes on a stage is the actor himself or herself. It is a role, a function, but that's all.

Ego is your face, form, and function. The *real* you is none of these. You are not the social face you wear, the form or body in which you temporarily live, or the function or role you perform in the world. These are all part of the ego.

Ego: Your Illusory Self

Ego is illusory in nature, shaped by your upbringing, decisions, and *karmic* experiences. *Karma* is a Sanskrit word that, in Eastern traditions, refers to the Law of Cause and Effect. In the Christian tradition, as I mentioned earlier, it's known as the Law of Sowing and Reaping or Planting and Harvesting (Gal 6:7).

> "The ego's fundamental wish is to replace God."
>
> —FROM *A COURSE IN MIRACLES*

In the Western world, this spiritual law gets expressed in a variety of idiomatic ways. Sometimes, for example, you will hear people say, "You reap what you sow!" or "What goes around comes around!" This is another way of describing karma.

Karma, says Lama Surya Das, "reveals all things as interdependent; every action has a reaction, and nothing exists in absolute isolation."[3] In reference to the ego, therefore, your karmic experiences give shape to your self-image. That is to say, all your life experiences contributed in scripting the narrative of your life, your life story. It is important to remember that, just as the ego is not you, the story the ego tells about you is not you either. Both may reveal you, but they are not you.

When you look at yourself in a mirror, for instance, the image you see is not you. It is a mirror image of you. Even then, you look only at your physical form, the body. It would be a mistake to confuse the form staring back at you as the real you. Yet, most everyone makes this fundamental error. We think we are the image we see, but the "you" you see is not the "you" you are. At best, it is what Albert Einstein called "an optical illusion of consciousness."

The real "you" is much deeper and far more significant than your body or any name, role, function, or story you tell about yourself. The deeper "you" comes from God. The Scriptures of the Old and New Testaments know this sacred self as the "soul," or "spirit." In the Book of Genesis, it is called the *breath of life*, or God's own essence within you. "God formed Man out of dirt from the ground and blew into his nostrils the breath of life. The Man came alive—a living soul" (Gen 2:7).

This breath of God, which was behind and beyond Adam's name, form, roles, or functions, is the real Adam. Of course, it is the same Divine breath, or life essence, that is the soul within you and me. This is who we truly are. As the Christian philosopher Pierre Teilhard de Chardin put it, "We are not human beings having a spiritual experience; we are spiritual beings having a human experience."

From the moment of your birth, you are a magnificent, living soul—a distinct creation of God. At the time of your birth, you have no ego, although you are born with the capacity to develop one. Normally, ego begins to take shape at about age two, which is why this period in a child's development is often known as the "Terrible Twos." As the ego develops, this self—or "little me"—starts seeing itself as separate from that which surrounds it. Every parent learns that the ego can be a little monster as it claims sovereignty.

Until ego develops, however, a newborn embodies God most fully, which is why, when you look into the eyes of an infant, you feel you may be observing the Sacred Presence itself. That's because, in a sense, you are. The state of oneness with God is the natural state of every child. Protestants call this the state of "innocence." It is the period of life prior to the emergence of the self, the ego.

The ego also steals away the state of innocence. Ego has one aim—to Edge God Out.[4] When God is edged out, so are joy and perfection, innocence and selflessness, and unity and oneness with God. What remains is an increasingly dysfunctional, disconnected, and problematic ego-self—a self that feels disconnected from the Source from which it emerged.

Ego: Your Temporal Self

The ego and its many identities, attachments, roles, and stories are not only illusory, but they are temporary. That is to say, no self-definition, self-identity, ego attachment, or social role will last indefinitely. Since everything in our material realm changes, the ego and any of its attachments, roles, or story-making will change, too, and ultimately disappear.

The real *you* is eternal, however. Eventually, everything but *you* will disappear. In other words, everything associated with the ego will die, including your form, but *you* will not die. There is no death to the essential self—the eternal *you* behind and beyond all that is transitory. How could your soul, your essence, ever die? That same essence is God. It is part and parcel to what is Eternal, the Unseen within all that is seen. While it is true that your form, the body, will one day breathe its last, the breath of God that is *you* will never expire.

You can observe the temporal nature of ego throughout your life. For example, your self-image as a child is not the same image you had as an adolescent. It changed as the former capitulated to the latter. It happened again when you became a young adult, a median adult, and so forth. Saint Paul expressed it this way: "When I was a child, I spake as a child . . . but when I became a man, I put away childish things" (1 Cor 13:1, KJV).

When I was young, I wanted to be Spartacus. In my mind, I pictured the folk hero as actor Kirk Douglas. He played Spartacus in Stanley Kubrick's Hollywood film by the same title. Boomers who saw the 1960 film will recall how athletic Douglas appeared in that film. If you could see me and my abs today—which, thankfully, you cannot—you'd see a caloric-induced abdomen no gladiator would have. They had near-perfect six-packs. My abs look more like six stuffed fanny packs with side pockets.

> "Sin in the sight of the Holy Spirit is a mistake to be corrected, not an evil to be punished."
>
> —FROM *A COURSE IN MIRACLES*

As a teenager, I laid down the sword and decided I wanted to be a disc jockey. Almost daily, I prayed to God to give me a rich baritone voice. In radio, it's all about the voice. Every week, I listened to Kasey Kasem and Wolfman Jack and longed for the day when I'd sound just like them. On many days, I took the bus downtown after school to the local radio station. I'd sit outside the studio and watch with envy and admiration as the jocks performed in the small room on the other side of the soundproof window. In time, I became friends with them so that, whenever I showed up, they waved me into the studio.

One day, the station manager offered me a Sunday morning job. I was surprised, given I was only fourteen years old. My parents were no less surprised when the station manager called to request their permission. I was the youngest disc jockey ever hired at the station. I remember wondering if they offered me the Sunday morning job because seasoned jocks with baritone voices wanted to sleep in after partying late on Saturday night.

With the permission of my parents, the station manager hired me. My dream had come true. I was a disc jockey. I'm certain the manager felt this was a win-win for everyone. He knew I was eager to be a jock, so he could trust that I would be a dependable employee. He also knew puberty was just around the corner. Had this been a choir, he knew that soon I would move from the soprano section to that of the bass. But, as with every role the ego plays, my career as a disc jockey was short-lived. It wasn't long before my voice changed. Instead of deepening, it went up two octaves. Almost as quickly as my voice changed, my employment was terminated. They said it was a change in the Sunday morning format, but I didn't hear any changes. I knew what it was: I had been fired. I went on to major in broadcasting and communications in college, although to this day, I still don't know why. The gig as a disc jockey was a performance, and, like all routines, the curtain eventually dropped.

There is a sense in which the ego is constantly dying and resurrecting in you, creating and re-creating itself. Over the course of a human life, it will do so multiple times, and none will last indefinitely. Anything associated with ego is transitory, subject to birth and death, appearance and disappearance. In other words, the ego is here today, gone tomorrow. But *you* are eternal.

Ego and Sin—The Same though Trivialized by Religion

The ego is dysfunctional, too. When correctly understood—and I say this because it rarely is—the biblical view of sin is contiguous to the ego. In other words, the way I use the word *ego* in this book is not dissimilar to the way the New Testament uses the word *sin*. Sin *is* the dysfunctional ego.

The word *sin* means "to miss the mark." It is a picture word, as many words are. The word picture here is that of an archer shooting an arrow but missing the bull's-eye. It is, therefore, a descriptive word that pictures the shared human condition. We all fail to reach our full potential. Saint Paul wrote, "For all have sinned and come short of the glory of God" (Rom 3:23, KJV). Why?

At the time of your birth, you appear in this world in perfect union with God. As ego emerges, however, and manifests itself, God is slowly edged out. The consequence is that you are left feeling separated from yourself, alone and cut off from others, and bereft of God. This is not something for which you should be punished, as many religions mistakenly believe. You did not choose this. It is your shared destiny by virtue of your participation in the human condition.

This deeply felt sense of disconnectedness gives way to fear, anxiety, self-obsession, self-centeredness, confusion, doubt, and so on. The list of dysfunctional consequences is virtually endless. Each person is left with what theologian Paul Tillich called "existential anxiety" and what Viktor Frankl, Jewish survivor of the Holocaust, called in his monumental work *Man's Search for Meaning*, the "trauma of non-being."

Sin actually means "to miss who you are"—who you *really* are. It is to be lost in the illusion that you are your ego. Regrettably, most people go through their entire lives and never realize this. They believe they are an illusory and temporary phantom. This is also why people experience life as an uphill battle. It is a journey beset with frustration and disappointment, with some successes but mostly failures. There is anxiety and fear or, to use the metaphor for *sin*, many missed bull's-eyes. The difference is only in degree and frequency. In all this, however, it is important to remember that these are mere symptoms of a condition shared equally by all.

Churches and church leaders often trivialize the meaning of sin. Instead of helping people understand that *sin* and *ego* point to the dysfunctional nature of the human condition, they typically associate sin with behaviors that are at best symptoms of the condition. Furthermore, there is no widespread agreement between Christian churches as to what behaviors are evil or how evil those behaviors are. The church's own cultural conditioning and provincial bias determine that.

For example, beyond such evils as murder, violence, killing, and stealing—wrongs that every sane person instinctively knows humanity can neither sustain nor tolerate—there is little agreement among Christians, or religious people in any tradition, as to which behaviors should be classified as sinful and which ones should not. Consequently, Christians and their leaders spend about half their time defining what's sinful and not sinful, acceptable and unacceptable, spiritual and unspiritual for their followers. The other half is spent sitting in judgment on those who don't measure up to these often arbitrary standards.

> "No tree has branches so foolish as to fight among themselves."
>
> —NATIVE AMERICAN WISDOM

The following is but one example. Many Protestant Christians, and almost all Evangelicals, believe drinking beverages containing any amount of alcohol is nothing short of a sin. But even here, there is little or no agreement as to the seriousness of this offense or whether it should be regarded as an offense. The issue is further clouded by the fact that, among Roman Catholic Christians, it is customary to enjoy the moderate consumption of beverages containing alcohol and even to use wine in the celebration of the Mass. Consequently, some Protestant and Evangelical Christians view Roman Catholics as sub-par Christians. Some Evangelical Christians even question, for this and other equally trivial reasons, whether Catholics are Christians at all.

On the other hand, some Roman Catholics believe this sort of standard for morality is responsible for the kind of judgmentalism that is itself a far more serious offense. Consequently, some Roman Catholics look with contempt on Protestants and Evangelicals as bigoted and backward stepchildren.

> "The world can only change from within."
>
> —ECKHART TOLLE

In the Muslim faith, you find a similar preoccupation with trivial matters. You discover widespread disagreement among its followers, too, as to which behaviors are acceptable and which are not. What's worse, if you look closely, you'll find that followers in both Islam and Christianity spend an inordinate amount of time and energy not only arguing and debating among themselves over insubstantial matters, but caricaturing each other, and even despising one another.

Again, I will limit my perspectives to what I know best, but the delusions among the faithful within both of these religions, as well as other religions, are too similar to ignore. Do you ever wonder, for example, how religions can become so "off target" with regard to the real nature of sin? How it is that they can become so "off center" from their own identity, purpose, and mission in the world?

The answer must be that they are lost in sin themselves, lost in a collective ego. Clearly, far more serious issues threaten the survival of life on this planet than some of the issues with which religions in general and Christians in particular preoccupy themselves. As long as these religions and their leaders remain unaware of their own collective ego, their own sin, they will continue to think their beliefs are truer than the beliefs of all other religions. Moreover, they will make a god of their beliefs while vehemently arguing that they have not done so. They will consider other religions inferior. They will debate, disagree, divide, and, depending on the degree of their unconsciousness or insanity, discredit, even destroy, those who disagree with them.

Moreover, they will confuse sin with behaviors each has deemed as evil instead of understanding that sin is a condition of the ego. Rather than helping people understand who they are beyond ego and live free of the consequences of that condition, they will remain obsessed with the consequences themselves. They will continue to view sin as an evil deserving punishment rather than a mistake that needs correcting.

They will dissociate from anyone whom they believe lives in darkness. Yet, what they will fail to realize is that they are themselves the ones who "walk in darkness" (John 8:12), as Jesus eloquently called them in his day.

The Awakened Religious Faith

When religions and their leaders awaken to their real nature, however, and no longer identify with the collective ego, they will experience a transformation, too. In fact, they will be the transformation they wish to see in the world. Religions and their leaders will die to the collective ego and live in a state of Divine-consciousness.

Within Christianity itself, you'll see the church become the "salt" and "light" just as Jesus predicted. They will encourage peace instead of making excuses for war. They will no longer feel threatened by belief systems different from their own. Instead, they will seek commonality and communal interaction with people of all faith traditions. Labels and distinctions—i.e., Baptist, Methodist, Catholic, etc.—will give way to a profound awareness of the interconnectedness of all living things, including all traditions. Of course, denominations will remain, for there will be no need for them to dissolve, but the present distinctions between them, on which each now depends for a sense of ego identity and survival, will either disappear altogether or cease to be a point of distinction or disagreement.

> "Enlightenment is the full awareness of who and what one is and one's true place in the world."
>
> —LAMA SURYA DAS

Furthermore, the illusion of separateness between all religions will dissolve. Instead of trying to convert everyone to a single way of believing, religions and their leaders will respect each other and be open to learning from one another. Leaders will acknowledge that there is one Vine but many branches, as Jesus put it (John 15:5), or one God but many ways to merging with Being itself. Consequently, their energies and efforts will be cooperative and collaborative instead of competitive and conflicting. Each will endeavor to preserve, protect, and promote the advancement of all life on planet Earth. This is the biblical view of the new heaven and new earth about which Saint John wrote in Revelation 21.

I am sure some readers think I describe some kind of impossible utopia. To the contrary, I have described a reality that many people already experience. It is a transformed state of consciousness where ego delusions disappear and people are free to experience life as God intended it—a God-realized life filled with joy, nurtured by tranquility, and blessed with a sense of unity with all other sentient beings.

If you have awakened, you are beginning to know this possibility, too.

Ego as an Insatiable Thirst

When I finally understood the human condition—what ego is, what it does in us and to us—it made sense that I felt so schizoid prior to the awakening. I was always out of sorts with myself, suspicious of others, and confused about my reason for being here. Like virtually everyone else, I searched for the right stream to satisfy my thirst for happiness, contentment, joy, and security. Since my religious tradition suffered from its own collective ego delusions, instead of helping me, it succeeded only in making my delusions more intense.

The American culture around me wasn't much help, either. It rewarded my ego-driven cravings for self-mastery, independence, personal achievement, and success. For example, whenever I achieved something that could only temporarily satisfy me, the culture rewarded me with a taste of triumph from a chalice called compensation. In the end, however, it was little more than a sip of satisfaction, just enough to make me crave more. I was like an alcoholic who can take one taste and the madness for more returns with vengeance. Just as the human body craves water in the blistering heat of a sun-scorched desert, it is the nature of ego to get thirsty. Whenever it does, you should expect that it will search for something more enduring and longer lasting.

When I awakened, however, I realized I no longer needed to look for an endless and satisfying reservoir. I was like the Samaritan woman who routinely came to Jacob's Well carrying a bucket with which to draw water. One day, however, she met Jesus at the well. As they conversed, something more profound than words could describe happened inside her. She tasted Living Water. When she left and returned to the city, she did so empty-handed and full-hearted. That is, she left the bucket and took the Well with her (John 4:28-30). A seemingly endless search finally ended. Or, as the Catholic mystic Anthony De Mello superbly expressed it, "The day you cease to travel, you will have arrived."[5]

> "When the pain of being the same becomes greater than the pain of being different, you change."
>
> —FROM *WHY IS GOD LAUGHING?* BY DEEPAK CHOPRA

> "Better to be hated for who you are than loved for who you're not."
>
> —AUTHOR UNKNOWN

Ego as the "Please Disease"

What follows are examples of our thirsts due to the insatiable nature of ego. These thirsts are responsible for much of the insanity with which I lived prior to my spiritual transformation. In varying degrees, they are familiar to everyone. Take note that I merely skim the surface. There is an endless number of ways the ego can manifest its delusional nature in you and through you. Allow the following examples to serve as entry points into your awareness of ego.

For much of my life, I lived with an insatiable appetite to please people. I suffered from what someone described as "the disease to please."[6] We could argue that some appetite to please is normal, but when it becomes obsessive, and it almost always does, ego makes us think we can only find ourselves in the affirmation and approval of others. In this respect, it interferes with the development of healthy self-respect as well as the capacity to develop a meaningful relationship with anyone else. When we always try to please others, we mistakenly think, "If I just try hard enough, I will succeed in making him or her happy." Whatever success we achieve will be as temporary as everything else associated with the ego. Sooner or later, we screw up, and the other person is displeased.

In my case, as long as I heard positive accolades on a regular basis, I functioned with some sense of emotional normalcy. I could deliver a sermon on Sunday, for example, stand by the door through which most worshipers exited, and hungrily gobble up their words of praise. As long as the appetite of my ego was satisfied, I felt okay.

In some ways, I was like an actor, playing a role for an audience whose applause was necessary but never enough. I'm sure some people said nice things to me after the morning homily, not because they were impressed by either my delivery or its content, but because they intuitively sensed my insecurities and were polite enough to accommodate.

In my situation as a minister, all it took was one critic calling attention to a grammatical error I made in a sermon, and the rest of my day was shot. In fact, I tortured myself over the mistake for several days thereafter, and vowed never to make the mistake again. I usually did not. I suffered from the compulsory need for perfection in everything I did, which is another consequence of the egocentric human condition.

I had to achieve perfection *and* have the approval of others, much like an addict needs a fix. Praise and attention were my alcohol, my drugs. Different only in the degree of insanity, and perhaps legality, we all have addictions. An addiction occurs whenever ego convinces you something is missing in your life. Instead of knowing your sense of worth within yourself, for example—which is part of what is restored in a God-awakened state of consciousness—you look for approval outside yourself. Since the approval you find wears off quickly, your life becomes one continuous audition where everyone is your judge. In time, this pattern becomes habitual and perhaps addictive.

When I look back now, I know much of my obsession for the approval of others stemmed from the desire to know the approval of my father. For whatever reason, I never felt that I had enough of either his approval or his attention. He was always busy and preoccupied. On the occasions when we talked, I usually felt that he wasn't listening or was thinking about something else. Only after my awakening was I able to admit that I repeated the same pattern with my own children.

Feeling I could never get enough of Dad's attention frustrated me. In time, the frustration turned to resentment. I envied the attention others gave to him, and he to them, as well as his ministerial successes. Hence, there were times I felt in competition with my own father. I was jealous of the recognition I felt too frequently came to him. I drove myself to surpass his achievements. I had to be more successful than he was, and that became the accelerator behind many of my early ambitions and desires.

I did not know how to handle the craving for attention, affirmation, and acceptance. I also did not know the ego takes the natural longing of a child to know the affirmation of a parent and corrupts it entirely. As it does, a child grows up with an obsession not merely to compete, but to win. It becomes important not only to know what others know, but to know *more* than they know. You must achieve more than anyone else has achieved, possess more than others possess, be better than, greater than, and so on. Below the surface of this compulsory need to win hides the fear of failure, the fear of being unrecognized, the fear of rejection, the fear of judgment or ridicule or some combination of the above.

Anxiety disorders, phobias, panic attacks, obsessive-compulsive behavior disorders, and even depression have become so commonplace today that many view living with these disorders as normal. The most common explanation by mental health professionals for the cause of mental/emotional disorders is biology, environment, or a combination of the two. There's plenty of conclusive research that your brain chemistry, genetic predisposition, and social environment affect your innate proclivity toward happiness or unhappiness.

What does not seem to be readily considered, however, by all researchers is the role the ego plays in the human drama. Perhaps this is because, until you are aware of your own ego, you will not likely see or acknowledge its impact on the mental/emotional disorders listed above. Ironically, ego may be the chief culprit in all of these disorders.

Ego, Self-Talk, Past and Future

Self-talk is the ego talking to itself. This kind of conversation goes on all the time. Perhaps you've noticed a person on a subway or street corner talking out loud to himself or herself. Unfortunately, our typical response is to regard such people as crazy, but the truth is that we all talk to ourselves. We're all crazy; the difference is only in degree. The more unconscious you are of your ego, the more self-talk typically takes place in your head or, you might say, the more insane you are.

Self-talk occurs in two directions—toward the past and toward the future. Here's how it works: Whenever the mind becomes preoccupied with what has happened in the past, it keeps the past alive by returning to it over and over again. Self-talk also occurs whenever the mind is preoccupied with what has not yet happened, as well as with what it imagines will happen. In other words, although Jesus counseled us to live in the present (Matt 6:34), the ego thrives by keeping us obsessed with either the past, the future, or both.

For example, the mind will recall a conversation, conflict, or an event or situation that transpired yesterday, last week, a few months ago, or even years ago. Whenever the recurring thoughts are accompanied by a comment, a complaint, judgments, or opinions (for example, what you should have said, what you should have done, and what she, he, or they should have said or done), the ego in you is talking or complaining to itself.

Conversely, the mind will also imagine a conversation, a confrontation, a situation, or an event that it anticipates happening in the future. The anticipatory imagination is usually saturated with ego, too (for example, what you should say or do and what he, she, or they should say or do). Whenever a thought about the past or the future morphs into a conversation in your head filled with judgments, comments, complaints, and worries, you should know that this is the ego in you.

When religious people, Christians in particular, express hope for eternal life or life beyond death and long for what is commonly called the Rapture or the Second Coming of Jesus, this, too, is the ego. *You*, eternal as you are, would wish for neither of these. Why would you? When you live in an awakened state of God-consciousness, for what more could you possibly hope?

Since the ego rarely feels safe or secure, its typical pattern is to manufacture a belief system around which it can attach its hope for survival.

One might wonder, "But isn't the *hope* of an eternal life taught in the New Testament?" Certainly, but the confusion for many Christians lies in the meaning and usage of the word *hope*. We come closer to the New Testament meaning of *Christian hope* when we substitute the English words *confidence, certainty,* or *guarantee* whenever we read "hope" in English translations.

Here's an example: "We were given this hope [*confidence, certainty, guarantee*] when we were saved [*awakened and enlightened*]. If we already have something, we don't need to hope for it" (Rom 8:24, NLT). Note my expansions of the word *hope* and for the worn-out and widely misunderstood word *saved*. The last sentence of the verse is the most important, and the following conversation illustrates why.

Whenever I make a routine visit to the dentist, my hygienist usually has a question for me about spirituality. Recently, for instance, she asked, "Do you believe in eternal life?"

"What is there to believe in?" I responded. "Isn't eternity now?" As I answered her, I thought of the beautiful words of William Blake, who wrote:

> To see the world in a grain of sand;
> And a heaven in a wild flower;
> Hold infinity in the palm of your hand,
> And eternity in an hour.[7]

What could be more eternal, more blissful than this?

At first, she made no response. I assumed she was mentally processing my answer. Later in the visit, our conversation turned to the Second Coming of Jesus. She asked, "Do you believe in the Second Coming?"

"If you're asking," I clarified, "if I believe in some future appearance of Christ, the answer is this: 'Why would I look for something that has occurred in me already?'"

Paul himself said we only look for what we haven't found already (Rom 8:24).

Ego, Faith, and Hope

Fear, even when cleverly disguised with religious words like *hope* or *faith*, is still fear. It's the opposite of faith. If a person lives in fear, she is most likely living from the place of her ego. For instance, you have perhaps met religious people who are vehemently passionate about their beliefs. When you first meet such people, you might assume they are devoted followers of God. It is possible they are, but it is equally possible and more probable that you meet a gathering of frightened little egos that perceive their beliefs as "under attack." Quite expectedly, they react in intense and often negative defense of their beliefs. If you look closely, you'll discover their passion is not charged by the higher-energy frequencies of faith and compassion, but the lower-energy frequencies of fear, negativity, and anger. They raise their voices, their faces flush with anger, and their conversations drip with negativity.

Moreover, the intensity of their reaction is related to the relative importance of their beliefs. For example, if you've ever felt perplexed by the loud, argumentative, and often angry preaching of some Christian ministers, here's the explanation: These ministers *are* their egos. Their egos are attached to their beliefs. Their beliefs have been given eternal, infallible significance. Believing their beliefs are under attack, they react.

This is an unfortunate way to live, and yet it is precisely the way I lived and the way many religious leaders and people live today. They live in fear. They are so identified with the ego that they *become* their fears. What's more, their beliefs morph into their god. Like a dog protecting its master, they attack anyone who threatens their beliefs.

An awakened person, however, is learning the difference between the ego-self and who he or she is beneath and beyond ego. Consequently, they fear nothing, feel no threats, and defend no attachments.

Ego and Mind Activity

The discontent, inner turmoil, guilt, regrets, and unhappiness you experience are the consequences of the ego and the place where it primarily lives—your mind. That is, the ego and the mind are virtually synonymous. The mind is the mechanism by which the ego-self talks to itself. Almost without exception, what the mind says to itself is tainted and untrue. Researchers tell us we have nearly 100,000 thoughts per day, most of them repetitive and useless. The thoughts we think today are the thoughts we thought yesterday, the day before, and so on. Furthermore, the thoughts are mostly initiated by the ego, which makes them suspect at best.

The spiritual teachings of Eckhart Tolle have affected my life significantly. If you're familiar with his work, you can see his influence throughout this book. He reminds us that the conversations in our heads, which for most of us go on almost continuously, are like mental noise or movies of the mind. For the most part, they are harmful. Since he has written extensively on this subject, it isn't necessary for me to go into detail here. However, I will say that when you know "you are what you think," you'll grow cautious about the thoughts you think.

> **If the chimney is full of smoke, how can the light be seen? If the mind is full of dirt, how can the soul shine?**
>
> —YOGASWAMI, SRI LANKA'S TWENTIETH-CENTURY SPIRITUAL MASTER

Have you noticed the recent escalation of social concern over chemical toxins in our food and water? What about the concerns about global warming, widespread pollution, and the likely extinction of some endangered species? Unquestionably, the human species ignores these problems to its own peril. What most humans do not know, however, is that outer pollution is a mirror of mental pollution. That is to say, external pollution can only ever mean one thing—*internal pollution*. No awakened person would intentionally pollute the environment. If the inner environment is clean, the outer will follow. If the inner environment is filled with negativity, complaining, fault finding, anger, and hatred, these will manifest in the outside world.

Enacting policies or passing laws that enforce environmental cleanliness may slow the self-destruction among humans who disregard the fragility of our world, but it will not approach the source of the problem. Pollution in the mind stream will always manifest itself as pollution in the mountain streams. When the inner world is changed, the outer world will change, too.

On an individual level, mind madness manifests itself in physical illnesses, premature aging, obesity, heart disease, and others. Our culture is not unlike the one Jesus entered. Ours may be more educated, but in many ways our culture is vastly more insane. People today, for example, are infinitely more concerned about what goes into their stomachs than what goes on in their minds or comes out of their mouths. Toxic thoughts, however, are far more toxic than the toxins in food. I find it interesting that Jesus himself said as much:

> Don't you know that anything that is swallowed works its way through the intestines and is finally defecated? But what comes out of the mouth gets its start in the heart. It's from the heart that we vomit up evil arguments, murders, adulteries, fornications, thefts, lies, and cussing. That's what pollutes. Eating or not eating certain foods . . . that's neither here nor there. (Matt 15:17-20)

Substitute the word *mind* for *heart*, and you'll translate the meaning of Jesus' words more accurately. The thoughts you think give birth to the emotions you feel. Your mental/emotional state impacts your physical health. If your thoughts are mostly negative, or if your mind is worried and anxious about anything, your emotions will be heavy and your body weak. A weak body is vastly more vulnerable and susceptible to illness and disease. Has not the medical community been telling us this for years?

Since I experienced my awakening, I have become more in tune with my inner world. Frankly, much of my thinking has been and continues to be repetitive, useless, and, given the previous discussion, even harmful in its effects. Thus, I'm making it my spiritual practice to stop thinking, to practice silence. It's harder to do than you can imagine. But with this practice, I have discovered something remarkable. Once I stop thinking, I start hearing the voice of God more clearly. (For more on this, see Part 3: Mastery of the Sacred Art.)

Ego, the Fate of Your Form, and Mohammad Ali

Most people think they are their bodies. They are not, of course. The ego attaches itself to the human form just as it attaches itself to other things (roles, functions, beliefs, a group—anything to give itself a sense of self, an identity), but the body is not you. Nor are you subject to the same decay and death that is the fate of the body. As I said before, and will likely say several times again, you are a spiritual being, and you will never die. Saint Paul put it this way: "For just as there are natural bodies, there are also spiritual bodies" (1 Cor 15:44). The natural body is mortal; the spiritual body immortal.

When you look in a mirror, you see your "natural body" the one that ages, decays, and eventually dies. The "spiritual body," however, is the part of you that is unseen, a kind of inner body. As your "essential self," or "higher self," it shares in the Divine essence. Even so, don't assign too much significance to any of these words. They are merely vehicles to help you arrive at the truth of who you really are.

To me, one of the interesting anomalies in our culture is this: People pamper and care for their external forms to the unfortunate neglect of their internal forms, as if they believe the exterior is eternal and the interior is not. There is one explanation for this oddity in human behavior: the ego in these people has so identified with body, and attached itself to it, that these people are confused. They mistakenly think they *are* their bodies. This explains the compulsive preoccupation in our culture with clothing, cosmetics, and calisthenics.

The objective behind these preoccupations is twofold: *to enhance the looks of the body and to extend its longevity.* There's nothing inherently misguided in either of these objectives, as long as you are aware that both are illusions of the ego. It is true that the care and feeding of the body can enhance and improve one's appearance. But changing the hands on the biological clock doesn't stop the clock from ticking. In other words, there's only so much that cosmetic surgery can stretch, alter, remove, or hide. All of us know of someone who has visited the cosmetic surgeon one time too many.

> "There's only one thing I can think of that's worse than death: that's living with the fear of it."

It is a mistake to think I make a case against exercising or looking and feeling your best. For more than twenty-five years now, I've made it a regular practice to run three or four times a week, three or four miles at a time. When I was younger, I ran six miles every day, and some of those years I never missed a day of running for the entire year. I am definitely an advocate of exercising, eating right, and trying to look and feel your best.

I'm simply offering another perspective. The fact is that the body is aging, which is a polite way of saying the body is dying. Our culture's obsession with looks and longevity is due to fear of death. The more you are identified with ego, the greater you will fear death.

Some think talking about death is morbid, but it is only so to those who *are* their egos and their bodies. There's nothing morbid about death to the eternal *you.* Death is natural. It happens to everyone, and it is part of God's plan for all living things, including humans. Contrary to what many people believe, especially Christians, death was not God's punishment for the sin of humanity. I believe it has always been God's intention that we show up, stick around for a while, and then return to our Source. I'll return to this matter soon, when I introduce you to the widely misinterpreted story of Enoch. For now, remember that if you die before you die, then death will no longer scare you. Ego-identification makes people frenetic, even fanatical, about their appearance, the aging process, and death.

Not long ago, I boarded a plane, and right after I sat down, I saw the flight attendants and ground personnel giving assistance to a passenger who struggled to get on board. When he finally appeared around the corner and began making his way up the aisle, two flight attendants flanked him on either side. I was amazed to see that the gentleman they assisted was none other than the Champ himself—the greatest boxer of all time, Muhammad Ali. At first, I thought he might take the empty seat beside me.

Could I be so lucky? I thought.

Not this time, but I got the next best thing. Ali sat across the aisle from me. I wanted to ask for his signature, but of course I did not because, while I remembered a time when he was strong and agile, toned and in superior physical shape, he did not seem so anymore. As we all do, he had aged, and his movements were slow and deliberate. Parkinson's disease caused him to shake uncontrollably.

Picture this: Here I am sitting beside the greatest boxer of all time, a human being whom I remember as an enviable specimen of the human potential. Now, however, he is aged, swollen, and in a vastly weaker condition, his hands and body shaking nonstop.

I wanted to ask, "Mr. Ali, what has happened to you? Did your years of boxing cause this? Do you ever wish you had quit boxing sooner? What drove you to keep pushing, to suffer the relentless pounding from your opponents, all of whom wanted nothing more than to take your title, surpass your accomplishments, or demonstrate their own invincibility? Is that it, Mr. Ali? Did you keep returning to the ring to prove something or to deny something? Can you appreciate, sir, that it's disconcerting to see you in this aging, declining condition?"

For obvious reasons, I did not ask these questions, but you can be sure that as I sat beside and observed the awkward and strained movements of the Champ, I did some sobering thinking. *Here sits the embodiment of ego itself— the man who used to boast to the world on national television, "I'm the greatest!"*

Now look at him.

He *was* the greatest. Ali backed up his boast with an unrivaled boxing career, and he was duly rewarded for it. Fame, fortune, good looks, stamina, a body of steel, notoriety, legacy. What more could anybody want? He had it all, including a museum built in his honor in my own city. People come from everywhere to see the Mohammed Ali Center and pay homage to the greatest boxer of all time.

Still, like everything else associated with ego—career, titles, accomplishments, fortune, the body, etc., it begins to fade away fairly quickly. Even a museum is no guarantee of a permanent legacy, no promise that people will remember you forever. A fading ego, a faltering body—the two make for a *breathtaking* pair. To those trapped in ego and its innumerable illusions, however, they're a mammoth pain in the you-know-what.

Consider visiting a cemetery. Recently, my wife and I visited a particularly special cemetery—Cave Hill, where my father's body is buried. Cave Hill is the Ritz Carlton of bone yards. Empty your pockets for a pothole or bungalow at Cave Hill and you'll have all the proof necessary that you've made it. It's astonishingly beautiful and brimming with life. Mighty oaks, sugar maples, pink and white dogwoods, crape myrtles, and evergreens are accented by a kaleidoscope of flowers that cover the crowded landscape, providing a lovely cover-up for the frightening reality of death.

As we drove through Cave Hill, I had the strange feeling that the ego tries to live even in death. In life, the ego competes to win. It feeds on the attention it receives. It tries to outdo, outlive, and out-perform everyone and everything else. The ego is just as eager when it comes to death. At Cave Hill, it seems that the bigger the ego in life, the grander the monument in death. You should see some of these statues, sepulchers, and crypts. It is egotistical madness. Imagine the expense involved, the wasted land and resources, not to speak of the formaldehyde, ethanol, methanol, and other solvents that seep through rotting flesh and cracks in crypts and coffins and then into the soil around it. For what? For respect? What could be more disrespectful of Life than the denial and desecration of death and the earth to which all forms eventually return?

It's none other than the little ego, terrified at the thought that it might not get its proper recognition, horrified at the thought of being forgotten. Ego does in life what it cannot do in death. It purchases for itself the best position, the most noticeable burial plot. It constructs a monument to itself. Then it draws imaginary boundaries around itself called a gravesite or burial plot. Finally, it surrounds itself with evergreens to foster its illusion of perpetuity.

In the grand scheme of eternity, you and I don't matter much and won't be remembered for long. This truth is offensive to no one but the ego—the little me. You, however, know the truth in these words. That's why, if you take an honest stroll through a cemetery and observe the beauty as well as the beast inhabiting the same sacred space, you will get the feeling that the stuff we do in life to hide ourselves from death is rather silly.

> As the ego dies, you live. Until it dies, you don't.

Seeing and observing Mohammed Ali was a superb reminder that our journey here is short. Only the ego makes living dreadful and dying dreaded. However, when you die before you die, that is, when the ego in you wanes and you wake up to Life, then Saint Paul's words will express for you a truth you've actually always known: "Nothing can separate us from the love of God" (Rom 8:31-39).

Die before you die, or you'll die a thousand deaths while you live.

Ego, an E-mail, and Fear

I received an e-mail one day, but I did not recognize the sender. As I read the message, I was perplexed, then startled by the following words:

> I feel very sorry and bad that your life is going to end like this, if you do not comply with my demands. I was paid to eliminate you, and I will do so within the next ten days, if you do not follow my instructions exactly. Someone you call a friend wants you dead by any means. This person has paid me a great deal of money already. Furthermore, this person has provided me your address and phone number. For the past week, I have been watching you closely. Here are my instructions . . . .

The writer gave me ten days to come up with $12,000. He also detailed how I was to deliver it. He warned me not to involve the authorities; otherwise, he would not only harm me but might also harm my wife or one of our four children. I have received strange e-mails before, but none this strange or unnerving.

I showed it to Pam, whose initial response was as impassive as mine. She did say, however, that the author was likely in a desperate financial state, a condition many face in today's economy. Perhaps after finding my website, where information about me is available to anyone, he sent the e-mail in hopes that I was gullible enough to take it seriously. Pam suggested I should ignore it.

> **Mental health increases as we pursue reality at all costs.**
>
> —M. Scott Peck

I did for the first couple of days. When a second e-mail arrived, though, and then a third and fourth in subsequent days, all saying essentially the same thing but demanding larger amounts of money, I became concerned. Additionally, the references to information about my family and me meant the e-mails were personal and not sent to thousands of addresses at once.

Understandably, I was anxious. Whoever wrote the e-mails took the time to gather enough information to make the threat seem real and serious.

Instead of ignoring it, I decided to send a one-sentence reply: *"You cannot kill someone who is dead already."*

I received no more e-mails from that individual, but I have wondered whether the author knew what I meant by these words.

Do you?

As we have learned from psychology, there are two kinds of fear. One is real fear, and the other is psychological or, as I call it, ego-driven fear. Real fear is the body's natural reaction to a threat. Let's say, for example, you're proceeding cautiously through the green signal at an intersection when the driver of another car suddenly disregards his red signal and drives through without stopping. Because you drive defensively, you are able to maintain control and avoid a collision. To do so, you slam on the brakes, turn the wheel, and steer your car into a nearby ditch. The driver of the other car never stops. In an instant, your life flashes before you. Your heart pounds rapidly. Your blood pressure skyrockets, and your palms sweat. Perhaps you even shout an obscenity or two at the driver and shake your fist at him for being so stupid and irresponsible.

What are you feeling and experiencing? It's what we might call real fear. After thousands of years of evolutionary history, the body instinctively knows how to respond in a threatening situation. It requires no preparation or planning. Instead, the body does what it's supposed to do when it's supposed to do it. Real fear is, therefore, the body's fight-or-flight response to a threatening situation. For as long as you live, you will occasionally find yourself in circumstances that necessitate an involuntary, automatic response to a real threat. This is normal and natural.

On the other hand, psychological fear is unnatural. If we follow the example above, this kind of fear is likely to appear later, when you have time to reflect back on a close call and imagine what might have happened had you not been in control. These reflections take on an added life when you share the story of the near collision with colleagues, family, and friends. You could almost think of psychological fear as *fear with an attitude*. An attitude emerges whenever fear ceases to be real fear and becomes psychological, or ego-driven, fear. As it reflects back, the ego is prone to develop an attitude and opinion about the real threat and relive it in countless ways. It manifests in anger, complaints, comments, and negativity.

Most little egos, however, don't lose control. They simply feel threatened, afraid, or offended and so comment and complain, sometimes for days. Basically, the ego turns what should have been a one-act play into a full-blown drama. The longer the ego thinks about the incident, talks to itself about it, shapes a victim identity around it, and fashions it into a story to tell to others, the more personal the story becomes and the more anxious and offended the ego feels.

Ego-driven fear is the anxiety you feel whenever the self talks to itself about things it wishes had happened, had not happened, or had happened differently; or the things it wishes will happen, will not happen, or is afraid might happen, but feels helpless to make happen or to keep from happening. In other words, your ego is as maddening as the sentence you've just read.

With regard to the threatening e-mails I received, I could have let my ego make more of them than I did. Instead, I chose to hear the comments my mind made. That is, every time my mind started complaining to itself about the e-mails, I stopped and listened to the conversation. As I did, I made an astonishing discovery. My thoughts about the e-mails, as well as the feelings of anxiety that accompanied them, began to vanish on their own. It was as if listening to my thoughts was enough to diminish both the thoughts and the anxious feelings. Although unclear to me at the time, this discovery was another of the benefits—or, as I like to think of them, Divine grace-gifts—I received as a consequence of my awakened state of consciousness.

> **All that we are is the result of all that we have thought.**
>
> —BUDDHA

When the transformation in me occurred, virtually all the fears that tormented me for most of my life began disappearing. They have left me and not returned, at least not to an unmanageable degree. If they show up, they are at best periodic, and their presence is so negligible I sometimes do not notice. Some fears, though, like fear of harm, fear of aging or disease, and mostly fear of death put up a stellar fight. They are disappearing more slowly. This is why the New Testament calls death "the last enemy" (1 Cor 15:26). The ego knows that, when your body dies, the ego itself dies. Physical death is its permanent end. So, during your life, it puts up a valiant, impressive fight for survival. Add to this the human, social, and cultural denial of death that has been our culture's *modis operandi* for decades, and it's not hard to understand why ego's fear of death dies hard.

Ego Death: Portal to Freedom from Ego

Most people think they are their thoughts, but this thinking needs to change. You are not your thoughts. You are the *awareness* behind your thoughts—the awareness that is aware of thoughts. Gary Zukav calls this awareness the *seat of the soul*.[8] Some spiritual teachers refer to it as *the witnessing presence*.[9] The book of Genesis calls it *the breath of God* (Gen 2:6-7). It is the essence of Being itself. It is who you truly are beneath and beyond your mind, your thoughts, and your body.

The first key to overcoming the ego is to know that you are *not* your thoughts any more than you are your body. Both the mind and the body are material, and everything material is subject to birth and death. You, however, are the *awareness*, the consciousness, beyond your thoughts. For example, you have perhaps heard someone say, "I caught myself thinking," before they proceeded to tell you what they were thinking. Perhaps you have said something like this yourself. This is a peculiar statement, but it is also quite revealing.

If I say, "I caught myself thinking," am I one or two persons? Who is the "I" who catches "me" thinking? By now, the answer should be clear. The "I" is the "real me" who catches "myself" (the ego) thinking.

> He who sees Me in all things, and sees all things in Me, he never becomes separated from Me, nor do I become separated from him. The one who has attained unity worships Me, who dwells in all beings.
>
> —*THE BHAGAVAD GITA*

It is awkward, but try it yourself and see if this is the way your mind works. The next time you catch yourself thinking, pay attention to your thoughts. Be the *witnessing observer*. The observer of your thoughts is infinitely closer to the truth of who you are than any of your thoughts about who you are. If you make this your daily spiritual practice, you will live freer of the ego and its dysfunctional nature. You will grow, as it were, in spiritual, or awareness, power. The stronger your awareness, the more cautious and suspicious you'll be of the thoughts you think. You will not trust your thoughts. Most of them are wrong, anyway, or, at a minimum, they are heavily biased by ego, the conditioning of your upbringing, and, most likely, both.

By being suspicious, I don't mean you judge your thoughts as good or bad or shame yourself for having them, even if they're somewhat shocking to you. To shame yourself for having a thought only means the ego has returned in a slightly different disguise. Simply observe your thoughts as you would watch a newborn whose movements are erratic and untamed. You do not judge the infant, saying things like, "What's wrong with this child? Why can't he better control his movements?" You simply watch. Sometimes you even laugh.

> "The relevance of Christianity to most Americans . . . has far more to do with the promise of eternal salvation from this world than with any desire to practice the teachings of Jesus while we are here."
>
> —FROM *AN AMERICAN GOSPEL* BY ERIK REECE

Do the same with your thoughts. As you do, you will become an expert watcher of the mind and much freer of ego's control over your thoughts and behavior. As your mind is purified, your life grows peaceful. The prophet Jeremiah said, "The mind is deceitful above all things . . . who can know it?" (Jer 17:9) That's a good question. Only *you* can know your thoughts. Since no one knows what you're thinking, then *you* must be responsible for your mind.

In *The Power of Now*, Eckhart Tolle wrote,

> So the single most vital step on your journey toward enlightenment is this: learn to dis-identify from your mind. Every time you create a gap in the stream of mind, the light of your consciousness grows stronger. One day you may catch yourself smiling at the voice in your head, as you would smile at the antics of a child. This means that you no longer take the content of your mind all that seriously, as your sense of self does not depend on it.[10]

Ralph W. Emerson said essentially the same thing: "The ancestor to every action is a thought."[11] By this, he meant all actions begin as thoughts. If you want your actions and attitudes to change, then change your thoughts. The fastest way to change your thinking is to watch your thoughts. This practice creates what Zen Buddhists call *a space of no mind.* Just as there are spaces between these words, there is a space as infinite as outer space between your thoughts. Whenever you pay attention to your thoughts, you widen the space between them. As this space widens, your inner peace deepens. Watching your thoughts is similar to pressing the "pause" button on a video player. The moment you do, you interrupt the "mind stream," as Tolle calls it. That space in the interrupted mind stream is the place of stillness, the Sacred Presence itself.

If you wish to know God, you must master the sacred art of mind observation. This is the way to human transformation. I believe this is the *only* way to what Saint Paul called "the renewed mind" (Rom 12:2, KJV).

The Ego in Everyone

I will mention only a few other ways ego might manifest itself. Sometimes the ego makes people feel incomplete, as if they cannot be happy until they find the right partner with whom to share human companionship. If this is you, you will look for your completion in a relationship with someone else. I call this the "Jerry McGuire illusion." Perhaps you remember this box-office hit that starred Tom Cruise, who played Jerry, and Renée Zellweger, who played Dorothy.

According to the storyline, following a tumultuous start to their relationship, Jerry falls in love with Dorothy. In a dramatic and memorable scene, Jerry says to Dorothy, "You complete me." When I first heard him say those words, I thought, "That has to be the most romantic thing I've ever heard!" As you might suspect, I tried repeating them to my spouse. It hardly had the same effect.

Soon after my spiritual transformation, I woke up to the realization that a significant reason for the failure of my first marriage was that I looked for completion in my spouse. I mistakenly thought it was my partner's responsibility to make me happy, to complete me and fulfill my life. That is ego.

If you look long enough, you will find someone with whom to share your life, but you will not find yourself or your happiness in someone else. You will only find yourself by looking within. I'll discuss this further in chapter 14.

Contrary to the fiction in most Hollywood movies, novels, and pop culture, there is not some individual out there who will make you happy or complete you. You are complete already. The ego in you makes you feel as if you're just half a person until you find the other half. It works overtime to make you believe something is missing. That way, you'll keep looking, searching, and hoping to find fulfillment. Unless you stop this madness, you'll make the same mistake as Rumi, the thirteenth-century Sufi poet who wrote, "I've lived on the lip of insanity, wanting to know reasons, knocking on a door. The door opens. I've been knocking from the inside."[12]

Looking for yourself, or happiness, in the perfect job, the ideal career, titles, degrees, accomplishments, or material possessions is equally delusional. The better house in the better neighborhood, the better-paying job, or the newest hybrid automobile will not give you what you long for. The same discontent from which you drove away in the last job will catch up with you at the new one. Until you are aware that this is how the ego manifests its insatiable wants and desires, it will continue to run your life and ruin it as well.

> "Excuse me," said one fish to another. "Where may I find this thing they call the ocean? I've been searching everywhere but to no avail." "The ocean?" responded the older and wiser fish. "Why that is where you are now." "This?" he asked. "But, this is only seawater. What I'm looking for is the ocean."
>
> —AUTHOR UNKNOWN

The things you may seek and find, pursue and achieve will reward you with a pleasurable feeling of accomplishment, but it will be temporary at best. When the good feeling disappears, then the feelings of incompleteness and discontent will return. If you remain unconscious to this cycle of ego-centrism, you will search and only find temporary happiness. It is madness to live this way, but, since virtually everyone does, everyone believes it to be normal. People have become the proverbial fish that swims in the sea in search of the ocean.

Ego and Your Christian Experience

Ego and grace cannot co-exist. Ego is into doing, grace into being; ego is a performance; but, grace? Well, grace is all about doing nothing . . . and getting everything.

Sometimes I wonder if being "Christian" for many people is little more than an ego identification, a role they play. It was for me. I mistakenly thought being a Christ-follower was subscribing to a certain set of beliefs, holding membership in a Christian church, or both.

> **I like your Christ. I do not like your Christians. Your Christians are so unlike your Christ.**
>
> —MOHANDAS GANDHI

When I awakened, however, this changed, as did everything else. In an instant, I was Christian in a way I had never been before. I became Christ conscious. I know this is infinitely more than a mere label of "Christian" or ego identification. In other words, I now realize there's a day-and-night difference between labeling yourself a Christian and living a Christ-conscious life, one in touch with what Buddhists call your "Buddha-nature."

You can know about Christ but not be conscious of the Christ within. When you are Christ aware, however, nothing is more important to you than this knowledge, and it changes everything about your life. For one thing, you look at the world differently. It becomes a sanctuary teeming with the Sacred Presence. You look at people differently, too. You feel an inner connectedness with everyone, regardless of his or her ethnic or religious background. The religious, racial, and cultural distinctions begin to disappear, too. You sense your eternal oneness with all living things.

You still have ambitions and goals in life, but they no longer carry the same degree of importance. The heaviness of life lifts as the struggle and stress disappear. Instead of feeling as if you're always swimming upstream and getting nowhere, you find yourself flowing with the River itself, confident that it will take you to your intended destination. You feel that the world is a temporary home, but you feel at home in this temporary world. You feel safe, too, unafraid, and at peace with yourself and everything else. You live with a conscious awareness of an Eternal Presence. Nothing else compares to this, and nothing else matters. Saint Paul described this life as follows:

> The very credentials these people are waving around as something special, I'm tearing up and throwing out with the trash—along with everything else I used to take credit for. And why? Because of Christ. Yes, all the things I once thought were so important are gone from my life. Compared to the high privilege of knowing Christ . . . everything I once thought I had going

for me is insignificant—dog dung. . . . I gave up all that inferior stuff so I
could know Christ personally. (Phil 3:7-10)

Among the many things Jesus did during his short stay on earth, he
sought not only to expose but to expel the hypocrisy he found in a religious
system overtaken by ego. Divine grace was reduced to something only a
deserving few were permitted to enjoy. What was intended to be free to all
from the Source of all, regardless of one's status in society, was replaced by an
ego-based religious system that depended solely on human effort and
achievement. This led to arrogance and pride, labeling and judgmentalism,
division and separation, even fighting and bloodshed. They took Divine
grace and turned it into an incomprehensibly complex ego-based system burdened by enough laws that it would rival that of the United States tax code.

Ego thrives in such an environment. No one could possibly remember—
much less obey—the plethora of cumbersome and complex religious rules,
but the ego drove people to try, nonetheless. This led to competitiveness as
devout people tried to outdo each other in terms of piety and performance.
In what has become known as his famous Sermon on the Mount, Jesus sum-
marizes the state of religious life and warns seekers of a spiritual life to avoid
it as one would avoid the Black Death itself. He says,

> Be especially careful when you are trying to be good so that you don't make
> a performance out of it. It might be good theatre, but the God who made
> you won't be applauding. . . . When you do something for someone else,
> don't call attention to yourself. You've seen them in action, I'm sure—"play
> actors" I call them—they get applause, true, but that's all they get. . . . And
> when you come before God, don't turn that into a theatrical production
> either. All these people are making a regular show out of their prayers,
> hoping for stardom! (Matt 6:1-5, The Message)

Jesus is speaking about the religious practices within Judaism, but he
could just as well be describing contemporary Christianity today. Even after
all these centuries, little has changed. As a consequence, it is no longer surprising when I read that believing people today are leaving the church in
staggering numbers. According to a recent report in the American Religious
Identification Survey (ARIS), virtually every Christian denomination in
America is losing members faster than it is gaining them.

The study offered this explanation: "The challenge to Christianity does
not come from other religions but from a rejection of all forms of organized

religion."[13] This raises an important question. What do believing people reject about "organized religion"?

Ego and the Decline of the Christian Church

The most obvious reason for rejecting the church is sheer disgust with a religious system that, as I heard one critic put it, "condemns homosexuals for coming out of their closet while hiding clergy pedophiles in its own."

Others leave because they no longer wish to be associated with a religion swallowed up in its own judgmentalism. The church preaches love, tolerance, and acceptance of all people, but in actual practice it loves, tolerates, and accepts those who conform to its dogmas and standards of morality. Religious bigotry and intolerance, as well as the more common practices of judgmentalism and condemnation, may be more prevalent among Christians today than at any other time in history. Ironically, Jesus said, "Judge not" (Matt 7:1, KJV). Here is poignant example of the judgmentalism pervading the Christian church today.

Judgmentalism

A married couple I know was once highly active in the church. Today, however, they rarely attend. Although they still consider themselves believers, they no longer turn to the church for guidance in their spiritual journeys.

Both the man and the woman were previously married and divorced, and they met as they neared midlife. They were instantly attracted to each other, began dating, and fell in love. A few months into their relationship, he proposed to her, and they planned to marry. At long last, the wedding date drew near.

They attended several different churches in their hometown in hopes of finding one they could join and attend together. After visiting several, they found a large church they liked, and one Sunday they joined. Requesting membership in this church required that they walk forward during the invitation time at the close of one of its many weekend worship services.

They walked forward as expected. At the altar, a minister warmly welcomed them and then passed them off to a church counselor. He led them out of the sanctuary and down a long hallway to a large, brightly lit room where others like them and their assigned counselors were gathering.

After a few brief words by the person whom they presumed was the lead counselor, the two were separated. Each was paired with a personal counselor whose job was to determine the candidate's Christian experience and readiness to join the church. While one counselor guided the man into a small room, a different counselor guided the woman to a room across the hall. As they already felt intimidated by the size of this church and its well-rehearsed operation, the separation was unnerving for them.

Later that day, as they shared their individual perceptions with each other, it was obvious that the counselors were well coached. Each asked the same questions, beginning with the expected ones—name, address, phone number, and so forth. Then the questions grew more personal and difficult. "Tell me about your Christian experience." "When did you join a church?" "What kind of church was it?" "Did they believe the Bible?" "Have you been baptized?" "Was your baptism 'believer's baptism'?" "Was it by immersion or were you just sprinkled?" "What are your spiritual gifts?" "Where do you see yourself serving in and through this church?" The interview surprised them, even offended them, but they persevered since they had achieved their objective of finding a church home.

A few days later, everything changed. The woman arrived home from work earlier than usual and fetched the day's mail. Buried in the carnage of junk mail was a letter addressed to her and her fiancé. She could tell by the address and stamp that it was not a form letter. She opened it and tried to identify the sender. She did not recognize the name, but the church was large, with a staff as numerous as the members of some smaller churches.

Assuming it was a welcome letter, she began to read. What she read, however, was anything but welcoming. She was shocked, embarrassed, hurt, and angered. The ego in her reacted in self-defense. She slammed the letter on the kitchen counter, reached for the phone, and dialed her fiancé. "Get over here now," she demanded.

"Why?" he asked, hearing the anger in her voice. "What's the matter?"

"Just get over here," she said.

He left his apartment across town and drove hurriedly to her house. When he arrived, she shoved the letter at his chest and said, "Here, read this." Before he could unfold the letter, she blurted out, "Did you give the counselor who questioned you my home address as if it were your address?"

"Well, yes," he said, "but what does that matter?"

"Well," she explained, "they think we're living together."

"But," he defended himself, "I didn't think anything of it. I just figured, since I'd be moving in after the wedding, I should give them your address instead of mine."

They debated the incident over dinner and wondered how to respond. Their first impulse was to call the church leaders and demand an explanation as well as an apology. The more they thought about it, though, the more convinced they became not only of the unjust nature of the letter, but that they had nothing to explain and nothing to defend.

"Who appointed them our judges?" they reasoned to themselves. "Besides, we're not two irresponsible teens, so what business is it of theirs whether we live together or not?"

They concluded that the assumptions church leaders made were ill informed and inexcusable. Instead of defending themselves or retaliating, they decided to ignore the letter and move on. In this respect, the couple acted more maturely than the ministers did.

This attitude of moral superiority is common in some churches today. Only a church confused about its real purpose would engage in such hypocritical and hypercritical nonsense. Given the church's own sordid and unremitting history of immorality and moral failure, it is hardly justified in setting itself up as anyone else's judge. However, this is how the collective ego works, and until churches and church leaders become aware of this, they will continue the madness of pointing out the toothpick in another's eye, as Jesus put it, while failing to see the two-by-four in their own (Matt 7:4).

People are leaving organized religion because they are tired of the negativity and warmongering both within churches and among churches and their leaders. It seems that many religious leaders are looking for a fight. It's as if the church has no identity without an enemy. To the uninformed, the bickering and fighting among churches and within churches may seem like a recent scourge to befall the twenty-first-century church. The fact is that churches and church leaders have been at war with each other, as well as the outside world, since the church's inception two hundred decades ago.

Disagreements, Debates, Doctrine, and Division

According to the Acts of the Apostles, shortly after Jesus' death, his friends and followers gathered in Jerusalem and formed a spiritual community. It was known as "The Way,"[14] most likely because Jesus himself referred to his spiritual pathway in this fashion (John 14). This is why Lutheran theologian Richard Hooper wrote, "The Way was a religion of Jesus, not the later religion about Jesus."[15] The "later religion about Jesus," as he puts it, is what we know today as Christianity.

The actual founder of Christianity was not Jesus himself, as almost everyone mistakenly assumes. It was Saint Paul. He is credited with authoring many of the books of the New Testament, and it was Paul who fashioned much of what we know today as Christian theology, soteriology, and ecclesiology.

Prior to Paul, however, the followers of "The Way" were a loosely knit group bound together by their common conviction that the way of Jesus would lead to salvation, or, as I call it, an awakening to the living Presence of God. When you read about these early followers of "The Way" in the Acts of the Apostles, for example, you discover that they were not only deeply devoted, but they were beset with struggles of the ego not unlike the ones we all face. A cursory reading reveals the repeated disagreements, debates, and divisions that took place among them, even among those closest to Jesus himself.

> If you meet a noble man, try to equal him. When you see an evil one, examine yourself carefully.
>
> —CONFUCIUS

As the followers of this pathway grew, so did their egos. Hence, they jockeyed for position, for authority over others, and for recognition within the community as well as control over the community. Luke records both this growth and these conflicts in what he might have more accurately titled Actions of Apostolic Egos instead of Acts of the Apostles. He spares no punch in showing his readers the early Christians both at their best, as in Acts 4, and at their worst, as in Acts 5.

At their best, he writes, "The whole congregation of believers was united as one—one heart, one mind! They didn't even claim ownership of their own possessions. . . . They shared everything" (Acts 4:32). Here, their unity, oneness, and generosity are abundant, as in the example he gives of Barnabas, who made a generous gift from the sale of his land, a gift sufficient to meet many of the community's most basic needs.

On the heels of this beautiful description, however, Luke shows the darker, egocentric nature that was also at work in the faith community. In Acts 5, we find the insidious actions of two insiders, Ananias and Sapphira.

Since there were no chapter divisions when Luke first penned his words, chapters 4 and 5 belong together. It is obvious that Luke places these two stories—that of Barnabas and that of Ananias and Sapphira—in striking juxtaposition. In graphic, even ghastly detail, Luke illustrates what happened when the egos in Ananias and Sapphira were inflamed with jealousy over the applause Barnabas's generosity received. Desiring their own round of applause, the egos in Ananias and Sapphira conspired to sell land, too. Instead of bringing all the proceeds to the community as Barnabas had done, though, they withheld a portion.

Ordinarily, there would be nothing wrong with this decision, since it was their property to sell and their choice as to how much of its proceeds to give away. They could give some of it or all of it. Either way, the followers of "The Way" would have appreciated it, and Ananias and Sapphira would have been duly recognized for it.

However, as any aware person knows, the ego isn't interested in mere recognition. It wants more of the applause that someone else may get. If Barnabas got an "8" on the applause meter, Ananias and Sapphira had to have at least a "9" and preferably a "10." Furthermore, given the state of the economy in the first century, the egos in Ananias and Sapphira may have been afraid of giving everything away. They might have been scared at the thought of turning over all the proceeds to the apostles.

> **Men never do evil so completely and cheerfully as when they do it from religious conviction.**
>
> —BLAISE PASCAL

Perhaps their egos whispered in their ears, "Sure, Jesus said, 'Seek the kingdom first and everything else will be provided' [Matt 6:34], but you've got to be sensible. Times are tough. Besides, God helps those who help themselves. You'd be wiser to set aside some of this. You might need it one day."

Ananias and Sapphira gave only a portion of the proceeds, but they let the community believe they were giving *all* of the proceeds from the sale of the property. Their deceit brought about their untimely deaths. The community was understandably shaken.

This story is only one of Luke's multiple examples of the ego-related challenges faced by the early Christian community. Though he did not know to call it ego, he describes its negative influence with amazing clarity. The pettiness among the followers of "The Way" who competed for recognition and position is apparent. While they began as a community committed to Jesus' pathway to knowing God, they quickly became a monolith of beliefs around which a hierarchy of control developed for the sake of survival. Over time, an institution emerged to manage the beliefs and the bickering and to discipline the aberrant. This gave birth to what we know today as the Christian church. The rest, as they say, is history.

From then until now, the Christian church has not only penetrated the world, but it has splintered into at least 20,000 different subsets. Today, each subset regards its beliefs, its understanding of truth, to be just a little more right than that of 19,999 others.

This is part of the reason many are abandoning the church. They have concluded that the continuous disagreement and fighting within every branch of Christianity is neither profitable nor necessary. For these Christ followers, the "what" about Jesus is not nearly as important as the "way" Jesus provided for knowing the Ineffable Reality. To know God and to walk in the joy of his presence is what they consider important.

It would be a misreading of my analysis to assume I suggest that all who leave the church today walk in the light of God's presence. It would be equally incorrect to assume I suggest that all who stay in the church remain in darkness. I only mean that, if you wish to know why multitudes are leaving the church *but not leaving their faith*, it is because they have moved on from the pervasive madness found in many churches. They wish to keep it simple. They wish only to do as Jesus himself said: "Come, follow me" (Luke 18:22, KJV). Nothing more. Nothing else. But certainly nothing less.

Involvement in Place of Intimacy

I wish to mention one other reason that many are leaving the church. Involvement has replaced intimacy. Participation in and support of religious functions and activities have overshadowed that which is superior—knowing God. Although Jesus said, "Be in the world but not of it" (John 17:16), most churches and church leaders are more interested in people being in church as well as *not* in the world.

The activities and programs, as well as the personnel and financial resources required to keep them going, are gargantuan in number and complexity. They demand increasing time and attention. It is not that these programs are harmful or serve no worthy purpose. The problem is that there is far too much going on in today's church. If seekers are not careful, the attention they must give to the plethora of programs competing for a slice of time ends up sucking the spiritual life from their souls. For many, it has already. They've grown weary of having no life, especially no spiritual life, outside of churchgoing. They feel empty, exhausted, and bereft of any sense of the Eternal Presence. Churches today boast of being a 24/7 operation. It's actually a warning signal to any serious spiritual seeker. Instead of finding communion with the Creator, most seekers find only a cauldron of endless and exhausting activity.

The healthiest and most spiritual action a church might take is to permanently shut down the majority of the time-consuming and energy-draining activities. The busyness in most churches today has nothing to do with the business of the church—which, again, is simply to serve as a guide in the quest to know God.

Instead of the church being a sanctuary into which people might enter to find quiet, reflection, and inspiration, the church has become a theater filled with noise. Instead of encountering the Sacred and Mysterious through solitude and stillness, church leaders have conditioned people to expect entertainment, and it had better be better than the competition down the street. Churches actually compete with each other for members. This is because the overwhelming majority of them are not reaching the ever-growing, unchurched population, so they have to compete for the few who remain.

The church has developed its own version of *Entertainment Tonight*. You don't have to be a statistician to know why mega churches, as they're called, are basically the only churches in America showing an increase in attendance. It is likely because they can afford to pay for the best talent and the most professional show in town. Who wants to watch a show on a ten-inch, black-and-white screen when the theater

> To live by Jesus' teachings would be to live virtuously as stewards of the land; it would be to create an economy based on compassion, cooperation, and conservation; it would be to preserve the Creation as the kingdom of God . . . But to believe in Jesus' death as an event saving us from this world makes the abuse of it that much easier to justify. We are no longer stewards of the natural world, but exiles waiting for release.

—FROM *AN AMERICAN GOSPEL*
BY ERIK REECE

down the street offers one in 3-D on an Imax screen, served up with a cappuccino?

I have a feeling the day will come, and there are signs of it already,[16] when people will tire of the hype, the noise, and the emotionally charged, superficial highs generated by religious professionals and their performances. People need substance, something more than a weekly fix that stimulates the emotions but does little to feed the soul. They're looking for Presence, for a deep and abiding connection to God.

If church leaders are motivated more by having the biggest crowds and the loudest applause, more by ratings and recognition and other egocentric ambitions, they should not be surprised when people eventually look elsewhere for God. Some have, and many others will. There are indications that many Christians have grown weary of the madness and are turning in great numbers to other religions to find what Christianity or, more accurately, the church's version of Christianity has failed to give them.

The notion among clerics that numerical growth is a sign of God's favor is as much an illusion as the idea that church decline is a sign of God's disfavor. A more telling sign is whether anyone is coming to know the transformative presence of God—a Presence that changes how people feel about themselves, how they treat others and especially their enemies, and how they care and show concern for creation itself. When being Christian is more about loyalty to an institution or to a peculiar way of believing than it is about a relationship with God, people will eventually walk away from such a church, either emotionally, physically, or both.

In short, American Christianity is as bigoted, busy, and misguided as the religious system Jesus encountered two thousand years earlier. Fortunately, people are discovering, due largely to the church's failure and to the rise of other religions in the United States, that Christianity is neither the only way to know God nor the only way to find and enjoy a worthwhile and fulfilling human existence.

> **How could eternity (or, heaven) be in the future? How could we wait for it or yearn to reach it, since we are in it already. He who lives in the present has eternal life.**
>
> —ANDRE COMTE-SPONVILLE

Perhaps you think I have something against the church. I don't. I've given my life to its work and ministry. I am not ready to give up on Christianity, either. To the contrary, I know that at the core of the Christian faith lies a pathway that will guide any person who wishes to connect to God into a transformative experience of Divine grace. I also know some churches and church leaders not only understand the real purpose of Christianity, but they seek to stay with it and to shape a church life around it. The church my wife and I call our spiritual home is just such a place to us.

The Christ Path as a Means of Knowing God

To those in his day, burdened by a religious system gone mad, Jesus offered this invitation:

> Are you tired? Worn out? Burned out on religion? Come to me. Get away with me and you'll recover your life. I'll show you how to take a real rest. Walk with me and work with me—watch how I do it. . . . I won't lay anything heavy or ill-fitting on you. Keep company with me and you'll learn to live freely and light." (Matt 11:28-30)

Jesus extends this same invitation to you. It is an invitation to follow his pathway, the Christ path, to knowing God. You don't have to believe a lot of stuff on this path. Deepak Chopra expressed it most accurately in *Why Is God Laughing* when he wrote, "Beliefs are just a cover-up for insecurity . . . you only believe in those things you're not sure about."

You don't "believe" in the sun, do you? Of course not! What's there to believe in? You know the sun. You see it every day. You feel its warmth and benefit from its intelligent placement at its strategic location in our galaxy. The same is true of gravity. No one believes in gravity. You know it for yourself. Though invisible to the naked eye, this energy field keeps everyone from floating off into galactic oblivion. Who worries about this ever happening? No one. We are certain not only of the existence of this force of nature, but of its dependability in doing what it is designed to do.

You will discover that this pathway to knowing God is not so different. It is a life lived by faith, not beliefs. What's there to believe? That God exists? When you live by faith, you do not believe in God; you *know* God. There's nothing to believe in. Attempting to prove God's existence will seem bereft of meaning to you, even needless. It will seem equally strange for someone to suggest there is no God. Instead, you will see all of this for what it really is: an ego-driven exercise in futility—little egos presuming to possess the capacity to defend or discredit, to explain or explain away the Intelligence that is both infinite and inexplicable, yet also individual.

You will feel God's warmth, love, and nearness. Because you do, you'll understand the immortal words of Walt Whitman in "Song of Myself":

> I hear and behold God in every object, yet I understand God not in the least,
> Nor do I understand who there can be more wonderful than myself.
>
> Why should I wish to see God better than this day?
> I see something of God each hour of the twenty-four, And each moment then,
> In the faces of men and women I see God, and in my own face in the glass;
> I find letters from God dropped in the street, and everyone is signed by name,
> And I leave them where they are, for I know that others will punctually come forever and ever.[17]

When I first read those words, I realized Whitman knew the Unknowable as I know the Unknowable. I can't explain who this is I know. I do not try. For me, awareness of this Presence, this "Holy Other," as Rudolph Otto called it, is enough. There's not much more I can say. There's not much more that needs to be said.

Beliefs won't cut it. On one side, you can have all the right beliefs but still feel lost, confused, and full of doubt and fear. I did. And many believing people are just like me. They hold to certain beliefs about God, the Bible, Jesus, and so forth. In reality, they live by their beliefs, bound to an ego that has found an illusory life in them, but they do not live by faith. They will defend to the death their beliefs about God without ever knowing the Reality toward which those beliefs point. Their "beliefs" are their surrogate God. They have made of them a mental idol.

In this regard, faith is the opposite of belief. Faith is a way of life. Since we have no verb for "faith" in the English language, we substitute the word "believe." Unfortunately, this oddity in our language has caused much confusion. People have confused "faithing" or "believing" with beliefs, but believing has little to do with *content*. It has infinitely more to do with *conduct*, though not in some morally superior way. It's not what you know that produces an inner transformation. It's Who you know and, as a consequence, how you go about living your life as well as facing your death.

It was all simple with Jesus, not complicated the way Judaism was then and Christianity is today. To his first followers, Jesus simply said, "Follow me." When you do, you make the wonderful discovery that he doesn't take you to God, as if God were out there somewhere waiting for the arrival of his elect. Instead, Jesus' path brings you face to face *now* with yourself and with God. You realize it doesn't matter if there's a kingdom in some other dimension where God is, and if one day you'll join him when you die. What's important is that you live in this kingdom now and in this Presence now.

The Eternal God, whom Jesus revealed, as well as his kingdom, is within you. Jesus said as much (Luke 17:21). In other words, you make the discovery that following the Christ path doesn't end up in some place where God is. The journey is itself—God. When you make this discovery, you will experience the transformation of inner consciousness. With this inner transformation, the world around you also begins to change. It is too remarkable to describe. It is too important not to try.

Have you ever prayed or pleaded for God's presence to be with you or to accompany you on your life journey? Until I awakened, I frequently prayed such prayers. Today, however, it would never occur to me to make such a request. Why would I ask God to be with me when I know God is with me already?

I think those who truly know God may pray little, at least in the conventional sense. Isn't it interesting that we only read a few accounts of Jesus praying—again, in the conventional sense? I have found this to be true in my experience, too. I meditate often. (In Part 3, I discuss the practice of meditation.) To awakened souls, prayer is not something they do; it's who they are. Their lives are prayer. They have what Easterners call "unity

> "Just do the steps that you've been shown,
> By everyone you've ever known,
> Until the dance becomes your very own . . .
> Into a dancer you have grown,
> From the seed somebody else has thrown . . .
> In the end, there is one dance you'll do alone."

—FROM "FOR A DANCER" BY JACKSON BROWNE

consciousness" with God. That is, they live in a state of unbroken communication with and connectedness to the Creator.

While most people look askance at what Saint Paul told the Thessalonians to do, to "pray without ceasing" (1 Thess 5:17, KJV), an awakened soul could not imagine doing anything else. When you live from a place of God-awareness, you pray for reasons different than you have ever prayed before. Prayer is not the grocery list of items you need or want. It's more often the blissful, silent awareness of Beauty, Presence, and Joy. What could you need that is greater than this?

> "There's a Hole in my Soul,
> that's been killing me forever;
> It's a place where a garden never grows . . ."
>
> —FROM "HOLE IN MY SOUL" BY AEROSMITH

You don't have much to worry about on the Christ path either. It's not that you suddenly face no problems or challenges. You may face more than ever before. The difference is this: your life will change on this journey, and perhaps the biggest change is how you look at everything. You'll find yourself regarding whatever happens in your life as a kind of "planned appearance," not a random accident. Rather than resisting what shows up, you will look for the lesson(s) you're supposed to learn. You'll feel as if God is using whatever comes into your life as a means of waking you up just a little more. You will know everything serves as an alarm to awaken you, while the ego is the snooze button to keep you asleep.

Your life on this path may appear complicated and difficult to others. To you, it will actually feel lighter, more enjoyable, and noticeably more exhilarating. You won't feel judgment either, at least not from God. You will realize that perfection was never a prerequisite for knowing Presence. Others may judge you, but their judgments will no longer matter. What critics think of you becomes none of your business. Bullies won't burden you. On this path, you'll know only understanding, self-acceptance, and serenity. The person with these non-material assets needs nothing else.

> "You have the choice of being host to God or hostage to your ego."
>
> —WAYNE W. DYER

You'll realize that salvation is not a future reward for which you endure the present in order to enjoy one day. Instead, you'll know what salvation really is: *the progressive waking up to Presence.* You only ever know this Presence in what Eckhart Tolle has popularly labeled, "Now!" In other words, you will not know God yesterday, nor will you know God tomorrow. Neither exists, except as a memory or as anticipation. God is only known *now.* If you live in the present, which is Presence, you know this already.

The Christ path will free you of ego. It must, or by the time you come to the close of your life, ego may edge God out completely. You can die a religious person, and many do. Or you can die a conscious, awake person. I believe only a few do.

The Christ path frees the religious world over which ego presently reigns supreme. The collective religious ego must die in Christianity as well as all other religions. It must die soon, or humanity cannot survive.

Ego is the principal culprit in virtually every problem faced in this world. Its death is a matter of grave urgency. When a critical mass in understanding is reached regarding the seriousness of this matter, and all religions and religious leaders return to the one purpose they share equally, then the collective ego will begin to diminish. When it happens, if it happens, you will see that the beliefs within each religious tradition, as well as the distinctions and differences that currently divide them, give way to mutual respect, unity, and a desire to work together—a united, cooperative effort to solve the global issues threatening the extinction of the planet.

For this vision to materialize, however, there must be a widespread "denial of self" (Matt 16:24, KJV), as Jesus put it, which is another way of saying the ego must die. The death of the collective ego begins with the death of your ego and mine. When you think that if you were a better Christian, you'd be closer to God, know that this is the voice of the ego. It will say things like this to you: "If you were only a little more sincere in your faith, a little more devoted to God and the study of Scripture, you'd feel more of God's presence." That voice is a lie, and the light of recognizing the lie is enough to plunge the ego into its own darkness.

My awakening made me aware that it takes no effort to know God. It was an inner knowing that I am one with God and that I could never be more so than I am now. In *A Course in Miracles*, it is expressed in this simple and inviting way: "It is quite possible to reach God. In fact it is very easy, because it is the most natural thing in the world. You might even say it is the only natural thing in the world."[18]

Do not listen to the voice of your ego. Do not wage war with it, either. There is nothing to fight. By virtue of your participation in the human family, you have what Saint Paul called a "carnal mind" (Rom 8:5-8).[19] The *carnal mind* and the *ego* are one and the same. You also have an inner desire to know God. Everyone does, although not everyone, as we have seen, knows that only the realization of God's presence will fill the emptiness within. This desire to know God can only mean you have awakened to this realization and now have what Saint Paul called "the renewed mind" (Rom 12:1-2).

An *awakened life* and *the renewed mind* are one and the same, too. "The renewed mind" is the Christ-conscious, transformational mind. It isn't a reward conferred on you for believing the right things. It isn't the consequence of your baptism, because you joined a religious community, or even because you recited what media ministers call "The Sinner's Prayer." The *renewed mind* is immediately yours whenever you act on the desire you feel to know the God who is. It's that simple.

Of course, the ego prefers to make a procedure of this, a spiritual checklist of the things you must do and believe in order to know God, but unless you're reading this book to find something with which you might disagree, you're probably already waking up to the most extraordinary life imaginable. You have the "mind of Christ" now (1 Cor 2:16; Phil 2:5)! You are awake. All that remains is that you stay awake. That is your spiritual practice, and this is how Jesus described it:

> You've been given insight into God's kingdom. You know how it works. Not everybody has this gift, this insight; it hasn't been given to them. Whenever someone has a ready heart for this, the insights and understandings flow freely. But if there is no readiness, any trace of receptivity soon disappears. That's why I tell stories: to create readiness, to nudge the people toward receptive insight. In their present state they can stare till doomsday and not see it, listen till they're blue in the face and not get it. I don't want Isaiah's forecast repeated all over again: Your ears are open but you don't hear a thing. Your eyes are awake. . . . (Matt 13:11)

Salvation, as it is called in the Christian tradition, or *Enlightenment*, as in Eastern traditions, is the opening of your spiritual eyes. Keeping your eyes open is knowing the benefit of an ever-expanding God consciousness. Again, Jesus puts it this way in the Gospel of Luke:

> Keep your shirts on; keep the lights on! Be like house servants waiting for their master to come back from his honeymoon, awake and ready to open the door when he arrives and knocks. Lucky the servants whom the master finds on watch! He'll put on an apron, sit them at the table, and serve them

a meal, sharing his wedding feast with them. It doesn't matter what time of
the night he arrives; they're awake—and so blessed! (Luke 12:35)

There are only two paths on this journey: the path of the *ego-driven, carnal
mind* that "leads to destruction" and the path of the *transformed mind* that
leads to life. Only a few people will know the path that leads to life. Jesus
predicted as much (Matt 7:13). However, it only takes a few or, as Saint Paul
put it, "a little leaven to leaven the whole lump" (Gal 5:9).

To live by the ego-driven, carnal mind is to live a self-centered and competitive life. It is to be obsessed with what Immanuel Kant called your
"precious little self." It is a lonely path, which is why those who follow that
path feel disconnected, separated, alone, and afraid. It is a path littered with
the refuse of frustration and burden. It is an uphill struggle, and if the
summit is ever reached, your only reward is the realization that you've
climbed the wrong mountain.

The preferred path is the one of self-awareness. It is the path of inner
wholeness and peace. It is one that liberates you from religion with its fanatical fundamentalism, arrogant liberalism, rules, beliefs, and dogmas, as well
as the disagreements, debates, and division that always result. On this path,
you know one thing only: what Romain Rolland, the Russian novelist, called
"the oceanic feeling."[20] It is a simple, uncomplicated path. You live in the
enjoyment of what St. Augustine called "the eternal present." To walk this
path is to walk with God. Jesus once asked his listeners, "Burned out on
religion?" Many were. Many are. To them, and to you, Jesus says, "Come to
me. . . . I'll show you how to take a real rest. Walk with me . . . and watch how I do it" (Matt 11:28-30).

"Watch how I do it!" That's what it means to be a genuine follower of Jesus. What you

> **We shall not cease from exploration,
> and the end of all our exploring
> will be to arrive where we started,
> and know the place for the first time.**
>
> —FROM "LITTLE GIDDING" BY T. S. ELIOT

contemplate, you imitate. What you mind, you mine; what you mine, you
mimic. Or, as we saw in the Law of Attraction, intentions are influenced by
attention. In older versions of Jesus' invitation, there is the more familiar

translation: "Take my yoke upon you. . . . For my yoke is easy and my burden is light" (Matt 11:28-30, KJV).

The Christian word *yoke* and the Eastern word *yoga* come from the same root meaning "union" or "connection." Give your attention to observing or meditating on Jesus' life and teachings, and I promise that, by a kind of magical osmosis, you will be transported continuously into Presence. You will live the most extraordinary and meaningful life imaginable. You will contribute to the positive transformation of this planet. Just as important, you will go daily into the world with joy, satisfaction, and even anticipation.

Notes

1. Martha Beck, *Finding Your Own North Star: Claiming the Life You Were Meant to Live* (New York: Three Rivers Press, 2001).

2. Eckhart Tolle, *A New Earth: Awakening to Your Life's Purpose* (New York: Penguin Group, 2005) 25–84.

3. Lama Surya Das, *The Big Questions: How to Find Your Own Answers to Life's Essential Mysteries* (New York: Rodale, 2007) 107.

4. Wayne W. Dyer, *The Power of Intention* (Carlsbad CA: Hay House, Inc., 2004).

5. Anthony De Mello, *Awareness* (New York: Doubleday, 1992) 146.

6. Das, *Big Questions*, 235.

7. William Blake, from "Auguries of Innocence," first published in Poems, ed. Dante Gabriel Rossetti (1863) (http://www.bartleby.com/41/356.html).

8. Gary Zukav, *The Seat of the Soul* (New York: Simon & Schuster, 1989).

9. Eckhart Tolle, *The Power of Now: A Guide to Spiritual Enlightenment* (Novato CA: New World Library, 1999).

10. Ibid., 17.

11. Ralph Waldo Emerson, from *Essays, First Series* (1841), part 4, "Spiritual Laws" (http://www.gutenberg.org/files/2944/2944-h/2944-h.htm#2H_4_0004).

12. From *The Illuminated Rumi*, trans. Coleman Barks (New York: Broadway Books, 1997) 36–37.

13. Barry A. Kosmin and Ariela Keysar, American Religious Identification Survey (Hartford CT: Trinity College, 2008).

14. For references to this earliest Christian community, see Acts 9:1-3; 19:9, 23; 22:4; 24:14, 22; Galatians 1:11–2:14.

15. Richard Hooper, *Jesus, Buddha, Krishna, and Lao-Tzu: The Parallel Sayings* (Sedona AZ: Sanctuary Publications, 2007) 28.

16. See "Americans are Exploring New Ways of Experiencing God," 8 June 2009, the Barna Group, Ltd., http://www.barna.org/barna-update/article/12-faithspirituality/270-americans-are-exploring-new-ways-of-experiencing-god.

17. Walt Whitman, lines 1278–1285 from "Song of Myself," first published in *Leaves of Grass* (http://www.bartleby.com/142/14.html).

18. Helen Schucman and William Thetford, *A Course in Miracles* (Mill Valley CA: Foundation for Inner Peace, 2007) 64.

19. Substitute the words "flesh," "carnal mind," "sinful nature," or "sinful mind" with the word "ego" as used in this book. These words all point to the same reality. Again, do not get hung up on the words used. Look beyond the words to the one universal truth toward which all of them point.

20. For an explanation of "oceanic feeling," see http://en.wikipedia.org/wiki/Oceanic_feeling .

Chapter 9

Death: Portal to the Awakened Life

"Something is missing in my heart tonight
That has made my eyes so soft,
And my voice so tender,
And my need for God so absolutely clear."
—*Hafiz, fourteenth-century Persian poet*
(1320–1388)

The year was 1994. Elton John sang "Circle of Life," Tom Hanks played Forrest Gump, and Nelson Mandela was elected the first black president of South Africa. As for me, I had been busy for several years in ministerial pursuits. Although a young minister at age thirty-nine, I already served as senior minister in a large Christian church in the south.

As do many others in our culture, I made the mistake of thinking my purpose in life was to find the right career that would fulfill me and make me happy. I believed if I were the senior minister in a big church and earned a big salary, I would find what I was looking for. Consequently, I always watched for the "right" church to come along, the one most ministers still define today by size, salary, situation, or location.

Since the "right" church is a figment of the ministerial imagination (or of the ego), I never stayed long at one church. To a discontented minister, the "right" church is never the one where you are. It's always the one where you are not. I spent a great deal of my

> **Why do we notice the speck in our eye but not the mountains, the fields, the olive groves?**
>
> —FROM *BY THE RIVER PIEDRA I SAT DOWN AND WEPT* BY PAULO COELHO

career looking for and competing with other ministers for the "perfect" church.

Occasionally, I got lucky enough to serve a church that seemed on the surface to be the perfect congregation, but soon I saw its many imperfections. At the time, I had no clue that what I disliked about the church, as well as what I disliked about other people, were the things I disliked or denied about myself. That understanding did not come until after my awakening. Before long, boredom sank in, and I grew displeased enough with my place of service to begin another search for the "right" church. I lived in this world of insanity for much of my adult life.

Titles and accomplishments were important to me, too. I worked hard to earn the professional doctorate—not quite the academic doctorate, but impressive nonetheless. To achieve this milestone, I was required to pursue theological studies, combined with practical experience, for at least eight years beyond college, or about as long as it takes to become a medical doctor. In spite of this achievement, my ego never let me forget that I failed to earn the more prestigious doctorate.

> **Nothing makes us so lonely as our secrets.**
>
> —PAUL TOURNIER

The ego always looks for ways to enhance its sense of importance. If it decides it must have an advanced degree, irrespective of whether it is earned or deserved, it motivates a person to do almost anything to have it. It doesn't matter to the ego from where the degree comes. It could come from a school with little or no accreditation, or worse, from a bogus school that awards doctorates for a donation. The ego is only interested in the importance that the title presumably supplies.

Earning an advanced degree, however, did not keep me from feeling inferior to others. My ego operated in a reverse fashion. In some people, on one hand, the ego is obsessed with its own importance. We know these people as egomaniacs. On the other hand, I lived with a deflated, even depressed sense of self. We know these people as those with low self-esteem. Some people think

> **How interesting it is that men seldom find the true value of life until they are faced with death.**
>
> —FROM *PLANETWALKER* BY JOHN FRANCIS

too highly of themselves; I thought too little of myself. Either way, it is the ego at work.

I never felt inferior to other ministers who served on the same church staff with me. As the senior minister, I had authority over them. However, whenever I was around colleagues who held the same position as I did, it was another matter. I worked hard to hide my feelings of inadequacy. I repeatedly told myself it was foolish to feel this way, but it seldom helped. I hated myself for feeling this way, and I hated myself for hating myself. I lived in a vicious cycle of frustration and negativity.

I'm amazed that I was able to stand before an audience of thousands, as I did hundreds of times, and deliver a flawless and inspiring speech. When it ended, I exulted for days in both the praise and applause of the people. However, when invited to address a small group of colleagues at a ministerial function, I was overtaken by panic. I felt sick to my stomach in the hours before any speech or presentation to my peers.

Merely standing in front of them made my heart pound and my palms sweat. At times, I thought I was having a heart attack, which gave me something else to worry about. It wasn't that I was afraid of dying, although I was. More often, I was afraid of what others would think of me if I suffered either a heart attack or a panic attack from imagining a heart attack. Consequently, one of the first things I did prior to any speech was survey the room, map out an escape route, and be prepared in case I felt I that I was losing control. When I remember the many years I lived with such self-loathing, it is not surprising that, almost all the time, I was on the brink of physical exhaustion.

I made a Herculean effort to overcome these negative self-assessments, but in the end only the awakening released me. Perhaps now you can understand why, whenever I recall the afternoon I woke up, an ocean of gratitude swells over me. I saw the real me on that day—the "me" beneath and beyond the image I wore in front of others. In an instant, I felt freed of the burden of make-believe living, and I felt infinitely worthwhile. I *knew* my life mattered. This radical reversal in how I felt about myself, as well as how I began observing everyone and everything else, was nothing short of a miraculous gift of Divine grace.

Occasionally, traces of the self-loathing thoughts return. When they do, I not only watch them, but I have learned to distrust them, too. I have seen that most of our thoughts are not only repetitive and harmful, but they are false or at least grossly biased. Fortunately, it is rare for such thoughts to appear anymore. This, too, is grace.

Thirty-nine and at the Top of My Game

At age thirty-nine, I knew none of the secrets of the awakened life that I share with you in this book. By the cultural standards of measurement to which most ministers today commonly subscribe, I was successful in every respect. Yet, in many ways, I lived two different lives. I can remember, for example, the occasions when I said to the congregations I served that I believed this or that about God, the Bible, or some doctrine, but deep down I wasn't sure I believed any of it. I could never admit my doubts publicly, however. That would have sabotaged my professional career. In the church where I grew up, few could stomach such a level of transparency and honesty. You were expected to be honest about your faults but never your thoughts, and even your faults had limits. If you went beyond those limits, you might not be outside the reach of God's love and forgiveness, but you were out of the church.

> "Today is a good day to die.
>
> —NATIVE AMERICAN WISDOM

Consequently, I felt trapped. On one hand, I knew what others expected me to believe. I understood the social and political positions I was expected to hold. On the other, I knew I did not feel right inside. My fear of confrontation and criticism forced me to conform. I lived in a duplicitous world for years. I think many religious people do, but especially ministers. I compensated for the internal madness I felt by telling myself I had made it. I achieved everything I had worked to achieve. I should be happy and content. Of course, the self-talk was hardly consoling.

I had been pastor of the last church I ever served only a few months when my parents retired and began attending. Though they lived across town, they came every Sunday, or as often as Dad's schedule permitted him. He was a successful minister in his own right. A great communicator, he was frequently invited to speak all over the country, and he honored those invitations whenever possible. When not traveling, however, my parents came to my church.

On more than one occasion, I told them they should find a church closer to their home, even as I hoped they would disregard the suggestion. I was proud they were coming. More than this, I wanted them to be proud of me. For the most part, I felt they were. I could never get enough of their approval, however. I lived for their words of praise, but especially the words of adulation that came from my father. I wanted him to tell me, for example, that my homilies were outstanding and that I delivered them flawlessly. If he did not offer a complimentary word on his own initiative, I could hardly relax on a Sunday afternoon until I called to ask what he thought. If he said anything critical, I felt diminished and demanded perfection of myself the next time. I usually achieved it.

> There will come a time when you believe everything is finished. That will be the beginning.
>
> —LOUIS L'AMOUR

During the singing of the invitation hymn one Sunday, Mom and Dad came to the altar where I stood. In a Baptist church, this is known as an invitation hymn, and it is sung after the sermon to give people an opportunity to become believers, to join the church, to seek help or prayer, and so on. As I think back, I find it funny. When they approached me at the altar, they pretended to be ordinary people seeking membership in our church.

"Pastor McSwain," they whispered, "we'd like to join this church."

I presented them for acceptance and confirmation to the rest of the gathered congregation. It was a day of celebration for me. For nearly half my adult life, I was the son of T. L. McSwain. Now I was his pastor. It is hard to put into words how I felt that morning. It was one of the happiest days of my life and career.

> You learn more at a funeral than at a feast.
>
> —ECCLESIASTES 7:2

That afternoon, I strolled around the neighborhood surrounding our newly built house. As I walked, I talked to myself. The conversation went something like this: "What more could you want? You're thirty-nine years of age, pastor of one of the largest churches in the city, and drawing the kind of salary you always wanted—a salary your dad could only imagine, since none of the churches he ever served paid a salary comparable to it. You have two beautiful children and a brand new house in suburbia. You're the envy of your peers, recognized, and admired everywhere you go. Everything you've ever dreamed of having, you have. You're at the top of your game, guy!"

I exulted in my accomplishments. Little did I realize, however, that before the close of that day, my world would unravel at every seam.

The Day My World Unraveled

I returned home and prepared for evening worship. Although they had joined that morning, Mom and Dad attended another church that evening. Dad was invited to be their guest speaker in a series of inspirational services, that is, revivals. During his homily, and as I delivered the homily in my own church, Dad had what we learned later was a cerebral hemorrhage.

The details of what transpired are sketchy. I remember a collection of snapshots, the kind of memories you might capture and put in a photo album. There's a snapshot in my memory, for example, of the interruption to our evening worship service that came from one of our members. I never discovered why he reclined in the church office while everyone else slept in worship, but suddenly there he was, standing at the entrance to the sanctuary. He called out in a voice loud enough to interrupt the preaching as everyone's heads turned in his direction.

"Pastor," he exclaimed, "I just took a call from a member of the Ralph Avenue Church where your dad has been preaching. Something has happened to him, and your mother has asked that you meet them at Baptist Hospital East!"

There are other snapshots in my memory. One is of our frenetic drive to the hospital. All the way, I tried to reassure myself that everything was going to be all right. "He just collapsed from exhaustion," I explained to my spouse. "You know how much the two of them have been traveling and speaking."

I remember the gurney on which Dad was harnessed as

> *Sometimes, those who have been deeply wounded, even broken, find that the cracks in their soul are really deep and endless caverns wherein the transcendent Presence abides.*

> *If you wish to see the truth, then hold no opinions for or against anything. To set up what you like against what you dislike is the disease of the mind.*
>
> —HSIN HSIN MING, THIRD ZEN PATRIARCH OF CHINA

they wheeled him into the emergency room. His mouth was drawn to one side, and while I don't remember his state of consciousness, I do remember this was my first indication that his condition was far more serious than I had imagined.

For the next ten days, a heart-lung machine kept Dad's body alive. Naturally, everyone wanted him to wake up from the stroke. We hoped he would, although I had doubts about this, too. I had witnessed this sort of thing too many times before. If our wishes and prayers had muscle, however, we figured we had the strength to pull him through.

The stroke was severe, and while we did not know this for the first few days, it was not because the doctors and nurses kept it from us. More than once, they showed us pictures of the brain scans and described the severity of his condition. If a picture could speak, his would have said the miracle for which we prayed would occur not here, but somewhere beyond. We were prepared to accept nothing short of a full recovery, however. A psychologist would say we were in denial. We said we were people of faith, and our prayers would accomplish what medical science could not.

Our religious tradition had taught us to pray and believe, and miraculous things would happen. Had none of us ever heard or witnessed a miraculous recovery, which we had, we might have accepted Dad's fate sooner. We prayed for the miracle. With every twitch or slight movement of Dad's body, we saw an answer to our prayers, a sign that they were working. In the end, though, the miracle for which we prayed never happened. Death won.

> "Death is very likely the single-best invention of life . . . life's change agent . . . clearing out the old to make way for the new."
>
> —STEVE JOBS, 2005 COMMENCEMENT SPEECH AT STANFORD UNIVERSITY

It was not only that we wished to believe our prayers could reverse his condition. We wanted also to believe Dad could hear our cries. There were times he seemed to respond when we pleaded with him to stay with us. Maybe he heard us. Maybe he didn't. I don't guess we'll ever know, but I will always believe he stuck around for as long as he did—ten days or so—because he knew how impossible it would be for us to see him go.

As nightfall approached on the final evening of Dad's life, my son Jonathan and I sat with him in the small room of the Intensive Care Unit. I stood beside his bed between a wall of monitors that flickered and made loud noises. Resuscitation devices, intravenous lines, and tubes that seemed to reach everywhere surrounded my father. Jonathan stood at the foot of Papaw's bed. Just prior to this, our family had granted the hospital personnel permission to turn off the heart-lung machine. While they did not expect him to breathe on his own, we held out one last hope. When the artificial support was terminated, however, he might have taken a few breaths on his own, but I couldn't tell. I had decided to stay with him. My son, Jonathan, reached somewhere inside himself to find the courage to stay, too. I will always be grateful he did.

If you knew Jonathan, however, you'd be no more surprised than I was. From the day he came into this world, he's always been a gift to me in some special way. That's the main reason his mother and I gave him that name. In Hebrew, it means *gift*. He's always seemed so grown up to me. I give the credit for this to his mother. She read to him incessantly. He was talking in complete sentences when other children his age were barely saying "Mom" or "Dad." For this and other reasons, I started referring to him as "Daddy's Little Man." At no previous time did he demonstrate his maturity more than on what turned out to be the darkest moment of his father's life.

My mother, wife, daughter, two brothers, their families, and a host of family and friends waited in an over-crowded room we had converted into a makeshift home, complete with a kitchen, sitting room, and even sleeping quarters for several nights. They were exhausted and ready for the nightmare to be over. Our relentless, weeklong prayer of "Please, Lord, let him live" became the silent cry of "Take him, Lord, and do so quickly."

In my mental scrapbook, I have a picture of Dad's final moments when I leaned over him and whispered in his ear, "We're okay with this, Dad. I'll miss you more than you'll ever know." Actually, none of us were okay, but for some reason I felt the need to say we were.

Dad had big hands and long fingers. They seemed bigger this day, swollen from fluids, loss of use, maybe both. When they turned off the heart-lung machine, I don't recall if he attempted to breathe, but at some point I knew he was gone.

One other picture memory sticks with me. Standing beside Dad's lifeless frame, I had the strange sensation that one day I would write this story. I had no clue what I would write, when I would write, or even why I would write about it. I just knew I would. There's something even stranger than this. As I stood there, I thought of a professor I had in seminary many years before. His name was Francisco. He was my favorite professor during graduate studies. After leaving seminary, I lost touch with him. A few years later, I heard that he had died. I remembered a lecture he gave years before about an enlightened mystic out of Jewish mythology whose name was Enoch.

Overall, it was an unforgettable lecture, but, as with any lecture, I had long forgotten the specific details—that is, until the moment of my father's passing. Surprisingly, much of it came back to me, along with a ubiquitous awareness that the spirit of Enoch was in the room with me. In fact, from that moment to the present, this awareness has never left me. Logically, I have no way of either knowing or explaining why I have this feeling. I do know that I find comfort it in to this day.

Jonathan and I stayed at Dad's side for as long as we could. In the background, nurses unplugged cords, removed tubes, and routinely prepared the room for the family's final viewing. As they worked, I stepped over to Jonathan, took him by the hand, hugged him, and cried. I don't remember if we exchanged any words. No words were necessary.

> "Just as you'll never understand the mystery of life forming in a pregnant woman, so you'll never understand the mysteries at work in all God does."
>
> —ECCLESIASTES 11:5

When the medical personnel finished, we made our way to the waiting room to inform the others of Dad's passing, and another wave of grief hit. This time, though, it left no wake, and we were thankful, for we had things to do. Several family members went in to say their final good-byes. Then we gathered the blankets and pillows of our temporary home and organized ourselves for what we knew would be a large memorial service.

We never would have imagined how large, however. On the day of Dad's memorial service, people came from everywhere. One elderly woman said it was the largest funeral service she had ever witnessed, and

> "Death is your guru. Let it teach you how to live."
>
> —BUDDHA

she had been a member of the church all her life. More than a thousand friends, family, and acquaintances filled the sanctuary. It seemed that everyone knew Dad. His influence had reached farther than any of us realized. My older brother gave the eulogy. My younger brother sang. I brought the funeral message. The whole thing was surreal.

The Portal Opens: Doorway into Presence

In the months that followed my father's death and burial, I felt confused, afraid, and lost. I tried to help my mother manage her grief even as I struggled to handle my own. To say that my life unraveled is an understatement. Within twenty-four months of Dad's death, I left the ministry, began a new career, and went through a divorce. Were it not for the fact that the new job involved consulting with churches across America, which was ironic given my mental and emotional state, I would not have been in church at all.

When I left the ministry and went through the divorce, I stopped going to church almost entirely. I had to get away. I had pretended everything was okay in my life when it wasn't. I was tired of playing roles. I once read the following line: "When the pain of being the same is greater than the pain of being different, you will change."[1] Change was coming, but not yet.

I began to reject virtually everything I said I believed. I questioned what I did not reject, and I carried a quiver full of questions: "Where are you, God?" "Why did you let my dad die?" "What am I supposed to do now?" "Where are you, damn it?" "Why don't you answer me?" "Do you even care?" "Does anything matter?" "Does my life matter?"

On hundreds of occasions over the years, I counseled others who faced similar circumstances to believe in a caring, compassionate God. When grappling with grief and doubts of my own, however, I found it hard to believe God cared about anything or anyone.

I even had a few questions I wanted to ask Dad: "Where are you?" "Are you dead or alive?" "If you're alive, where are you?" "Will I ever see you again?" "I tried all my life to talk to you, to feel that you were listening to me, and on the day you join my church, you die? What the hell is that?" "Is this whole thing a cosmic joke, or just an illusion?" "What was it like to die? Painful? Fearful?" "What will death be like for me?" "Will I be afraid?"

I lived in a spiritual limbo for several years following Dad's death. Not until the afternoon of my awakening did I begin to see how his death, indeed how everything in my life, had been a portal into Presence. The words of Jesus finally made sense then: "I am the door" (John 10:7).

Though at first we typically resist them, any crisis is a doorway Life opens to us. Given the nature of our conditioning, however, it often takes a crisis to awaken us. For some who are deeply entrenched in conditioned religious thought and expectation, or whose egos are fixed and strong, it may take a series of crises to wake them up. Perhaps you know someone who experienced a crisis only to have it followed by a series of additional crises of equal or greater severity. Maybe he or she needed them. Yet, even with crises, some people never get it.

Pam, my wife now of several years, insists on setting her alarm clock to wake her up at 6:00 A.M. She seldom plans to get up, however, until 7:00 A.M.

I have often asked her, "Why not set the clock for 7:00 instead of being awakened several times, only to hit the snooze again and again?"

Her typical response is, "Because it takes four alarms to fully awaken me."

Next time you hear of a four-alarm fire, know that the severity of fire is so great that more than one truck and one team of firefighters is needed. In the same way, know it took both the death and the resurrection of Jesus for those closest to him to wake up to his spiritual identity and to that of their own. Although he had said, perhaps over and over again, "I am the light of the world" (John 9:5) and "You are the light of the world" (Matt 5:14), none of this began to dawn until the darkness of his death.

As my own eyes began to open, I noticed a profound difference in how I responded to every event in my life, no matter how inconsequential. For example, I used to resist anything I interpreted as an

> "Nothing is ever really lost, or can be lost, no birth, identity, form —no object of the world. Nor life, nor force, nor any visible thing."
>
> —FROM "CONTINUITIES"
> BY WALT WHITMAN

> "Everything and everyone who has ever come into my life has come with a purpose . . . to teach me a lesson about something."
>
> —WAYNE W. DYER

obstacle that upset my happiness or interfered with the pursuit of my goals. Shortly after the awakening, however, I boarded a commercial airline destined for Atlanta. It was 7:45 A.M. and we were already behind schedule by thirty minutes. The pilot informed us that, due to an electrical problem, the plane would be delayed even longer and could possibly be grounded altogether.

Before the awakening, I would have been frustrated by this kind of minor disruption, and even inclined to take it personally, as if airline officials plotted a way to complicate my life. The resistance would have manifested itself as complaints. If none of that was sufficient, I would call someone on my cell and complain.

This time, however, I didn't resist. Nor did I complain. I was noticeably surprised. I saw it as an opportunity, almost as if it was supposed to happen, the reason for which was mine to discover. I watched and listened. I became present, so to speak, and looked for the message from beyond or for a stranger I was supposed to meet. I reached for my notepad and began writing about my experience. You are reading its results. Perhaps this happened to me for no other reason than you might read about it now. If you watch, you are likely to see what you're destined to see. Who knows? If you are awake, you will know.

Where could you possibly go to find a healthier, happier, and more stress-free way to live than this? Perhaps many of my words seem odd to you. You perhaps feel resistance to some of them, but as you awaken, you will know for yourself the truth in these words. You will cease to resist what is given to assist you in knowing God.

By resistance, I am not suggesting that you lie down and let life step on you. Nor am I saying you pretend to be happy about everything that shows up, although the New Testament says, "In everything give thanks" (1 Thess 5:18, KJV). Some things are difficult to accept. On the spiritual path, though, you begin to know instinctively that since nothing is ever accidental, anything may serve as a portal into Presence. Your destiny could not unfold without the appearance of these circumstances. In other words, everything serves a higher purpose. Eckhart Tolle makes this point in a beautiful way

> "The things that make you weep contain something you need to know about."
>
> —CHRISTIANE NORTHRUP

in *A New Earth.* He writes, "Life will give you whatever experience is most helpful for the evolution of consciousness. How do you know this is the experience you need? Because this is the experience you are having at this moment."[2]

More profound words have seldom been spoken. When you remember them, as well as apply them to your life, they have the power to transform both how you receive and how you respond to everything. No less equal in beauty, and more familiar to Christians, are the words

> Joy and woe are woven fine,
> A clothing for the soul divine.
> Under every grief and pine,
> Runs a joy with silken twine.
>
> —FROM "AUGURIES OF INNOCENCE" BY WILLIAM BLAKE

of Saint Paul: "All things work together for good to those who love God" (Rom 8:28, KJV). If this is true, why resist what happens to you?

The sudden and unexpected end of my father's life was the surprising and unanticipated beginning of my own. How could I resent something as amazing and perfect as this? My confusion, as well as many of my questions and doubts, have disappeared. Sure, I still ask questions, but with none of the background cynicism, the latent resentment, or the existential fear I had before. There is only a profound awareness of Presence and, with it, gratitude and joy.

Notes

1. Deepak Chopra, *Why Is God Laughing? The Path to Joy and Spiritual Optimism* (New York: Harmony Books, 2008) 80.

2. Eckhart Tolle, *A New Earth: Awakening to Your Life's Purpose* (New York: Plume, 2008) 41.

Part 2

Archetype of the Sacred Art

*"And Enoch walked with God: and he was not; for
God took him."*

—*Genesis 5:5*

*"An infinite God . . . does not distribute himself that
each may have a part, but to each one he gives all of
himself as fully as if there were no others."*

—*A. W. Tozer*

A God-awakened life is a transformational shift in consciousness that brings
the sacred Presence into immediate awareness. In this awakened state, there
is a ubiquitous awareness that Intelligence suffuses all living things. This
awareness is not hypothetical or speculative. It is real. Awareness of
Intelligence or Presence makes you conscious of the fact that what seems
real—the material world around you—is actually a passing illusion, and
what seems unreal—the spiritual world—is actually what's real and eternal.
That is, it's not what's seen, but what's unseen that is most real. Saint Paul
expressed it beautifully: "The things we see now are here today, gone tomorrow. But the things we can't see now will last forever" (2 Cor 4:18).

As you wake up, a shift takes place in your consciousness. You become
more and more aware of yourself—that is, of your own feelings, hopes, and

dreams as well as disappointments and failures—and you accept it all. You feel no need to argue with what is. Rather, you are at peace with yourself and your reason for being in the world.

"The truth is, God talks to everybody."

—FROM *CONVERSATIONS WITH GOD* BY NEALE DONALD WALSCH

You've ended the madness of looking for yourself outside yourself—in things, relationships, a career or calling, roles, functions, a belief system, and so on. You know that any of these has the capacity of adding richness to your life, but none of these could ever *be* your life. Furthermore, instead of just one or a few other persons, you sense a deep connectedness to all sentient beings. The prejudices, stereotypes, opinions, and beliefs about others, part of your conditioned upbringing, come into the light of your consciousness. You are more aware of your conditioned responses to people and circumstances and therefore capable of changing what needs changing. What should disappear fades away. What should expand does so, too. None of it happens overnight, but on the awakened, spiritual path, you are amazed at how much more at peace you feel with life itself. You live what Jesus described as "the abundant life" (John 10:10, KJV).

The abundant, God-aware life is perfectly illustrated in the life of Enoch, an enlightened spiritual master who perhaps lived thousands of years ago. Early Jewish and Christian saints, including many of the early Church Fathers, regarded Enoch as an enlightened soul whose writings were sacred. In spite of this widespread acknowledgment, however, by the fourth century, his works were excluded from the canon of Scripture, or what we know today as the Bible. This is regrettable, as Enoch's example of the enlightened life holds the secret to life and death. Enoch lived as God desires all to live. He died as God desires all to die. Because his writings are not widely accessible, however, his example has been virtually hidden from countless generations.

Enoch has much to share with us. Our Jewish ancestors knew this, which is why, long before Jesus and for many years after him, Jewish and Christian saints venerated Enoch. This is accentuated by the fact that only two persons in the Bible are credited with having "walked with God." They are Noah and Enoch. That alone is puzzling enough to warrant an investigation.

What does it mean *to walk with God*? Is this simply an anthropomorphic way of describing a spiritual life? In part, yes, but it is patently more than this, too. The inference is that a depth of intimacy existed between

Enoch and God that was unknown to almost everyone else, either before or after him.

There was a time when intimacy prevailed between God and humans and between humans and all other sentient beings. In Jewish mythology, something was lost in creation. When the serpent, whom legend calls Satan but we also know as ego, lifted its noxious head, its toxic venom contaminated human consciousness of the Divine. Ego severed what was once a magnificent, effortless attachment to God. God was successfully edged out of human consciousness.

The story of Enoch is a story of recovery. What Adam and Eve forfeit in the creation narratives is reclaimed in Enoch. The writer of Genesis makes this point with the words, "Enoch walked with God" (Gen 5:24). The previous reference to "walking" in the book of Genesis tells us God walked alone. While God once walked in harmony with Adam and Eve, separation became the order of the day (Gen 3:8).

Enoch broke that cycle, however. What his predecessors and contemporaries could not do, and most of his successors have not done since, Enoch did. He lived in spiritual union with Eternal Presence. He walked with God. The good news is this: if he did, others may too.

Enoch is a universal archetype of the sacred art of knowing God. If anyone was ever awake, it was Enoch. The remarkable way he lived and the equally remarkable way he died hold the secret to living and dying today. Though relegated to a place of obscurity for centuries, his legacy is instructive to the spiritually discerning. Your interest in him is the next step you're destined to take in your journey of awakening.

Enoch lived as God would have you live—in unity with Being itself. Enoch died as God would have you die—with satisfaction, contentment, and no fear.

Enoch was born, lived, and died the way God originally planned for everyone—that is, until the ego contaminated the human condition, making birth painful, life problematic, and death what the New Testament calls "the last enemy" (1 Cor 15:26, KJV).

In the Bible, Enoch is mentioned only three times: in Genesis in the Old Testament and in Jude and Hebrews in the New Testament (see Gen 5:18-24; Jude 14-15; and Heb 11:5). Most of what little we know about him comes from Rabbinic, Islamic, and ancient Greek traditions as well as the few books attributed to his authorship.[1] One such book is known as *The Book of Enoch*.

One day recently, I had the amazing opportunity of observing an ancient, second-century copy of this book. Though not the actual parchment on which Enoch wrote, it is more than 1,500 years old, making it one of the oldest known manuscripts in the world.

I was traveling on business trip when I received a message about this remarkable discovery.

Note

1. The books attributed to Enoch are known as *1 Enoch* (or *Book of Enoch*), *2 Enoch* (or *Secrets of Enoch*), and *3 Enoch* (or *Mystical Enoch*). Early Christians of the second century were familiar with these writings, and many considered them sacred, including Church Fathers like Justin Martyr, Irenaeus, Origen, Clement of Alexandria, and Tertullian. By the fourth century, however, the *Book of Enoch* was excluded from all Christian lists of books that would comprise what is commonly known as the Bible today. In no way, however, does this discount the significance of Enoch's life or his death. In fact, his experience of death was so rare and different that virtually everyone since then has mistakenly concluded he did not experience death at all. He did die, however, just as everyone dies. But the way he lived and the way he died were preserved for a reason. In the story of Enoch, we find the secret that can transform the quality of our lives and solve the quandary of our deaths.

Chapter 10

A Visit to Remnant Trust

"Coincidence is God behaving incognito."
—Author Unknown

I called home one morning to wish Pam a good day. We spoke briefly, and then she said, "Oh, before I forget, you'll never believe what I saw in the newspaper this morning."

Pam is an avid reader. She still gets all her news the old-fashioned way—in the newspaper.

"What was in the paper?" I asked.

"There's a place nearby, some museum or something, that has a copy of a book by Enoch," she explained.

"What's the name of this place?" I asked.

I could hear papers shuffling in the background as she looked for the story.

"Here it is. Looks like the name of the place is Remnant Trust."

"Never heard of it," I responded. "What is it?"

"Well, says here, it's located across the Ohio River on the Indiana side and it's some kind of library or museum. It's an educational foundation that archives original and first-edition works that deal with a variety of topics, mostly liberty and stuff from American history."[1]

"I see, but what's that got to do with Enoch?"

"Well," she continued, "it seems they've picked up an actual copy of a manuscript called *The Book of Enoch*."

> **Your passage through time and space is not at random. You cannot but be in the right place at the right time.**
>
> —FROM *A COURSE IN MIRACLES*

"You're kidding me." I knew she wasn't, but I needed a response in which to package my excitement.

There was a long pause as I pondered the news. My mind took an instant detour, and the word "synchronicity" came to mind. Swiss psychologist Carl Jung coined this word to describe meaningful coincidences that occur in our lives. I've always wondered why he did not label all coincidences as meaningful. It seems to me that they are. In this instance, I knew the discovery of the article was no accident. While writing a book on Enoch, I learned that one of the oldest manuscripts ever found about him showed up fifteen minutes from my home.

"Incredible!" I exclaimed. "Cut out the article for me, would you?"

"Doing it as we speak," she answered.

We talked about a few other things, but I could not stop thinking about the discovery she'd made. It was no accident. I tried to remain cautiously excited in case the prized find turned out to be off limits to a history novice like me.

I flew home the next morning, and as soon as I arrived I called and made an appointment to visit the Remnant Trust. I could hardly wait to see firsthand this pre-1500 Ethiopian manuscript of *The Book of Enoch*. It was the only known copy of its kind in either the United States or Europe. Not long ago, in fact, a professor of Hebrew Scriptures at Notre Dame inspected the book and estimated it to be one of five manuscripts holding the distinction as the oldest known texts of its kind in the world.

On the day of my visit, I was amazed at the security of the place. I was more amazed, however, that they gave me permission to hold and closely inspect the wood-bound book. It was written in red and black ink on animal-skin paper. Surprisingly, given its age, the text was much clearer than I expected. The fact that I could not understand the Ethiopian language in which it was written diminished neither its significance nor the mystery associated with it.

As I observed the book, turned the pages, and held it like one might hold a newborn, I suddenly had the same feeling I had at the bedside of my deceased father. I felt a presence. Maybe it was Enoch's presence. I do not know, but I knew this rendezvous was not random. After all, there are only 17,500 museums in America, yet *The Book of Enoch* showed up in my hometown. I took it as a sign that the desire I felt to reintroduce Enoch into the mainstream of contemplative, spiritual thought was part of my human destiny. You feel a great sense of peace when you observe your destiny unfold before you. It's not something you conjure up or control. You watch, instead, and you marvel at the ease and perfection of it all.

I stayed at the Remnant Trust for about an hour. Surprisingly, the curator left me alone to visit with Enoch and his book. She must have sensed the sacredness this moment held for me. When I finished, I replaced the book in the display container, expressed my appreciation for the rare opportunity, and returned home.

The mysteriousness of this experience underscores the seriousness of my writing task—a task I consider a sacred appointment. As you contemplate Enoch—who he was, how he lived, and the manner in which he died—you'll know why God preserved his legacy.

Enoch's example of living and dying is *The Enoch Factor*.

Note

1. The article was by Peter Smith, "Rare Religious Text on Loan," *Courier-Journal* (Louisville KY), 16 February 2008, B5.

Chapter 11

Professor Francisco and Mr. Enoch

A Prayer of Mary Davis

I am the place that God shines through.
He and I are one not two.
He needs me where and as I am.
I need not doubt, not fear, nor plan.
If I but be relaxed and free,
He'll work his plan of love through me.
                    —*From* Awakening to the Sacred
                              by Lama Surya Das

"The invariable mark of wisdom is to see the mirac-
ulous in the common."
                    —*Ralph W. Emerson (1803–1882)*

I first met Enoch during the year of the hostage crisis in Iran. Saddam Hussein had just risen to power in Iraq. The Village People were singing "YMCA," and the Charlie Daniels Band was chasing the devil somewhere down in Georgia.

Kate Hudson and Pink were born that year, too. John Wayne died of lung cancer. I'm sure other notables appeared and disappeared from the scene. My meeting with Enoch took place in 1979. I was twenty-four years old, a first-year seminarian, and studying to enter the professional ministry.

One beautiful fall morning, I was in a hurry to get to a class in Old Testament interpretation. Many students regarded courses in Hebrew and Old Testament history as tedious and boring. Had it not been for the professor himself, Clyde T. Francisco, I might have, too.

I kicked my way through the freshly fallen leaves covering the lawn that separated the parking lot from the administration building. By now, many of the leaves had succumbed to the changing season. They cracked under the crushing weight of my feet, as if to voice a loud and final objection to their irreversible fate.

Professor Francisco was one of the most popular on campus and, if you did not arrive early, you had to sit in the back or, worse, stand along the walls. His lectures were always inspiring, and often students who were not enrolled in his class showed up just to hear him speak. I was intent on finding a seat front and center.

Francisco loved to play golf, too, and it was not uncommon for him to arrive at class wearing a golf shirt and pants. On this day, he added a pair of golf shoes. I remember thinking he must have been on the fourteenth tee preparing to drive the green when he remembered he had a class to teach at the seminary. Hurrying to get to class, he forgot to change his shoes.

We had just finished what Scripture scholars call source theories on the origins of the book of Genesis. *Source Theory* is the study of the text and stories of the Old Testament that were passed orally from one generation to the next. They are known as *oral traditions* because, long before the stories were written down, they were shared verbally, or orally. They came from many different sources, too, which explains why, if you read any of them carefully, you sometimes find discrepancies between them.

For example, in Genesis 6:19-20 (which is known as the "P" source for *Priestly Source*), God instructs Noah to take one male and one female of every kind of animal into the ark with him. Then, one chapter later, in Genesis 7:2-3, (which is known as the "J" source for *Yahweh Source*), Noah is told to take *seven* of every clean animal and two of all unclean animals. Which was it? One male and one female? Or seven clean and two unclean of each?

Here's another example. For many years, I wondered, if Adam and Even were truly the first two homo sapiens to inhabit the earth, then how did Adam understand the admonition in Genesis 2:23-24 to "leave his father and mother and cleave unto his wife," since Adam presumably had no mother or father?

Discrepancies like this used to disturb me. They disturb most religious people who were raised as I was to believe the Bible is "perfect," meaning it contains no discrepancies or errors. Of course, those who taught me to think of the Bible in these ways were sincere but misguided. They thought that by telling us the Bible is "inerrant" and therefore error-free, they respected the Bible and helped protect its place of authority. In fact, they innocently disrespected the Bible and undermined its credibility as well as its authority. Only a blind and weak, even if innocent, faith would tell a person to believe something that simply is not so.

Once I gave up my illusions about the Bible, I was drawn into the richness and beauty of its spiritual message. Rather than a rulebook of "dos" and "don'ts," it became a spiritual guide for my life. I also figured out why there were apparent discrepancies like the one above. If Adam and Eve were the first two people, how did Adam understand the instruction to "leave his father and mother" and be joined to Eve, his wife? I think this is not a reference to Adam and Eve. Although the advice is given in the context of the story of the first marital pair, Jewish elders were giving instructions to all succeeding generations. It was a wise bit of advice they were giving to new families, too. The counsel could be described as the *principle of colonization.*

In ancient Jewish families, it was assumed that a girl would leave her parents, her family of origin, and give her loyalty to her husband and their new family. It was not always assumed, however, that a guy would leave his family and make the new colony his priority. For partners in any relationship who are serious about the long-term survival of their union, this is some of the wisest counsel they could receive. The new household takes preeminence over the old. This is the *principle of colonization.*

This same principle or standard is what gave birth to our nation. When the Europeans came to the New World, it wasn't long before they faced a question of epic proportions. Were they going to give the colonies in the New World their loyalty, or would they remain loyal to their native homeland? As we know from history, they chose to give their loyalty to the new colonies, and America was born.

Professors like Clyde Francisco helped young seminarians like me both to see and love the richness of wisdom that is the Old and New Testaments. Rather than "destroying" the Bible for me, which many in my tradition warned would happen if I went to seminary, the scholars with whom I studied only deepened my love for the sacred writings. Contrary to my misguided contemporaries, my professors didn't have to believe a lie about the Bible to help me see, know, and revere the truth within it.

On this day, as Francisco walked into class, he stepped behind the lectern, grinned, and confessed, just as I had suspected, that he had been on the golf course when he remembered he had a class of students to teach.

Without missing a beat, and perhaps to return quickly to the golf course and finish his game, he said, "We'll begin reading at the fifth chapter of the book of Genesis."

This is what he read:

> And all the days that Adam lived were nine hundred and thirty years: and he died. And Seth lived a hundred and five years, and begat Enos: And Seth lived after he begat Enos eight hundred and seven years, and begat sons and daughters: And all the days of Seth were nine hundred and twelve years: and he died. (Gen 5:5-8, KJV)

At the risk of losing readers, I intentionally limit the verses of this chapter, which can be tedious to read. Some passages of the Bible, even some books, are hard to read and harder still to understand. The book of Leviticus holds this distinction, as does the fifth chapter of Genesis.

Professor Francisco spared us nothing, however. He read every word of every sentence. As he did, my mind wandered. I looked out one of the floor-to-ceiling windows that opened onto the leaf-covered promenade outside. There were always students skipping class and playing football, kicking a soccer ball, or pitching a baseball. Today was no different. I wondered if they had not made a better choice.

I looked at other students, and I think the same question was on their minds: "Where's he going with this?"

Reading through a monotonous list of Old Testament names wasn't interesting. None of us could pronounce their names. Their life spans were highly suspect, and their historical significance was of little consequence. So little, in fact, that all the historical record remembered about any of them is that they were born, begat, and died.

Today's lecture had gotten off to a slow start. I remember thinking, *If his golf game began today the way this lecture has begun, he probably needed several mulligans to rescue his game from embarrassment.*

As if he were inviting our bewilderment to be certain of our attention, he continued reading. Just when I thought he might never stop, he did. He looked at us and began to speak of things that I could tell were sacred to him. Maybe it was the words he used or the seriousness with which he spoke. Or maybe it was the fact that he spoke with a soft voice and a slight stutter, characteristics that accompanied each other whenever he spoke of things mysterious.

"Uh . . . uh . . . students," he began, "Today, I . . . I . . . I . . . want to introduce you to an ancient mystic who may just be the most significant person in all th . . . th . . . the Old Testament. What he will teach you—if you ever really ge . . . ge . . . get it—will change everything about your life."

With that introduction, he returned to the text and began reading again the verses he had read already, only this time with the intention of drawing our attention to the meaning behind the words.

> And Enoch lived sixty and five years, and begat Methuselah: And Enoch walked with God after he begat Methuselah three hundred years, and begat sons and daughters: And all the days of Enoch were three hundred sixty and five years: And Enoch walked with God: and he was not; for God took him. (Gen 5:21-24, KJV)

"Did you catch it?" he asked, as if he thought we might have but wanted to make sure we did.

"Catch what?" I wondered, because I did not.

I think he heard my question because he continued, "The fact that Enoch's appearance interrupted the birth, begat, and death cycle? Why do you suppose the writer does this?"

A cascade of other questions followed that one, each with comment and commentary, and by the time he finished, he had painted a masterful portrait of this mysterious saint out of Jewish antiquity. From that day to the present, the portrait he painted of Enoch hangs in a sacred room in my memory.

"Who was Enoch, anyway?" asked Francisco. "Why do we know so little about him? He is said to have 'walked with God.' Only two persons have ever been so described. Why only these two? And what could it possibly mean to 'walk with God'?"

He paused again, only longer this time. At one moment, I thought he might close his notes, turn, and walk out of the lecture hall. But then, he presented another round of questions: "How do we explain that Enoch and his contemporaries lived to be hundreds of years of age? Was time calculated differently? Or did they somehow pull it off? And if so, how did they do it? Furthermore, why can't we live to be this old today?

"Virtually everyone wants to live to a ripe old age. What if this story is suggesting there is a secret somewhere to the fountain of youth? What if people could live to be three or four hundred years of age? Wouldn't they eventually find the happiness they can't seem to find in the seventy-five or so years they have now?

"Finally," he concluded, "what are we to make of the words, 'and he was not, for God took him' [Gen 5:24]? Does this mean Enoch did not die? If he did not, how did he escape death? Isn't death something everyone will experience? Is the writer hinting at the possibility of avoiding death altogether? Or is he saying there's a way to die that's qualitatively different than the way most people die?"

As any reputable scholar would, Francisco gave us the background information—such as the reason Enoch's story was preserved and why history all but ignored him. He gave us the varied speculations surrounding Enoch's appearance and sudden disappearance from the biblical record. It was the personal way he spoke of Enoch, however, that I found most fascinating. You would have thought the two of them were on the fourteenth tee together when Francisco remembered he had a class to teach.

These memories came back to me, and brought comfort with them, on the day I stood at the bedside of my father. That's also when I knew these stories were somehow inextricably tied together. Somewhere in them was the secret to the meaning of life and death. Somewhere in them was the secret to the necessity of my own death if I was to know Life.

In the academic world, Francisco was a highly esteemed Old Testament scholar, but it was not his intelligence that attracted me. I had known many smart people over the years. Instead, his wit and wisdom drew me. He loved life, and anyone who knew him knew this. But he was real, too, and genuine. When he spoke about the meaning of life, you did not question whether he had found it. You knew he had. When he spoke of death, you did not wonder if he feared it. You knew he did not.

During this lecture, I first heard Francisco speak of death, but it would not be the last time. In fact, I heard him speak of it on many occasions. It was as if he was totally at peace with death and, therefore, comfortable in its presence. On at least one occasion, perhaps more, I heard Francisco tell us how he would one day die. He described it in such precise detail that you would have concluded he had either lost his mind or experienced his passing already.

This is essentially what I remember him saying: "Someday, I will stand behind a lectern like I am doing today, open my notes to begin a lecture, and, at that precise moment, God will call me home. I will slump behind the lectern, my body, that is, while I make the transition from the material dimension to that of the spiritual."

The first time I heard him say this, I scoffed and thought, *What is he talking about? He cannot be serious. Who can predict how they'll die?*

You can imagine my consternation, however, when some ten years later, I heard that Francisco died. He did not die just any death. He died in the precise manner he had predicted years before.

Like Enoch, Francisco was not, for God took him.

Chapter 12

A New Perspective toward Aging and Death

"We are not human beings having a spiritual experience; we are spiritual beings having a human experience."

—*Pierre Teilhard de Chardin (1881–1955)*

Dying and death are not the consequences for the first couple's sin in the Garden of Eden. While this has been the traditional position of the Christian church for centuries, an alternative perspective is not only possible but preferable. This perspective is more consistent with what the Bible teaches about the two inescapable realities we share with all living things—birth and death. It is also more consistent with what other faith traditions taught about death centuries before the advent of Christianity.

The Meaning of Spiritual Death

As the legend goes, Adam and Eve disobeyed God and ate the fruit of the forbidden tree. At that moment, ego was born and they began to die—spiritually speaking, that is. They did not die physically, as they went on living long after their "eyes . . . were opened" (Gen 3:7). Though this phrase about their eyes being opened is frequently overlooked, it holds the key to interpreting the meaning of the story. Believing the serpent's lie, Adam and Eve ate the forbidden fruit thinking they would see more as well as know more. In other words, they thought

> While I thought I was learning how to live, I have really been learning how to die.
>
> —LEONARDO DA VINCI

they would become the beneficiaries of greater insight, understanding, and awareness, as well as completeness and fulfillment.

The serpent, representative of the ego, spoke to Eve. This is a mythic way of describing a conversation Eve had with herself. Eve debated within herself—that is, the ego had a conversation with itself—about whether something was missing from her life. Her thoughts were mixed with doubts. She wondered whether there was more insight, knowledge, and awareness beyond what God had given to her already. These thoughts were laced with suspicion that God might be holding out on them. The longer she lived with her suspicious thoughts, the more they shaped her feelings and attitudes toward God. It was a matter of time before her thoughts translated into actions that had dire consequences. Eventually, she ate the forbidden fruit.

This is how sin, or the ego, progressively materializes in every human being. You can observe this progression of thoughts to actions in the chart below. What begins as a thought becomes a feeling that, with more time, ultimately manifests in a behavior or action.

Thoughts	Feelings/Attitudes	Actions/Behaviors
Can I trust the universe? Does God have my interests at heart?	Doubt, Suspicion, Fear, Distrust, Despair, Discouragement	Isolation, Independence, Self-sufficient or Tentative, Withdrawn
I'm not happy. Life's unfair. God's holding out on me.	Frustration, Disappointment, Anger, Discontent	Greed, Ambitious, Selfish, Competitive, Compulsive
I'm not enough. I don't have enough. I'm missing something.	Ashamed (Naked), Inadequate, Incomplete, Incompetent, Sad	Driven and Competitive or Lazy, Jealous, Miserly, Selfish, Egocentric
I'm a failure, a royal screw-up. I never do anything right!	Guilt, Remorse, Sadness, Anger, Hatred, Disappointment	Blame, Accuse, Attack, Deny, Defend, Label, Judge, Criticize
I can't please God. I try and try but can't quite make it with him.	Sadness, Frustration, Despair, Hopelessness, Guilt	Driven, Competitive, Rules, Laws, Dogmas, Doctrines, Burnout

When you look at each of the thoughts or questions in the first column, you realize any one or all of them might have been on the minds of Adam and

Eve. When reading the story of their rebellion, the mistake we often make is to assume it occurred in a matter of minutes. It is more likely, however, to have taken place over a significant span of time.

It's not the random thoughts that get you into trouble. It's what you do with the thoughts once they appear. When thoughts linger, usually actions result and consequences follow. Since Adam's and Eve's thoughts were primarily of a negative nature—doubt, distrust, discontent, and so on—these thoughts manifested themselves in destructive actions.

Essentially, this is the Law of Attraction I discussed earlier in Part 1. Since everything is energy and information, as Albert Einstein's famous formula $E = mc^2$ reminds us, we know that thoughts vibrate at varying energy frequencies. Had the thoughts of Adam and Eve vibrated at higher energy frequencies—that is to say, had their thoughts been filled with confidence, trust, contentment, and so on—perhaps the history of the first family might have been written differently. But, since their thoughts vibrated at lower energy frequencies—that is to say, since their thinking was filled with doubt, distrust, discontent, and so on—their resulting actions, as symbolized in eating the forbidden fruit, severed their natural feeling of felt oneness with God.

James, the New Testament writer, points to the same progression from thinking to feeling to living, showing how an innocent lust can become an insidious act of sin. Though the words he uses are different, the reality toward which he points is the same: "Every man is tempted, when he is drawn away of his own lust, and enticed. Then, when lust hath conceived, it bringeth forth sin: and sin, when it is finished, bringeth forth death" (Jas 1:14-15, KJV).

Substitute the word *thoughts*, or even the word *ego*, for James's word *lust* and the point he makes, as well as the progression he illustrates, is unmistakable. All negative and aberrant behaviors, all unhealthy and unproductive activities, and all dysfunctional and destructive actions, whether on a global scale between nations or individually between persons, start as thoughts. As I have said already, when you know this, you'll be more cautious about the thoughts you think.

Instead of being the beneficiaries of greater insight, awareness, and completeness, Adam and Eve got the opposite. Their actions left them feeling "naked," which is another way of saying ashamed, vulnerable, bewildered, or even separated, fearful, and alone. The "I" in Adam became the "I" and the "Myself" to which I referred earlier. This is how the ancient world explained the appearance of egocentricism, a condition it described as "fallen" or as "sinful," by which they meant humans "missed the mark." They failed to remain connected to their spiritual center.

From that point on, everything changed. Their thinking became more and more negative and filled with doubt, their feelings and emotions dysfunctional, and their actions often regrettable. Lost was the feeling of oneness and unity within themselves, with each other, and with God. The natural intimacy they once knew with each other and with their Creator disappeared. Consequently, they spent the remainder of their lives looking for what was missing, which was their awareness of the ineffable Presence. This is what the sacred Scriptures mean by spiritual death.

Birth and Death

Spiritual death is *not* physical death. It's a misreading of the ancient record to conclude that physical death was the punishment God inflicted on Adam and Eve because of their rebellion in the garden. While it is true that physical death became problematic for them and everyone else who has followed them, it was not a penalty for their sin.

> The quality of your life depends on how you resolve the question of your death.

Birth and death have always been part of the Divine plan for the human family. It was never God's original plan that Adam and Eve, or anyone else for that matter, live forever on this earth or in this physical form we call the body. Such a belief is, in fact, indefensible either in Scripture or in nature itself. Saint Paul said as much when he likened the human body to a house made with hands that would eventually dissolve and disappear (2 Cor 5:1). Moreover, since the opposite of birth is death, just as you are born, you can be certain you will die. That's the only thing about which you *can* be certain. It's the destiny of every living thing.

Separation within and without was the consequence of Adam and Eve's actions. In other words, what died in them was their mental-emotional relation to themselves, to each other, to all other living things, and to God. This loss of the natural state of felt oneness with the Creator is why they and everyone after them look for what they feel is missing from their lives. Unfortunately, most people spend their lives looking in the wrong places. They search outside themselves to find what lies only within them.

In this regard, Adam and Eve represent every human being. You are yourself Adam or Eve. Try reading the story from this perspective and see what happens.

The Creation Story . . . Your Own Story

There was a time when I debated whether the Genesis account of creation was true and whether Adam and Eve were the first two people. On this side of a radically different spiritual experience, however, I am sometimes amazed at the depth of insanity in which I lived. To argue the scientific viability of the creation account, or to debate the efficacy of Adam and Eve, is to miss the point of the Genesis story altogether. The creation narratives work much better for us if we read them as a mythical tale of our own story.

The word *genesis* is the Hebrew word *bereshith*, which literally translated means "in beginning." Virtually every modern translation mistakenly adds the definite article "the" between the words *in* and *beginning*. That mistranslation has misled countless religious people who have assumed the point of the story is to give a scientific account of creation, as in "the" beginning. It's not, however, a story about *the* beginning. It is, instead, a story about *your* beginning. It's a story about what went wrong in you and me and how it might be corrected.

Since it's the story of your beginning, here's how it might go:

When you first appeared—that is to say, at your own creation—you entered this world and enjoyed, as did Adam and Eve before you, a deep, felt sense of connection to the Creator. Of course, you did not know this just as you knew little else. But those around you knew. They could see the Divine in your eyes. You may have felt they were simply amazed at how cute you were when they held you up, giggled at your smiles, and made funny sounds at you. The truth is, though, they could see in your eyes what they had lost in their own.

Then, one day, your serpent appeared. Call it the self, the ego, sin, whatever works for you. These

> "Humans and animals come to the same end —humans die, animals die . . . We all end up in the same place —we all came from dust, we all end up as dust."
>
> —ECCLESIASTES 3:19-22

are only words, pointers to a condition whose complexity requires many words to explain. As your serpent emerged, this connection to yourself, to Cosmic Intelligence, seemed to fade away, even to disappear altogether. At least, it felt as if it did.

Suddenly, your world, once friendly and joyful, now seemed hostile, lonely, and insecure. While you made grand self-discoveries, you made other discoveries, too, more secretive in nature. These discoveries you made through childhood and adolescence were too embarrassing to admit. At times, it was as if you felt naked, vulnerable, and insecure, but in the competitive, hostile environment in which you grew up, helplessness was not a weakness you could freely admit. You pretended to be stronger and more secure than you felt. In fact, you learned to do a lot of pretending.

There were other secrets, too, but you seldom talked about them. Many were frightening, some perplexing, and all made you feel alone and afraid. Even so, you were never alone. You simply thought you were—an innocent mistake of consciousness. God was still there within you. It's just that you became busy with yourself, your own interests, ambitions, accomplishments, and pretensions. Everyone around you seemed pleased by your emerging independence, self-sufficiency, and determination. They duly rewarded you for it.

However, when the activities of life lagged long enough for you to be alone with your thoughts, a sense of emptiness, even confusion, surfaced inside. Everyone around you seemed to have an opinion about how to take care of such feelings, but since most of them seemed as dispossessed and confused as you, you realized that following their advice would merely give new meaning to the proverbial "blind leading the blind" (Matt 15:14).

You searched for something that, like a dimmer switch, would turn up the Light of Consciousness within you. You wanted to bring wisdom back into your life and restore a sense of spiritual vitality that you'd lost long ago or never realized you had.

I absolutely believe that what you thought was lost isn't lost at all—that your relentless searching isn't necessary. It seems too simple, doesn't it?

"But isn't there something I have to do?" you might wonder.

I would say to you, "Yes, of course, you can do everything and be nothing. But hasn't that been your routine for years? You have everything but feel as if you're nothing. Wouldn't you prefer to do nothing and be everything—everything that matters, that is? Be still; have a look within; and enjoy. Don't make this into a problem, some effort, something else you must do in order to be. There's nothing to do, nothing to find. God has done it all—that's why it's called grace. The Light you seek is still burning within you. Otherwise, you'd have no interest in spiritual things. Have a look and see for yourself. *This* is your Divine purpose, the reason for which you're here. If you miss this, you've missed the point of your own life."

You decide to "let go and let God," as they say, figuring you had nothing to lose, anyway. What you find is a bottomless well, an Infinite Wellspring deeper than the universe beyond you. Grace dawns. Your search ends. It is Genesis, your *Genesis*, all over again.

Birth and Death: A Shared Reality

Humans share two realities with all other living things—*birth and death*. No other animal but the human animal travails in birth, trembles at death, or finds life and living troublesome. This is precisely because no other animal has an ego-driven nature. If you observe nature, for example, you'll witness animals willingly embrace the pain associated with birth and live out their existence, however short or long it may be, never complaining about either. In absolute peace with life itself, they consequently exhibit no phobia about dying or death.

Watch the human animal, however, and you observe the opposite—the unnatural repudiation of all pain; a stubborn resistance to the aging process; the feeling that life is an indecipherable riddle; and a loathing of death itself. You will never see a bird rant or rave because its feathers wilt, fade, and fall out. You will never observe a tree, shrub, or flower fretting and worrying whether the sun will shine or the rains will fall. Only humans wage a futile war with wrinkles, worry about life and living, and writhe over death itself.

The reason for this? Unlike the world of nature, humans have lost their natural bond to Life itself. The ego has erased God from consciousness. Animals and plants instinctively know, as Jesus eloquently put it, that the Father clothes and cares for them. "Look at the birds," said Jesus. "They don't plant or harvest or store food in barns. . . . Look at the lilies of the field. . . . They don't work or make their clothing yet Solomon in all his glory was not dressed as beautifully as they are" (Matt 6:25-29, NLT).

The human ego is the guilty party. That's why it is important that ego die in you before you die—that is to say, if you'd like to raise the quality of your life and solve the quandary of death, you have no choice but to rid yourself of ego. Until you do, it will be as a flaming sword "guarding the path to the Tree-of-Life" (Gen 3:24), the garden of God's Presence. Ego must die. Jesus said as much on several occasions (Matt 16:24; Mark 8:34; Luke 9:23).

Only the ego in you has trouble with living, aging, and dying. The real *you* has no difficulty with these. Your ego knows, for example, that when the body dies—which is but one of its many attachments—it will die, too. It naturally panics. The more identified you are with ego—your mind and thoughts, roles and functions, beliefs and opinions, and so forth—the more anxiety you feel about living, aging, and dying. On the other hand, the more in touch you are with the real *you*, the more comfortable you'll be with life and the more confident you'll feel in the face of death.

> To see a world in a grain of sand
> And a heaven in a wild flower,
> Hold infinity in the palm of your hand
> And eternity in an hour.

—FROM "AUGURIES OF INNOCENCE" BY WILLIAM BLAKE

Immortality or Life beyond Death

Humans share uniquely with each other, but not with other living things, an insatiable curiosity with or desire for life beyond death. This desire is also fabricated by an ego wishing for its own survival. Since the real you—beyond form, thoughts, identity, and so on—is timeless and eternal, it could never desire what it is already—eternal. You are in your essence what your ego desires to be—complete and eternal.

Many religious people are unaware that the ego is running their lives. Consequently, they confuse their longing for and belief in immortality with what the New Testament calls Christian *hope*. From a scriptural standpoint, however, *hope* is neither a belief in eternal life nor a wishful longing for it. It is instead the quiet confidence in the eternal present, the *Now*, as Tolle calls it, an inner knowingness and resolute assurance that eternity is the timeless now. When you are in union with God, you know, as Saint Paul said, that "neither death, nor life, nor angels, nor principalities, nor powers, nor things present, nor things to come . . . shall be able to separate us from the love of God" (Rom 8:38-39, KJV).

When the ego still runs your life, this kind of quiet confidence escapes you. You may say things like, "I believe in heaven" or "I believe in eternal life," but the ego is still tormented by doubts about living forever. It trembles at the thought of having to die to find out. The ego mistakenly thinks its belief in eternal life is enough to secure its eternal destiny. This is its supreme delusion—a delusion under which I lived half my life. I rehearsed and could recite as well as any Christian the beliefs of my Christian faith regarding heaven and eternity, but doing so neither assailed my fears nor changed anything about my life. I remained terrified of death and equally troubled by life.

I now know, however, as I said earlier, that the ego in us only believes the things it's uncertain about. If it knew Life Eternal, what would ego need to believe? In other words, ego can make all the pompous pronouncements it wishes to make about spiritual things, but the ego has no connection to Transcendence. Its declarations, no matter how religious they sound, are deficient of meaningful substance. We, on the other hand, share in the eternal nature that is God.

The goal of the ego is survival. It thrives by making life a pain, death a predicament, and aging a problem. Why else do you think the collective ego in our culture is obsessed with pharmaceutical drugs to alleviate all pain from life—as if all pain were evil? What else would explain our culture's preoccupation with pleasure—the next party, the most exotic trip, or the newest toy? And how would you explain what Liz Kelly, *Washington Post* columnist, calls "celebritology," or celebrity obsession in our culture? The interest in who is dating, marrying, or cheating on whom? What they eat and wear? Where they live and vacation? Isn't the fascination simply envy (a function of the ego) behaving as a curiosity? A socially acceptable pastime that masks the meaninglessness you feel about your life by the imagined meaningfulness in someone else's?

Why is it that people in the United States obsess over food and fitness? What we eat, as well as what's in what we eat, how much we eat, how little we eat, even how quickly we eat? Isn't most of this obsession a cloaked fear of aging and dying?

Everyone talks about the importance of good health, but who talks about the importance of a good death? Ego loves to deceive people into believing they're wise to say, "Today is

> "The end of illusion—that is all that death is . . . painful only as long as you cling to illusion."
>
> —FROM *THE POWER OF NOW* BY ECKHART TOLLE

> "Even death is not to be feared by those who live wisely."
>
> —BUDDHA

a good day to live!" Wouldn't it be wiser to be able to say, as did the sages of old, "Today is a good day to die"? Wasn't Leonardo da Vinci correct when he purportedly said, "When I thought I was learning how to live, I was really learning how to die"?

In the "birth, begat, and died" cycle that is the fifth chapter of Genesis, it's as if the ancient storyteller wanted us to sense the repetitiveness, as well as the meaninglessness, in how people lived in his day. The irony is that, after all these centuries, little has changed. If the most that may be said of your life—the brief blip between your birth date and death date—is that you begat offspring who ended up repeating the cycle of madness that was your life, then what's the point of either your existence or theirs? Both are futile indeed. What could be more insane than to be born, begat, and die but miss Life itself?

Enoch's life interrupted the insanity. He showed his contemporaries and all who followed them a better way. Even though ego altered God's original design, making aging terrible, dying dreadful, and both so unthinkable that people would do anything to avoid them, Enoch came along and broke this cycle. He demonstrated an alternative way to live and die. Enoch showed how death could be the uninterrupted translation from one dimension of existence (material and physical) to another dimension (spiritual and metaphysical). It is precisely because Enoch had died before he died that he realized there was no death. His death was little more than an illusion of the mind. In realizing this, he was freed of the compulsive clinging to his own body, other people, things, the past or future, ideas and beliefs, and even his own life. He was free to live and die, and so he did, in the joy of God's ineffable presence.

> "There is only one cause for unhappiness: the false beliefs you have in your head, beliefs so widespread, so commonly held, that it never occurs to you to question them.
>
> —ANTHONY DE MELLO

Enoch's Translation or Spiritual Transformation

"By faith Enoch was translated that he should not see death" (Heb 11:5, KJV). Many Christians misunderstand this statement from the book of

Hebrews. They assume the words "he should not see death" mean Enoch never died. However, the writer of Hebrews means that when Enoch *was translated*—"transformed," "awakened," or "lifted up from one dimension of existence to another"—this spiritual transformation enabled him *to see*, meaning *to know* or *to experience*, death in a qualitatively different fashion from others. Translation, transformation, awakening, change—these are merely different words describing the same reality. An awakening changes not only how you live but also the way you view dying and death.

Death was not the problem for Enoch that it was for others. While others approached death with resistance, regrets, and even revulsion, Enoch approached it with acceptance, even with joy. Consequently, it was as if he had not died at all. That is, in fact, the legend that grew up around him. In the Kabbalistic mystical texts of Judaism, Enoch is frequently thought of as becoming the angel *Metatron* after he was "translated" (*metetethē*).

> He who lives in the present has eternal life.
>
> —FROM *THE LITTLE BOOK OF ATHEISTIC SPIRITUALITY* BY ANDRE COMTE-SPONVILLE

Instead of embracing what I've called the *Enoch Factor*, which is to die before you die, the collective ego in Enoch's contemporaries found a way to survive by saying Enoch never truly died. By making him into a legend of folklore, they were able to regard his life and death as not only a little different from everyone else's but *impossibly* different. Enoch became a kind of death-defying superhero who is impossible to emulate. I have long suspected this may be the real reason why the early Church Fathers did not include Enoch's books in the canon of Scripture. It had less to do with the esoteric nature of Enoch's writings and more to do with the ego in themselves.

Instead of exploring the nature of Enoch's *translation* or transformation, the ego succeeded in doing what the ego does in all religions. It makes heroes and heroines of those who, like Enoch, have mastered the art of "overcoming the world" (John 16:33; 17:16). In this way, their followers get the mistaken idea that their leader was not actually human at all. They think what their spiritual leader achieved was so remarkable that it escapes everyone else. Many followers of Hinduism, for example, believe *nirvana* is attainable only after the wheel of *samsara* ends or only after a person has cycled through many lifetimes. Some Buddhists believe *enlightenment* was enjoyed by the Buddha but is not something they should expect to attain in their lifetimes.

You find this perspective in any religion. It is true that Enoch, Buddha, Muhammad, Abraham, Jesus, and others were rare souls, but not because they were superhuman. They were simply human beings who lived in a higher state of consciousness. By dying to ego, they were free of narrow thinking, self-interests, self-obsessions, fears, anxieties, and so on.

In Christianity, some traditions have done this with Mary, the mother of Jesus. She is no longer simply the mother of Jesus, but the mother of God. It's as if the ego has found a clever way of making her into some kind of mythical character whose spiritual awareness and accomplishments are out of reach to ordinary people.

In believing in the "inerrancy of Scripture," my own tradition spends an inordinate amount of time trying to make Saint Paul's words, which were frequently inconsistent and contradictory, appear to be otherwise. Why can't we let people be people? Why must we make them infallible? Isn't it just the ego in us that does this? By dragging us into meaningless debates over the spiritual things biblical writers said, the ego manages to keep us from knowing the efficacy in what they did say.

It is my intention neither to disparage any spiritual master nor to detract from their extraordinary contributions and accomplishments. I only offer a perspective that I hope challenges the assumption that extraordinary people come into this world and live at a level of God awareness that is out of reach to others. If that is true, why do their words, as well as their teachings, invite those who come after them to know what they knew or to live as they lived?

This is precisely what is wrong with the Christian church in America. It is also what goes wrong in virtually every religion. Every weekend in the Christian church, pews, bleachers, and folding chairs are occupied by people who revere a Jesus they do not know. They can recite the creeds of their churches. Many of them are closely identified with the beliefs and traditions of their faith and are passionately loyal to the institution wherein their egos have found an identity or sense of self. They give and attend regularly. Some of them are highly involved in the programs and ministries of their churches. The fact is, however, that multitudes of them are clueless when it comes to following the path of Jesus and living a transformed, God-aware life. I know: I was one of them. The overwhelming majority of them know little of either what Jesus said or how he lived. What they do know is more academic than transformative. They know what their church believes, but as we have seen already, much of what the church obsesses over today has little, if anything, to do with living a Christ-conscious life.

The real followers of Jesus are not those who believe in Jesus and not even those who regularly attend or serve a church that believes in Jesus. Followers are those who take seriously what Jesus said, who deny self—die before they die—which the New Testaments calls "taking up their cross," and follow after him (Luke 14:27). That is to say, they are those who travel a path of ego denial and God realization. In other words, they walk with God.

Enoch, Jesus, Mary, Paul, and a host of others too numerous to mention, but found in all spiritual traditions, lived a God-aware life. They walked with God, but their awareness of Presence wasn't exclusive to them. It is true that you and I may never raise children who become the next Mother Teresa, Mohandas Gandhi, or Dalai Lama. We might never write hallowed epistles that one day get included in the canon of Sacred Scripture. We may never die a martyr's death. Still, we can live at the same level of God realization that will transform not only us, but the world around us.

This is the real meaning of salvation, conversion, enlightenment, or the awakened state of consciousness. This is the *Enoch Factor*: the sacred art of knowing God.

Chapter 13

Premonitions, Intuitions, and Hyperlinks to the Eternal

"It is better to travel well than to arrive."
—*The Buddha*

Before closing Part 2 and turning to how one might experience an awakening and so live and walk in the Sacred Presence, I want to address one more aspect of Enoch's life, or better, his death, as well as that of Professor Francisco.

I've lived long enough to know that many people have predicted not only when they would die but *how* they would die. They had a premonition or intuition or whatever, but, interestingly, it turns out that they died just as they said they would. Recently, for example, Senator Ted Kennedy died. Weeks before his death, he wrote a letter to Massachusetts governor Deval Patrick, House Speaker Robert DeLeo, and Senate president Therese Murray, encouraging them to move quickly to find a replacement for his seat should it soon become vacant. Did he have a premonition that within weeks of sending the letter he would be dead? Perhaps so!

As I write this, the daily news is obsessed with the death of Michael Jackson. It has been ruled a homicide. I doubt, however, that they will discover it was premeditated or planned. The prescription drug, Propofol, the kind administered only by professionals and only in a proper environment, was found in his body and likely played the primary role in his unexpected death. But then, his death may have been unexpected only to the public. In an interview hours after his death, Lisa Marie Presley, to whom Michael

Jackson was married for a brief period, made a comment that suggests Michael might have had a premonition of his death.

"He knew," said Lisa Marie.

When asked to explain, she said that one day, during their relationship, they talked about the death of her father, Elvis Presley, and Michael told her of a premonition. Elvis died in 1977 at the age of forty-two. Although his death was believed to be caused by a cardiac arrest, at least one post-mortem report indicated there were as many as fourteen different drugs in his system at the time of his death.

As Lisa Marie and Michael discussed Elvis's death, Presley explained to the reporter, "At some point he [M. Jackson] paused, stared at me intensely, and stated with almost calm certainty, 'I am afraid that I am going to end up like him, the way he did.'"[1]

Is there something to this? Can a person anticipate, even predict, his or her death? Perhaps. No one knows for sure. If it is possible, however, it may be related in some way to the mechanics of the mind or to another dimension of consciousness altogether, or it may have some connection to the Law of Attraction discussed earlier.

Our local paper carried a story recently of a mother who died six days after seeing her last wish fulfilled. Years before, she was diagnosed with terminal breast cancer and given six months to live. As you might imagine, the diagnosis was both shocking and devastating to her and her family. To die within six months would mean she not only died young but, more important to her, she would miss out on the high school graduation of her two daughters.

She made up her mind to live long enough to share their high school experience and to witness their graduation. Consequently, rather than dying in six months, as others unsuccessfully predicted, she lived six more years. Not only did she beat the medical odds, but she saw her wish fulfilled—almost, anyway.

A few months before their actual graduation, her condition worsened. When it became apparent that she would not likely make it to the actual commencement exercises, family and friends held a symbolic graduation complete with speeches, gowns, diplomas, and applause. It was a special affair captured in pictures and published in our local paper.[2]

When I read the story, I thought, *Though she missed their actual graduation by a few weeks, who can say that her death wouldn't have come sooner had she not decided how long she would live?*

Can you choose how long you'll live or when you'll die? I don't know. Sometimes it seems so, and I'm not referring to those who commit suicide. I'm talking about ordinary people in everyday circumstances. Almost everyone knows someone, or has heard of someone, who reports having had a premonition about their death or that of someone else. They seem to see, sense, or know something that transcends what we know and even logic itself.

Many years ago, while I was in seminary, I became friends with a student who remains a dear friend to this day. Although we live in different parts of the country and rarely talk, whenever we do, it's as if no time or distance has separated us. We pick up the conversation where it ended last.

During our seminary days, he met a girl who was studying for the ministry just as he was, and the two of them fell in love and got married. One day, during our last year of studies, they shared the good news that she was pregnant.

> "The breeze at dawn has secrets to tell you . . . Don't go back to sleep . . . Don't go back to sleep!"
>
> —RUMI

Several months passed, and one night I had a dream. I woke up shortly before dawn and sat straight up in bed, with the images of the dream still vivid in my mind. I looked at the alarm clock and, though it was still early, I knew I had to get dressed and go to the hospital in downtown Louisville.

As I shuffled about in the dark, my wife woke up and asked what I was doing.

"I just had the strangest dream," I explained, "and I must go to the hospital."

She rubbed her eyes as if that would make the situation clearer. "What are you talking about?"

"My dream," I responded. "I know it's weird, but in my dream I saw David and Linda. As you know, she's been expecting, and I saw the two of them in my dream walking into the hospital. I know it seems unbelievable, but I know they will be there when I arrive."

"You're making no sense whatsoever," she exclaimed. "Get back in bed!"

"I can't," I objected. "I know it makes no sense, but I saw the two of them in my dream, and they're either there now or they will be there shortly. I must go."

"That's the craziest thing I've ever heard," she responded, pulling the covers over her head and turning over. "Besides," she mumbled, "I can assure you, you're the last person Linda wants to see at a time like this."

I suspected she was right about that.

I finished getting dressed, and then, as I exited the bedroom, I said, "Look, I can no more explain this than you can. All I know is my dream was as real as I'm standing here. Under any other circumstances, I would wait until morning, but for some strange reason, I'm compelled to go."

> **What could you not accept, if you but knew that everything that happens, all events, past and present, and to come, are gently planned by One whose only purpose is your good?**
>
> —FROM *A COURSE IN MIRACLES*

What makes this story stranger is that, while I knew David and Linda expected a child, I did not remember the due date. Nor did I know what hospital they planned to use for labor and delivery. Yet, in the dream, I not only saw them walking down a corridor of the Norton hospital, but I also saw the precise corridor and the exact birthing room where Linda would have the baby.

I got in the car and drove the fifteen minutes from our home to the hospital. I pulled into the parking garage and took one of the two available parking spaces for ministers. Although I had never been to the maternity ward of this hospital, I instinctively knew from the dream which escalator to take, what corners to turn, and what corridor to follow. Presently, and as expected, I saw a sign hanging from the ceiling that confirmed the accuracy of my choices.

As I turned the last corner, I saw David walking beside Linda, who was riding in a hospital wheelchair. He was holding her hand but saying something to the nurse who pushed the chair. I was speechless at first, but just as the nurse pushed the oversized button to open the doors into the private area for women, I called out.

"David! Linda!"

David stopped and turned. The nurse turned, too, and as she turned, so did the wheelchair. Linda strained as she looked to see who called them.

I'm certain that hearing someone call out their names was enough to startle them. I learned later from them that they had called no one when it became apparent that Linda would soon give birth. Instead, they had hurriedly left their apartment and headed for the hospital.

> **"Truth is perspective; absolute truth is ego."**
>
> —AUTHOR UNKNOWN

"Steve," David responded, clearly surprised. "What are you doing here?"

"I'm not sure, David," I cautiously responded, not knowing whether to tell them of my dream.

We shook hands. I spoke to Linda, who looked as if she were in terrible pain. I remembered what my wife had said minutes before, so I instinctively sought to diffuse the situation. "Come on, Linda, seeing me can't be that painful!"

She must have read my thoughts because she said, "I can't believe it's you, and sometime you'll have to tell me the details. Right now, just give me the edited version. I'm ready for this to be over."

I briefly shared the dream as we walked toward her room. We laughed, and marveled, too, at the absurdity of the whole thing. Then I offered my best wishes and left them alone. Later that day, Linda gave birth to their first child.

To this day, we can't help laughing every time we recall the episode. Neither of us has a clue as to why I had the dream or if there was any significance to it. But, as you've learned about me already, I no longer view anything as accidental, random, or meaningless. To me, everything is inexplicably tied together in some mysterious way. I can't prove it, but I no longer feel the need to try. Instead, I regard this, just as I do all of life, as one of the mysteries whose purpose is to remind me of the ubiquitous Mystery that is God.

In this book, I attempt to reveal candidly my spiritual path and the perspectives toward life and death I have now embraced. I do not expect everyone to agree with my conclusions or to accept what is "my higher truth," or *dharma* as a Buddhist might call it. You will know the path you are to follow for yourself, but if what I share assists you in understanding your *satori* or serves as a guide to your awakening, then the book accomplishes its purpose. How could I be anything but grateful for this?

If you have ever sat in front of a computer and navigated the Internet, you are likely familiar with the term "hyperlink," or "link" for short. A hyperlink is the connecting point between two web pages. It is like a single thread in a spider's web of silken threads. Hyperlinks make it possible to connect with what has become an inconceivably vast network of international webpages. Without these threads, these hyperlinks, the web would not exist. With them, you have at your fingertips an infinity of connections, a colossal web of a countless number of connections that encircle and unite the global community.

With a little imagination, think of yourself as a website. As a webpage, your principal aim is to anchor yourself to the target, the bull's-eye, which is God. I know of nothing more significant than this and nothing that will reward you with a greater feeling of importance. Miss this hyperlink, however, and the web of your life will remain hidden from you. You will neither sense nor see the interconnectedness of all things and all people. Instead, you will feel alone, separated from Source, others, and even yourself. Life will seem chaotic, random, sometimes completely out of control, and like a virtual web of meaninglessness.

> "My conversion, and with it God, is not a thing I can live down, but something I'll always have to live in, through and around. The very fact of it, that it happened at all, is a proof for its own ongoing existence."
>
> —NATHAN SCHNEIDER

When the hyperlink between you and Source is reached, however, you will live with an intense awareness of Life itself. Though you may never see or fully understand this Source, you will know that every other hyperlink is neither random nor accidental, but essential to the evolution of your destiny. Although you may not know how or why an experience or an encounter, a conversation or a relationship, a success or a failure, a challenge or a defeat may cooperate in the manifestation of your destiny, you will nevertheless trust that it does. While there is great mystery to this Life, life itself will not frighten you. To the contrary, Life will make your journey all the richer and more meaningful. You'll no longer feel the need to explain everything that happens to you, but you'll enjoy every step you take on the path you follow. You'll resist nothing, and because of this, you'll miss nothing. Since you are wide awake, you'll remain alert to everything and everyone around you. As Hafiz, the Sufi poet, put it, "Since everyone is God speaking . . . be polite and listen to him." You'll listen and you'll hear, as well as see, the God who is in everyone and in everything.

As you live life in this way, everything and everyone will be another hyperlink to the Eternal. The link might be a conversation you have today with a friend, a colleague, or, for that matter, a complete stranger. It might be an event, an experience or several experiences that are mysteriously linked together. While all of these links may not be clear to you at first, you will in time see and know how they have worked in concert with each other to produce the splendid destiny that is your life.

From this vantage point, I can now see how all of my life experiences prepared me for the spiritual awakening. As far back as those first trips overseas, to the relationship with my father and his unanticipated death, to the professor in seminary who introduced me to Enoch, who's been my travel companion now for three decades: these and a host of other life experiences have enabled me to wake up to who I am—"a spiritual being," as Teilhard de Chardin put it, "having a human experience."

Your journey here is temporary. You won't think about what lies beyond much anymore. I don't because it doesn't matter anymore, at least not to the degree it used to matter. It's only the ego that worries about the future, that longs and hopes for an eternity. *You* aren't interested in either the past or the future. If there is an afterlife, fine. If there isn't, well, that's okay, too. As far as I'm concerned, and I think it must be the same for other awakened souls, what matters to me is *this life*, this moment. It's like my favorite atheist André Comte-Sponville, says. (Coincidentally, he may have renounced religion, but if you ever read his writings, you'll quickly discover that he hasn't renounced a spiritual life.) Quoting Ludwig Wittgenstein, perhaps the greatest philosopher of the twentieth century, Comte-Sponville writes, "he who lives in the present has eternal life."[3]

What else truly matters?

It took half a lifetime, but I now get it. I was born to walk with God. This knowledge is the only thing that satisfies and the only thing that really matters. Career, calling, accomplishments, recognitions, and so forth are as temporary and fading as the body in which you walk around. Everything is destined to fade away and die. Consequently, the ambition of my life is to be free of ego, or to die before I die. My spiritual practice is to observe the ego and die to it every moment. As I do, the fear of death dies with it. What could be better than to be free of all suffering, resistance, and fear? What more could salvation, enlightenment, give you?

In Part 3 of *The Enoch Factor*, I show you what I'm learning about walking with God. Since you can know God only in this present moment, then what's important is that you give your attention to the step you're taking now. Or, as Lao Tzu put it in the *Tao Te Ching*, "The journey of a thousand miles begins with a single step."

Are you ready to take that step?

Notes

1. "Lisa Marie: Jackson Foresaw His End," CBSNews.com, 27 June 2009, http://www.cbsnews.com/stories/2009/06/27/entertainment/main5118362.shtml.

2. Chris Kenning, "Mother Dies after Last Wish Fulfilled," Courier-Journal: (Louisville KY), 11 July 2008, A1, A5.

3. André Comte-Sponville, *The Little Book of Atheistic Spirituality*, trans. Nancy Huston (New York: Penguin Books, 2007) 173.

Part 3

Mastery of the Sacred Art

"It's not a matter of faith; it's a matter of practice."
—Thich Nhat Hanh

As with most religions, Christianity has its share of anomalies. For example, consider the widespread disregard for Jesus' explicit words regarding public and private prayer. Here is what he said:

> And when you come before God, don't turn that into a theatrical production either. All these people making a regular show out of their prayers, hoping for stardom! Do you think God sits in a box seat? Here is what I want you to do: Find a quiet, secluded place so you won't be tempted to role-play before God. Just be there as simply and as honestly as you can manage. The focus will shift from you to God, and you will begin to sense his grace. The world is full of so-called prayer warriors who are prayer-ignorant. (Matt 6:5-7)

These are brutal words for public prayer and beautiful words for private prayer.

Go into almost any church in America on any weekend, and you'll hear multiple public prayers but almost no provision for private prayer, or what I think of as silent intimacy with God. In fact, not only do most churches provide no room in worship for quietude, silence, or stillness, but most churches and church leaders do not even teach, most likely because they do not know, what this kind of prayer is. Yet, ironically, this is the only kind of praying Jesus does in the Scriptures.[1]

As I noted earlier, most Christian worship services are a frenzied chase from start to finish. It is not hard to understand how a congregation might be manipulated into an emotional frenzy because of the incessant noise that feels more like a rock concert or a sports event than a hallowed hour of worship. Getting an emotional kick from a worship experience, however, hardly means you've experienced a transformational shift in how you think and live at other times.

In recent years, worship styles have undergone enormous changes. Many of them have been long overdue. It is a misreading of my words here to conclude I'm a disgruntled traditionalist who resents changes or prefers traditional styles of music and worship to contemporary styles. To the contrary, no one likes music that reminds a Boomer of Woodstock more than I do. I simply offer the perspective that religious people frequently mistake an

> **Atheists are as liable to be virtuous as believers are not to be.**
>
> —Pierre Bayle

emotional lift for a spiritual transformation or awakening. Doubtless they did when traditional styles of worship were the norm, too, but the problem seems vastly more acute today.

Many people come to a church, mosque, synagogue, or temple searching for spiritual completeness. What do they receive from worship?

• A transformation of how they think, live life, and treat themselves, others, and all living things?
• A realization of who they really are, of how the ego functions, of where their conditioned thoughts come from and how those thoughts give birth to destructive attitudes and actions?
• The knowledge of what happiness *really* is and their real purpose beyond career choice or calling?
• Encouragement to cultivate their inner world, the only place where human transformation *is* possible?
• Acceptance and respect for all people—black/white, yellow/red, straight/gay, Republican/Democrat/Independent, Christian or Buddhist, Jewish or Muslim, atheist or agnostic, single, married, or divorced, addicted or challenged, and so on?

• Guidance to be generous in spirit and resources with all people and nations, but especially the poor, the displaced, and the oppressed of this world?

• A sense of quietude, awe, reverence, and humility in the presence of this inexplicable Mystery whom Christians and Jews call God, Muslims call Allah, and so forth?

Is attending your church, synagogue, mosque, or temple helping you be a better and more compassionate person, spouse, neighbor, employee, and employer? Is it leading you to understand yourself, to know what ego has done and is doing in you, your thinking, your relationships, and so forth, to experience a transformational shift in consciousness, "to overcome the world," as Jesus put it? If not, then my advice is this: *Stop going!* Go somewhere else or find another religion altogether.

> ## A World of Contradictions
>
> People are afraid of war; yet, they prepare for it with frenzy.
>
> They produce in abundance, but distribute miserly.
>
> The world becomes more crowded, but humans become more isolated and lonely.
>
> People live close as in one big family, but each individual finds himself more separated from his neighbor than ever before.
>
> —*THE WAY A BUDDHIST THINKS*
> (SOURCE UNKNOWN)

Better yet, give up on religion entirely. Don't let this madness masked as worship, no matter how emotionally packed or perfectly packaged it may be, rob you of the joy of walking in an enlightened state of Christ-consciousness. If you must, do what those did whom my tradition too quickly labeled as *backsliders*.

To the Baptists with whom I grew up, a backslider was any person who had either given up on the church or wished he or she had. While many of them remained members of the church, they seldom attended. Instead, backsliders went fishing, played golf, or simply stayed at home and watched *Meet the Press* on television during the worship hour. Had there been a Starbucks in those days, you'd have found many of them, just as you do today, sipping cappuccinos on couches and reading the Sunday comics.

Today, they're called *nones*. They number an estimated 35,000,000 in the United States alone. Many of them are former churchgoers who still regard themselves as religious or spiritual, although they define that in various ways. All of them have given up on organized religion, offended by the hypocrisy found in virtually all religions but especially Christianity.[2]

Backsliders were usually adept at defending their choice of non-church-related activities on Sunday. They'd say things like, "I can worship God in nature" or "I don't have to go to church to be a Christian." The guilt-driven and habitual "never-miss-a-worship-service-on-Sunday" folks, however, were bothered by these explanations of absence. They dismissed backsliders as bound for hell or, if they were Catholics, bound for purgatory, where they'd be cleansed of their waywardness before entering the Pearly Gates.

The backsliders had a point. You *can* worship God through nature, and churchgoing isn't a prerequisite to knowing God. I may be a rebel, but I am not a union steward calling for a strike on churchgoing. Further, I'm not advocating for a widespread walkout on religion. I am simply acknowledging the candor in the comments of those who are frustrated by organized religion today. Ask almost any person who has given up on the American version of Christianity, and you'll hear some or all of the following in their explanations:

• "I don't need the busyness found in church, nor the busybodies, either; my life is cluttered enough. I need freedom, not more neurotic attachments."
• "I don't care for the incessant bickering and backstabbing in church; there's enough conflict in the world without it."
• "I'm tired of the judgments, the critics, and their criticisms; I'm down on myself enough; I don't need any help; I can do without the sanctimonious stares, too, for my screw-ups and mistakes, especially by people just as screwed up as I am."
• "I'm tired of pretending what I believe is right, what others believe is wrong, and that I have all the answers when I'm not sure what the questions are. I'm tired of the narrow-mindedness in religion; I'm ready to live in peace, openness, and respect for all people and all faiths."
• "I've had it with the weekend religious performance. I'm tired of what it has made of me—a critic—a kind of worship blogger who comments on everything. I'm tired of measuring how good worship is by how it compares

to the week before, the church across the street, or the one I used to attend. I need more than a show; I need substance. I want peace, not more noise, chaos, and confusion. The emotional high is fine from time to time, but I actually need a total makeover. Only one thing matters to me. I want to know God, to walk in the presence of my Creator. Frankly, I'm not sure the church is the place to know God anymore."

When you can't know God at church, where do you turn?

Notes

1. See Matt 14:23; 26:36; Mark 1:35; 6:46; Luke 5:16; 9:18; 22:45.

2. For more on this rapidly growing segment of the population worldwide, read the 2008 ARIS report (American Religious Identification Survey) found at the following web address: http://www.americanreligionsurvey-aris.org/.

Chapter 14

Going Within: Taming Self . . . Touching Source

"The kingdom of God is within you."

—*Jesus*

"God requires no synagogue—except the heart."
—*ancient Hasidic saying*

To know God, *Go within.* That's the real tabernacle, temple, or worship center. Jesus said, "The kingdom of God is within you" (Luke 17:21). You will not find this kingdom anywhere else. Channel the desire you feel to know God into a journey to the inner shrine of stillness, meditation, and peace. "You are the temple of God," said Saint Paul, "and God himself is present in you" (1 Cor 3:16). Words do not get clearer than this. In the unseen temple of the heart, you touch Source and tame your ego self. All outer temples, shrines, churches, and altars are mere reminders that *the pathway to Life is the pathway within.* There, within, you enter the real sanctuary, experience real Sabbath, and enjoy Source itself.

> "Who looks outside, dreams; who looks within, awakes."
>
> —CARL JUNG

Just as you cannot know God in a collection of beliefs or doctrines, no matter how "right" your religious tradition insists they are, so you cannot know God in a church, temple, or mosque, no matter how emotionally uplifting the place may be. It is true that God may visit, surprise, or awaken within you in any of a million different ways—in a worship service, through the reading of sacred Scripture, during a confession, or as you ponder a religious doctrine or belief. It is also true that God may awaken in you on a golf course, in the midst of a crisis, or as you do nothing at all, except recline on a couch watching television.

Waking up to God is one thing; staying awake is another. It's like two sides of the same coin, and both sides are important. If you have awakened to Presence and wish to remain awake, the rest of this book is for you. Just as Enoch walked with God, so may you, but the first place the path leads you is inward— to the deep, dark places of your soul. If you wish to walk with God, you will have to take this journey often. The inner world is as mysterious as the world beyond, and it may be just as infinite and as expansive. By *going within*, you meet yourself and your Source, and from there you emerge to walk in unbroken union with this ineffable presence we call God.

> "Where there is silence, one finds the anchor of the universe."
>
> —FROM THE
> *TAO TE CHING*

Jesus and the Journey Within

Just like the Buddha before him and Saint Paul after him, Jesus took his own journey within. For the Buddha, the journey occurred over several years, culminating in a forty-day state of silent meditation under the famous Bodhi Tree.

For the Apostle Paul, it took place suddenly and unexpectedly on the road to Damascus as he actively sought the prosecution of Jesus' followers (Acts 9:1-10).

For Jesus himself, the journey within took place over a forty-day period while he sojourned in the wilderness. The Gospel accounts tell us that, when he entered the wilderness, Jesus was tempted by the Devil (Matt 4:1-11; Mark 1:12-13; Luke 4:1-13). There are several noteworthy points about Jesus' journey to the wilderness within.

It is said that Jesus was *driven* by "the Spirit" into the wilderness (Mark 1:12). Life, or Spirit if you prefer, will lead you to "whatever experience is most helpful for the evolution of your consciousness," according to the spiritual teacher Eckhart Tolle.[1] In other words, since God desires not only that you wake up but that you walk in union with him, every life experience is choreographed to help you in this regard. If you resist the natural unfolding of life, you will experience what the Buddha called *dukka*, or suffering. All resistance is negativity toward life. When you refuse to accept what is, you suffer, and the natural evolution of your spiritual life is thwarted. But you get a second chance.

The destination of Jesus' journey was the wilderness. While Jesus most likely took his journey into the desert because that was the nature of the environment around him, this is not a mere reference to the outer world. It refers instead to his inner world. You wake up to God in the outer world. You learn to walk with God in the inner world. Only by *going within* do you come face to face with yourself. Only by *going within* do you emerge hand in hand, so to speak, with Source.

The duration of Jesus' journey was forty days and nights. You perhaps know that the forty-day cycle, and sometimes forty-year cycle, occurs frequently in the Old and New Testaments. What you may not know is that this same phenomenon occurs in other religions. In Islam, for example, Muhammad is said to have been forty years old when he received his first angelic communiqué. In Buddhism, Siddhartha Gautama spent forty days and nights in a state of inner silence before he awakened as The Buddha. Rather than referring to a literal period of time, however, the forty-day or forty-year cycle refers to a significant life transition or paradigm shift in a person's thinking and living. In other words, only by *going within* will you change and, therefore, "be the change," as Gandhi put it, "you wish to see in the world." You can only ever change from within.

Jesus encountered the demonic on his journey within. Again, the Devil here was not an evil, external being dashing about in a red suit with horns. Temptation does not come from without. It comes from within, as Saint James reminded us (Jas 1:13-15). If you wish to overcome temptation successfully, you must go where it is—within. As you do, you will make an interesting discovery. You will discover that the Devil was to Jesus' inner life what the ego self is in you. When

> I count him braver who overcomes his desires than him who conquers his enemies; for the hardest victory is the victory over self.
>
> —ARISTOTLE

I finally understood this, the temptations of Jesus took on an entirely new and substantially greater significance to me. See if they do so for you.

Note

1. Eckhart Tolle, *A New Earth: Awakening to Your Life's Purpose* (New York: Plume Book, 2005) 41.

Chapter 15

The Temptations of Jesus

"What lies behind us and what lies before us are tiny matters compared to what lies within us."
—*Ralph W. Emerson (1803–1882)*

To Live from the Place of Ego

One of Jesus' wilderness temptations was to turn stone into bread and satisfy his material hungers (Matt 4:3-4). This is perhaps the most basic temptation everyone faces. As we saw in Part 1, the ego edges God out early in life, but since virtually everyone is unaware that this happened to them, humans typically waste much of their lives trying to satisfy their inner hunger with something other than God. Some people try to fill it with religion or a belief system. Those not raised in a religious environment try to fill it with other attachments—such as their roles or functions in life, their ambitions and accomplishments, their relationships or career, and so forth.

Nothing could ever fill this Divine vacuum, except temporarily. The temptation, however, is to believe that if we try hard enough, we will eventually succeed in turning stone into bread, something material and transitory into something spiritual and satisfying. It cannot be done. These temptations are
• to forget the nature of reality—that what's real is not what's seen but unseen;
• to live at the surface level of existence;
• to be devoid of a spiritual connection to Source;
• to look outside to find the happiness we could only ever find inside;
• to live an ego-driven rather than a God-grounded life;
• and to look for God in a religion outside of you instead of in a relationship within you.

In Eckhart Tolle's book, *The Power of Now*, he writes about a beggar who had sat by the side of a road for more than thirty years. One day a stranger walked by.

"Spare some change?" the beggar mumbled, holding out his baseball cap.

"I have nothing to give you," responded the stranger. "What's that you're sitting on?"

The beggar said, "Oh, nothing. Just as old box I've been sitting on for as long as I can remember."

"Ever looked inside it?" asked the stranger.

"No," responded the beggar. "Why would I? There's nothing inside it."

"Have a look and see," insisted the stranger. The beggar managed to open the lid of the box. To his disbelief and amazement, he discovered the box was filled with gold.

Tolle writes,

> I am that stranger who has nothing to give you and who is telling you to look inside. Not inside any box, as in the parable, but somewhere even closer: inside yourself. . . . Those who have found their true wealth, which is the radiant joy of Being and the deep, unshakable peace that comes with it, are beggars, even if they have great material wealth. They are looking outside for scraps of pleasure or fulfillment, for validation, security, or love while they have a treasure within that not only includes all those things but is infinitely greater than anything the world can offer.[1]

Everyone faces this temptation. Who has not looked for happiness—for God—outside of himself or herself? Who has not settled for scraps of pleasure outside the house when God has prepared a banquet table on the inside?

The question is, "Are you ready to come in and enjoy?" If you *go within*, you will enter into God and emerge to walk with him.

To Live in Fear instead of Faith

In another temptation, Jesus imagined that he stood on the pinnacle of the temple. The ego whispered, "Cast yourself down and so test to see if God will send angels to rescue you." In other words, just as the ego does in everyone, it reasoned within him. "The world is an unsafe place. How can you be sure God will take care of you? Why not ask God to do something extraordinary, even miraculous? That way, you'll know, before taking this big step, that all will go well for you!"

This is the temptation to live not only from a place of fear, but of sinister fear, one dressed up to look like faith. There are only two ways of living your life—from a place of fear or from a place of faith. When you live with fear, as virtually everyone does before awakening, you live under the control of your ego. When you live by faith, however, you are connected to God and trust the universe to provide for you just as it does "the lilies of the field," as Jesus put it (Matt 6:28). In other words, you walk with God and trust your future to him.

Most people are unaware they are living in fear. There are two fundamental reasons for this. For one thing, humans have lived in fear for such a long time that virtually everyone thinks it is normal. They do not recognize that fear dominates their thinking. Second, fear and its culprit—the cunning ego—have assumed many aliases. Since the ego cannot admit to being afraid, it has led us to develop many different names for it—sometimes we call fear *stress*; at other times *nerves* or *nervousness, anxiety, worry,* and even something seemingly benign like *concern.* These words may seem less toxic, but what's behind them isn't. They are, according to the Dalai Lama, "destructive emotions," and when you live in fear, even fear you describe as stress or anxiety or concern, you cannot walk by faith. In other words, when it comes to living your life, it is not a "both/and" proposition; you either live in fear or you live by faith.

As I wrote about earlier, apart from the involuntary fight/flight response whenever threatened with bodily harm, virtually all other fear, regardless of the label you may give to it, arises whenever the ego in you is threatened or burdened. This is why, the sooner you die to ego, the sooner you will live free of any trace of anxiety, worry, or stress. It is not more complicated than this. Yet, the ego will cloud, complicate and confuse people about this for as long as it can get away with it, which is why some will vehemently object to what I say. They will insist that most of our anxiety, nervousness, depression, and so forth is genetically based, the consequence of some kind of chemical irregularity within the brain.

They'll get no argument from me because I know, just as the geneticists and medical scientists have told us, that genes play a major role in what some call the brain's "set point" for happiness or "genetic predisposition." On one

> "Unfortunately, illness is the only acceptable form of western meditation."
>
> —CHRISTIANE NORTHRUP

side, for example, there are people who seem wired to be happy, positive, and optimistic no matter what's happening. They look at failure, whether the failure of others or their own, not as a catastrophe but as an opportunity.

Other people, however, seem wired to be unhappy, negative, and pessimistic. Instead of seeing opportunities, virtually everything is a challenge or a difficulty to them. In the more acute expressions, their unhappiness becomes depression, even despair. Until recently, the two most common ways of managing the severe instances of unhappiness were prescriptions and psychotherapy. In the last couple of decades, scientists and researchers have made an interesting discovery. Meditation, or the practice of *going within*, is often just as effective as medications but without the side effects.

A few years ago, I had anxiety attacks that escalated beyond my control. My physician gave me a prescription from a family of drugs known as *serotonin reuptake inhibitors*. The drug helped. I was able to manage better both the frequency and severity of my attacks, but I had no interest in taking a prescription for the rest of my life. Eventually, my body would adjust to it, likely compromising its effectiveness. Even so, apart from taking the drug for as long as it was effective, or sitting in a therapist's chair on a regular basis, I knew of no other alternatives that might be available to help me.

The awakening, however, and the subsequent discipline of *going within*, changed this. Instead of *medication*, I found that *meditation*, something Easterners have done for thousands of years, worked for me in ways nothing else did. Today, this is my spiritual practice, and not only does it enable me to manage my fears—the ego-driven phobias that have plagued humanity for eons—but it is the way I stay in touch with my deeper self, the real me, which is always in uninterrupted union with Source itself. Furthermore, the flaws in my character—that is, the things about me I wish to change—seem to change all the more naturally, with no effort or struggle whatsoever.

When I meditate, I enter to observe the ego; I exit to walk with God. Observing the ego alone reduces its power over me. Ego is tamed; Source is

> "Every night and every morn,
> Some to misery are born,
> Every morn and every night
> Some are born to sweet delight.
>
> —FROM "AUGURIES OF INNOCENCE" BY WILLIAM BLAKE

touched. The consequence is that I am whole and at peace. Practitioners of *holistic* or *integrated* medicine call this the "mind, body, spirit" connection. For me, it's simply the connecting link to Love itself. By *going within* and watching the dysfunctional ego—the principal cause in the "disconnect" between mind, body, and spirit—I find that the ego has no other choice but to dissolve. With continued practice, I am confident that the ego will ultimately die. As Atman—the name Buddhists give the ego—dies, you live. Meditation is, therefore, my key to living a healthier, happier, and more sacred life.[2]

Notes

1. Eckhart Tolle, *The Power of Now* (Novato CA: New World Library, 1997) 9.

2. Those interested in reading more about the medical research into this phenomenon associated with alternative methods in the practice of medicine can consult the Journal of the American Medical Association. Search "Alternative Medicine," "Mindfulness and Medicine," "Mind, Body, and Medicine: An Integrated Approach," http://www.mindfulnesscds.com/ Mindfulness_in_Medicine_JAMA_9-16-08.pdf (accessed 31 March 2010).

Chapter 16

Michelle, Manhattan, and Mad Movies of the Mind

"With senses, mind, and intellect under control;
having liberation as the prime goal;
free from lust, anger, and fear;
such a sage is verily liberated."
　　　　　　　—Bhagavad Gita (Hindu Scriptures)

As you have likely detected already, one of the consequences of my spiritual awakening is a belief that the experiences of my life conspire to create yet another opening through which my connection to Divine Source might be more fully realized. What was lost in me soon after my birth—namely, the sense of union with God as the ego in me edged God out—is destined to be completely restored through the various portals Presence opens up to me. Death is the final portal. But, between birth and death, there are a myriad of other portals. In fact, every new day provides more portals into Presence.

This is the point Jesus was making when he said, "I am the door" (John 10:9). To debate endlessly whether Jesus is the *only* door is to risk missing the Presence who resides beyond it. My aim is to know this Presence and so walk in it. For me, that's the principal point of human existence and, as a result, it's the primary purpose of my life. Nothing else matters. Strangely, though, everything (and everyone) has become, or is becoming, increasingly sacred to me.

The spiritual transformation that began in me one Sunday afternoon continues to this day.

How is this working in my life? Walking with God is not something you are rewarded with one day, after rigorous spiritual discipline and difficulty. There is no effort in it. Effort is ego and is born of a stubborn determination to achieve something and so be duly rewarded for it. With an authentic spiritual life, however, in an awakened state of Divine awareness, it's altogether different. God has done everything for you. Since God's way is the way of grace, then to do nothing and be everything is the ultimate expression of an awakened life.

What began in me on that Sunday afternoon continues to the present. Each new day, indeed each moment, is just the next step into the Divine presence. Not all of my steps are taken perfectly. I am like a child who is learning to walk. I stumble and fall, and there are times I'm still afraid or that I cry and get mad. What's different today is that I no longer step all over myself when I do. The judgment, as well as the guilt, is gone. I accept my stumbles and sometimes I even laugh. But, in every instance, I forgive. When you can forgive yourself, you can forgive others. Until you can forgive yourself, you can never forgive others. Or, forgive God.

What took me half a lifetime to learn is that Life is not a journey to God. It is instead a journey with God. When you know this, and this awareness is what the awakening did for me, you stop going through the motions of believing *If I just live a decent, moral, upright life, one day I'll make it to God and be in the Presence forever.* To the contrary, you will know this Presence now and so walk in the joy of it. What could be grander than this? There is nothing in eternity that could be more precious than walking in Presence now. How could there be?

Given this, I thought I'd bring this book to a close with a demonstration of how the portals into Presence open for me daily, just as they do for everyone, even those who are as yet unaware. I view every experience in my life as a door, a challenge, even a choice, to go deeper into Presence or to remain at the surface of life. Some of these doors I step through easily; others with more difficulty. Sometimes a few I miss altogether, but I don't despair (not anymore, anyway) or denigrate myself for missing a door. I know that Life is grace and, if one door is missed, another will open. I know this much, too: it will be the same for you. Why? Because the Shepherd won't sleep till the sheep have been found (Luke 15:3-7).

My daughter Michelle graduated college mid-year, at Christmastime. Over the holidays, Pam and I helped her move to New York City. At the time, I had no idea of the mental, emotional, and physical impact her move would have on me. A few months earlier, she mentioned to us that, upon graduating college, she would move to the big city. I disregarded her comment, assuming she wasn't serious. Besides, I knew she dated a young man in our city, and the two of them spoke frequently of getting married. I assumed they would follow through on those plans soon after graduation.

When the subject of New York came up again a few weeks later, I challenged her with questions about what she would do there—whether she had secured a job or even found a place to live. That's when I discovered how determined she was to follow this path. Not only had she been offered a coveted internship in her field of fashion photography—one that, if she performed well, would likely become a real job with real pay—but she had met a girl online, and the two of them planned to room together somewhere in middle Manhattan.

> **For the raindrop, joy is entering the river.**
>
> —MIRZA GHALIB

The proverbial red flags went up. I imagined and feared a plethora of unfavorable scenarios transpiring in Michelle's future. Almost daily, my mind created these horror movies as it imagined the menaces that awaited her. I feared, for instance, that she would not be able to make it financially, especially when she informed me that the rent on the apartment for her and her would-be roommate totaled nearly $3,000 per month—utilities not included. I feared another disaster in Manhattan similar to the attack on 9/11. I also imagined her abducted on a subway train and harmed in unimaginable ways. In my uncontrolled mind, her "supposed" roommate was not a girl she could trust. In fact, she was not a girl at all, but the subway abductor who posed online as a hometown girl looking for a roommate in Manhattan.

I managed to hold at bay these imaginary fears, at least until the morning after we moved her into the comfortable but costly Manhattan high-rise. Since Pam and I had an early morning flight, we were up before sunrise. After packing, we stood at the door to say our final good-byes. I looked across the darkened room at Michelle, who was still half asleep. Enough light from the streets filtered through the sheers to form a soft glow on her cheeks. In that instant, I was transported back twenty-plus years to the day when her mother and I brought her home from the hospital. She was a tiny, helpless infant, so full of life and yet so vulnerable and fragile.

I do not have the words to describe the tsunami of anxiety that swelled over me as I stood looking at her. I grieved. I cursed time for stealing the years from me. I trembled at leaving my little girl in such a big, busy, and terrifying city. I started crying right then, and for all practical purposes I did not stop crying for weeks thereafter. I didn't cry constantly, of course, but the

tears came with no warning, and their sudden appearance was never convenient. I could be anywhere and abruptly start crying with such intensity that
I'd have to bury my head, walk out of a room, or dismiss myself from a conversation to keep from being an embarrassment.

During these crying spells, not only did I wonder about Michelle's
safety, but I was also overcome with guilt and shame. Even then, after my
awakening, I carried an ego identity of being the "great" or "perfect" father
to my children. Since I had not lived up to that image, I constantly berated
myself for not being more available to them; for not modeling a healthy and
loving relationship to their mother; and, worse, for dragging them through
our painful divorce. So great was the intensity of this suffering that at times
I was physically immobilized and thought I might go mad.

Winston-Salem and the World Within

Once, for example, I was invited to bring the keynote address at a conference
in Winston-Salem, North Carolina. After arriving by plane, I picked up a
rental car and headed toward the conference hall. Without warning, the tears
came suddenly. I'm sure I was thinking about my daughter and wondering
whether she was safe, scared, broke, or, worse, something bad had happened
to her. After all, it had been two long days since I last spoke to her. I could
tell myself not to imagine such horrible things, but no inner sermon, regardless of its persuasive power, converted my thoughts or feelings. They seemed
only to become more entrenched and unmovable instead.

On this occasion, the thoughts and feelings were severe enough that I
was tempted to drive past the conference hall. Given my state of mind, I
could not bear the thought of standing before an audience and trying to
speak. I looked for a way to escape the situation. I wondered what would
happen if I didn't show up, if I continued driving until I got far enough to
leave my suffering behind.

Fortunately, I knew the source of this fear
and angst. It was the ego in me. Even though
this incident occurred after I awakened, I still
had "me" to deal with. The only difference was
this: if Michelle's graduation and move to New
York had occurred prior to my spiritual awakening, I would have returned to my physician
and requested a prescription. I could not have
coped either with my thoughts or the feelings
that accompanied them. Thankfully, however, I

> The journey of a thousand miles begins with a single step.
>
> —LAO TZU

was growing, not only in God consciousness, but ego awareness, too. I had already experienced enough freedom from its enslaving presence to know that more freedom was near. I hoped as much, anyway.

Ego and fear are two sides of the same coin, just like faith and freedom. I had tasted enough of the freedom associated with an awakened life—life lived in faith and by faith—that I was determined to press on "for the prize of the high calling of God" (Phil 3:14, KJV), as Saint Paul put it. I was not going to let anything, especially my ego and its neurotic tendencies, keep me from knowing "the peace of God . . . which passes all understanding" (Phil 4:7, KJV).

By this time, too, I regularly practiced the art of *going within*, of meditating. Admittedly, I was still a novice, and my successes were sporadic at best. Most of the time, whenever I tried to meditate, instead of experiencing the silencing of my mind, the mind grew busier, burdened, and occasionally besieged by an army of thoughts. I could scold myself, and often did, for not having more control over the mental movies, but no reprimand seemed to help. My mind was as busy as Paramount Pictures, producing not full-length horror shows but something more akin to a preview of coming attractions. The mental images were brief, intrusive, sometimes scary, and seldom related to each other.

On this day in Winston-Salem, I wasn't sure it would do much good, but I had to stop the car and try to *go within*. "Maybe," I reasoned, "I can find relief from this insufferable ego mind."

I stopped the car, perhaps an exit or two from the conference site. I pulled into the first parking area I could find. It looked like an abandoned gasoline station, the kind you might see in deserts where cactus plants grow and tumbleweeds blow indiscriminately in the wind. A large part of the building was missing, as if struck by high winds. The corners of the building were rounded and rusted, and all the windows were shattered like someone had held a grudge against the garage. The only signs of life were in the pavement crevices where grass and weeds flourished but not with obvious effort. I sat there for a long time as the tears flowed and the urge to flee raged on.

"What am I going to do?" I asked myself. "I can't speak to this audience in the shape I'm in." As I contemplated my few options, I remembered something one of my spiritual guides had said,

As you are learning to *go within*, and so be free of the enslaving power of the ego, remember that there will be occasions when the ego puts up one hell of a fight. It will not die easily. Believe nothing the ego says in your mind. Just watch your thoughts, without judgment or self-recrimination. There is no battle to fight; it ended long ago. Just be the observer, the witnessing presence, and you'll see a space of stillness between you and your insufferable mind. It is there you'll move, slowly but certainly, and it is there you will know the peace that passes all understanding.

So I did. I wiped away another tear, laid the car seat back in a reclining position, stretched out my legs, and placed one palm in the other, my thumbs softly touching each other. For me, this posture of meditation had worked, though maybe the Buddha would have preferred a more proper posture in the pursuit of meditative mind. By letting my thumbs slightly touch each other, I signaled my desire to see the self in me in unity with itself. I closed my eyes and began the journey within.

In previous meditations, I had made it my practice to picture myself climbing a staircase of some twenty or thirty steps. To this day, I don't know why that was the mental path I took to the inner garden, but it worked. There in my own Garden of Eden, I met the Gardener and was learning to walk with him. This inner garden has become to me what I imagine Eden was to the first couple or the kingdom of God was to Jesus. It is my inner world and there I meet and so walk with the Gardener herself. But be advised: it is also the garden where you meet yourself—your serpent self—the ego that hangs like a snake from a tree. Make peace with this serpent, and you've made peace with yourself.

> "We don't sit in meditation to become good meditators. We sit in meditation so we'll become more awake in our lives."
>
> —FROM *WHEN THINGS FALL APART* BY PEMA CHÖDRÖN

Although rare, whenever I was successful at *going within,* I came out refreshed with noticeable changes in my demeanor as well as in my character. Throughout the day, I would be more awake and aware, tranquil, and at peace. I was more observant of nature, too, inspired by it, and kinder to myself and to those around me. Most important, however, I was conscious of the Sacred Presence in everyone and everything. Even in the early days of meditation, I remember thinking, *What could I ever fear when I see God everywhere? How could I judge anyone else, be prejudiced toward them, or have an enemy anywhere in the world when I see the God I'm coming to know, both in me and in everyone else?*

At the top of my mental stairwell stood two heavy wooden doors that opened and closed like the doors of an elevator. I gave my attention to the closed doors even as I made my way up the stairs. Then, after reaching the top, I concentrated on the doors until they opened, yielding to the infinite space of stillness that lay beyond.

On the door to my left, I pictured the word "Be." On the door to the right was the word "Still." "Be" to the left, "Still" to the right. Back and forth I moved my attention slowly, like an observer of a tennis match might watch the ball volleyed by players back and forth, only in slow motion. After focusing for a few seconds on each word, I started again with different words. On the door to the left, the word "And." To the right, the word "Know." I continued this practice until I completed the sentence "Be still and know . . . I am God" (Ps 46:10, KJV).

By the time I got to the word "God," my attention was centered at the precise point where the two doors met. There I left my mental gaze on "God" and patiently waited for the doors to open. When they did, I stepped to the edge, observed, and, almost instantly, was drawn into the infiniteness of inner space—as someone put it, the very "body of God."

If you are a Jew or Christian, you most likely know that the words, "Be still and know . . . I am God," come from the ancient psalmist. This phrase and others like it from the sacred Scriptures of both Jews and Christians is for me what a *mantra* is to practitioners of Zen Buddhism. *Mantra* is a Sanskrit word made up of two others, the root word *man* meaning "mind" or "thought" and the suffix *tra* meaning "instrument" or "tool." A mantra, then, is "a tool of the mind" or "an instrument of thought." The suffix can also mean *guardian* or even *liberator*. A mantra can be "an instrument that guards the mind" or "liberates the mind" from itself and from the world.

Christians will recall that Saint Paul essentially said this when he admonished, "Think on these things" (Phil 4:8, KJV), with the promise that if we do, then "the peace of God . . . will *guard* [our] hearts and [our] minds" (Phil 4:7, KJV). A mantra, therefore, can be a sound or sounds, a word or group of words that are repeated over and over. By repeating them, we focus our minds and free them of the many thoughts that constantly interrupt them.

The Benedictine monks may have been some of the first Christians to use mantras as words or passages from Scripture in what became known later as a *lectio Divina*, Latin for "Divine reading." These words or passages from

Scripture were their prayers and mind meditations. Like everyone who practices meditation, the monks made the wonderful discovery that, by *going within*, they drove insanity out. They were restored to their natural state of felt oneness with God.

If at any time I lost concentration on the words, "Be still and know . . . I am God," the instant I realized I had lost consciousness, I would start the meditation again. Eventually, this rigorous discipline paid off, but, as you might imagine, in the early days of my meditative practice, I spent much of the time simply climbing the mental staircase. I seldom made it to the top before my mind wandered in another direction. This was at first frustrating. What should have been a liberating practice was a laborious problem. Brother Lawrence said, "Practice the presence of God." What he did not say was to make a problem of it, but that's precisely what I did.

Today, however, I reach the top on a regular basis and enter into that blissful state of eternal stillness almost effortlessly. On the occasions when I don't, I no longer judge myself or make a problem of it. I simply accept it. As it does in all of life, acceptance implies forgiveness. Your spiritual life is never to be a struggle.

When you accept yourself, and so forgive yourself for your limitations and your failures, you can accept others who have limitations and failures, too. Until you accept yourself, you can neither accept others nor forgive them of their failures. This is so important to understand, especially in our culture where the ego in each of us masquerades as our friend when really it is our greatest enemy. Not only this, but the ego is prone to clustering in groups of likeminded egos so as to strengthen itself. Further, it loves to make enemies of others. And, yet, Jesus said, "Love your enemies" (Matt 5:43, KJV), which really means, "Have no enemies." Until you learn to *go within*, however, and make peace with your greatest enemy—your ego self, Jesus' injunction will make no sense whatsoever, which explains why it is almost universally disregarded by Christians and the church. When there is no longer an enemy *within*, there will be no more enemies *without*.

You only attract enemies when you have not made peace with the one within. Most people in the West have not yet learned this spiritual truth, which is one explanation for the number of America's enemies in the world. I've always considered it a strange irony that the United States is one of the most compassionate nations on one hand, offering relief in staggering amounts to countless people and nations around the world, yet, on the other hand, it is resented and even hated, often by the peoples and nations it helps the most.

Why is this? The explanation may not be too difficult to understand when you remember how the collective ego works. Frequently, the aid the United States gives to other countries is anything but altruistic—that is, free of ego or self-interest. Instead, our aid is often given to protect our interests or to maintain our superiority as a nation. If philanthropy is not selfless, however, with no strings attached, it may be generous and look compassionate, but it's actually convenient and self-serving.

This is what Jesus meant when, regarding giving alms to the poor, he said, "Let not thy left hand know what thy right hand doeth"(Matt 6:3, KJV). He was not saying, as many Christians mistakenly assume, that charity given in church on Sunday should be known only by the bookkeeper and the IRS, but that charity must be guileless, or without expectation of anything in return. Jesus observed the Pharisees giving alms to the poor with their left hands, while with their right hands they held trumpets to blow in the streets. In both instances, their objective was the same: to feed their egos, or, as Jesus put it, "that they may have the glory of men" (Matt 6:2, KJV).

Others may receive this kind of charity, but they eventually resent it. The ego in the giver hooks the ego in the receiver. Only when a recipient of charity has no idea of the origin of the gift, which is the point Jesus made about secrecy in charity, is there no room for ego in either the giver or the receiver. Again, the ego in everyone, giver or receiver notwithstanding, is interested in one thing only—itself. Until the people of the United States understand this, politicians and citizens will remain perplexed as to why a people or nation to whom Americans have given aid would then support camps where terrorists are trained to hijack commercial airlines and attack our cities and allies.

> Enlightenment is not changing your outer world, it's changing your inner world.
>
> —WAYNE DYER

It's not as perplexing as it may seem, however. One hand will turn against the other hand whenever a heart full of ego extends either hand. The resentful ego in the receiver inevitably reacts or attacks the self-serving ego in the giver. To put it another way, the enemy within will always have enemies without.

Doorway into Inner Space . . . the Place of Stillness

Sitting in the abandoned parking lot outside Winston-Salem, I noticed something different as I made my way up the mental staircase. Instead of the doors being closed, awaiting my concentration to make them open, today they were wide open already. I was surprised and also afraid they might close before I reached them. I hurried up the staircase, scaling two stairs with each step.

When I reached the top, I stepped quickly to the edge and looked out at the vastness before me. It was as before, but this time it was more beautiful than ever. In an instant, peace came over me. The chaos that swirled around me stilled like a summer pond at sunrise. The scene reminded me of the times I gazed at the stars and planets on a clear night and wondered at the depth of space itself. For as long as I can remember, I have been fascinated by the midnight sky, its unimaginable depth, where stars too numerous to comprehend sparkle like diamonds against a black velvet canvas.

This day, however, I wasn't looking upward into outer space. I was looking inward at what seemed to be just as infinite, inviting, and inexplicable in beauty. All of the anxiety, worry, and grief I had battled for weeks melted away. I felt nothing, and yet I felt *Everything*, too. Had I any say in the matter, I would have stayed there indefinitely, speech or no speech. Yet I knew I could not remain there any more than Peter, James, and John could stay on the mountaintop of exhilaration they experienced with Jesus (Mark 9:2-8).

This was one of many mountains I climbed or steps I took—one of many spiritual lessons I learned. There will be others, each taking my awakened state of consciousness to its next level of awareness. If I keep up this spiritual practice, and I cannot imagine doing anything less, I believe I will one day know an uninterrupted state of Divine consciousness not unlike that of the remarkable spiritual masters before me.

Just as I grew comfortable in the bliss of this peaceful state, however, a sudden and intrusive voice jolted me.

"Leap!" it cried. I jerked myself into an upright position and looked around,

> When you tire of suffering, you stop resisting. When you stop resisting, you step into the Eternal Presence.

certain a stranger had approached the car, but I saw no one—only the empty, abandoned gasoline station.

I relaxed and lay back, shutting my eyes simultaneously. This time, I didn't have to climb the stairs again. The moment I shut my eyes, I stood at the precipice, doors opened to the infinity of inner space. Then, just as I began to relax in a state of peace and tranquility, the voice cried out again, only louder, "Leap!"

"I can't," I objected, knowing now that the voice I heard was not outside me, but within me. The peace I felt only seconds before was gone. The panic returned, but not as severely, and probably because I recognized the voice. It was the voice of the serpent in the inner Garden of God—the voice of my own ego. I had heard it before.

"What's out there to catch me?" I asked. "You know I hate heights!"

"Jump!" the ego suggested, providing no explanation.

"But if I jump, which I won't, who will catch me?" I could hear the distrust in my own discourse. "Will God?" I asked.

"Jump and find out for yourself," the ego replied as it crawled out of the darkness and to the edge where I stood. I dared not look or take my eyes off the vast space of stillness before me, but I could feel his stare and breath against my clammy, cold arms.

"To jump would be insane!" I said.

"Really?" he asked.

"For God's sake," I argued. "Promise you'll catch me. Or give me something I can take hold of or something I can be sure will take hold of me. You just can't expect me to leap when I can't even see what's out there! "

I thought, *This is a test, I know.* At the time, though, I wasn't sure how. That understanding came later. I was only aware enough to know that this pertained to my fears on one hand and my faith on the other. I had the feeling that, if I did not face my fears head on, they would return later and be more difficult to face. Frankly, I had suffered enough. I wanted freedom from the mind.

Whatever else might happen to me, I knew I had to look my fears in the face and be done with them once and for all. I knew I had to take this step into the unknown, even though I vehemently insisted I would not. If I did not step into the unknown but shrank back in fear instead, as I had done many times before, if I insisted on some assurance, a sign, or anything tangible that would prove to me that a leap into uncertainty would not be disastrous, I knew I might never get another chance or be free of ego.

Later, I learned that this isn't necessarily true. The Universe, this One Song whose voice silently rings throughout the heavens, will always give us a second chance and even a third, a fourth, and perhaps an infinite number of chances not only to awaken, but to stay awake. Again, in Christianity, it's called *grace* or *good news*. Although I held a graduate degree in theology, wore the proverbial sacred collar, and told others about grace for more than thirty years, not until my awakening did I know Divine grace for myself. I have long suspected that church pews are filled each week with people who have neither experienced grace nor know what's good about it.

For all of my life, I had looked outside myself for inner confidence and assurance that everything about my life would work out; that the choices and decisions I had made—or would ever make—would not be wrong or cata-strophic; and that what was dear to me, as well as those who were dear to me like my daughter, Michelle, and Pam, Phillip, Jonathan, Allison, and others would themselves be safe from harm, secure, and successful in all their endeavors. In other words, I was scared, and ego fear kept me, as it had done all my life, from taking risks or trusting the Universe to provide, protect, and prosper my life as only the Universe can. I had confused cowardliness for cautiousness, and, although a person of faith, I was most possessed of fear.

I found comfort in the thought that Jesus was likely just as afraid as I was. Standing on the precipice of his own inner temple, he reasoned that a little reassurance wasn't unreasonable. As it had done in me, the ego likely whispered in him, "Are you sure this will go well for you? Don't you deserve to know? But, of course, you do. After all,

> **When you finally tire of self-inflicted, egoic suffering, you will transform.**
>
> —AUTHOR UNKNOWN

given the task that lies ahead of you, you have a right to a little reassurance. Go ahead. Jump. Make God show you he'll take care of you!"

Jesus wanted to know that his efforts would meet with success. What could be wrong with that? He thought of asking for proof, for some sign on which to hang his fears. That way, he could proceed on his faith journey free of the anxiety of not knowing what the future held for him.

But could he really? Is it possible for anyone to know with certainty what the future holds, or was this just another of ego's tricks?

My suspicion is that if Jesus was already confident that God would walk with him, protect him, and provide for him, he wouldn't have been tempted to ask for a sign, for proof that God would take care of him. That's the point. Had he been confident, it would never have occurred to him to seek a sign. He was no more certain of his future than you and I are.

That's it! I thought. *Jesus was a chicken, too, no more confident than I am. Afraid, like me. Wow! That's the kind of spiritual master I want to follow. He faced the test, and this is my test, too!*

The test/question Jesus faced was this: "Will I make this journey by faith, or will I hide my fear behind some proof of the Divine Presence, some sign that God will indeed guide me on the path I will follow?"

If you know the ending, you know Jesus passed his test; he did not leap in order to test whether God would be with him. But I have often wondered if that means he didn't leap at all. I'm not certain. We assume he didn't, but there may be another perspective on this story. When Jesus looked at the tempter and said, "Don't . . . dare test the Lord your God" (Matt 4:7), he may not have turned and walked away. He may have jumped anyway, but for different reasons. I suspect, in fact, that he did jump, the primary difference being that he neither expected anything nor demanded anything. Instead, in an act of complete surrender, *which is what real faith is,* he abandoned any attempt at the control of his life or destiny and trusted whatever the Universe held in store for him. He leaped into the confidence that everything would be okay!

Isn't this the highest kind of faith? Authentic faith? Isn't this what it means to know God and walk in the bliss of God's Eternal Presence? I think so. It is total surrender to what is. No guarantees. No proof. No sign of assur-

> Listen in deep silence. Be very still and open your mind. Go past all the raucous shrieks and sick imaginings that cover your real thoughts and obscure your eternal link with God. Sink deep into the peace that waits for you beyond the frantic, riotous thoughts and sights and sounds of this insane world.
>
> —FROM *A COURSE IN MIRACLES*

ance that things will go well for you. If they do, that's fine. If they don't, well, that's fine, too.

In such a state of complete surrender, there's no such thing as good or bad, except in some relative sense. When you've relinquished all control and all judgment, and have surrendered to this present moment, you are not only completely free of ego, but there is only what *is*—Presence.

In this Presence, you give up the control of your life entirely, your future as well as your past. Both are inconsequential, anyway. In a state of surrender, what matters is falling fully into the joyful embrace of Presence itself. Here, there is no place for ego, and when ego is absent, Presence is present. Where Presence is, there is only ever peace. There can be no panic, no fear, no anguish. Saint John said beautifully, "Perfect Love casts out fear" (1 John 4:18, KJV).

Jesus leaped, but not to test whether God would take care of him and remove his doubts and fears. He leaped in an act of total surrender. By turning loose of ego, he fell into Presence. To all who would follow his spiritual path, Jesus demonstrated the primacy of living by faith, not by sight (2 Cor 5:7, KJV). By taking his leap into uncertainty—expecting nothing and demanding nothing—he trusted and touched Source itself and was freed of the burden of ego. Though it would return again later, for now he took the most important step in his spiritual evolution.

What could be more important to the evolution of your consciousness—than to let go of the past, to give up all attempts to control the future, and instead embrace the present and, by implication, Presence? To experience the joyful freedom from ego enslavement?

For me, I cannot imagine a more significant and fulfilling purpose to human existence. I searched for years for what I was supposed to "do" with my life. Until this day in Winston-Salem, however, it had not occurred to me that there was nothing I was supposed to do. I was everything already. I was one with Source. I could not imagine anything greater than this. To *do* nothing and *be* everything, all at once! What could be more blissful, more blessed, more eternal?

The Leap into Life Itself

I stepped as close to the edge as I could. The toes of my shoes were beyond the ledge, touching nothing but empty space. My heart pounded like a loud drum in my chest. I looked up and then down, to the right and to the left. In every direction, infinity of space awaited me, as inviting as it was revolting, as tranquil as it was disturbing.

This much I knew: whatever awaited me in the infinite unknown would be resolved today. No longer would I live in fear of the future. I had made my peace with the past, but now I would make my peace with tomorrow. I would throw myself into the present—into Presence.

I, too, would ask for nothing, demand nothing. I would seek no sign, no promise on which to hang my hopes and dreams. I would live my life knowing that the God in whose Presence I had awakened would let nothing happen to me that would surprise him. I would trust the Universe to be a friendly place, knowing that everything is perfect and just as it's supposed to be, even if I do not understand it. Just as I had found freedom from the guilt of the past, I would know freedom from the fear of the future, too. I would walk in the stillness of God's Eternal Presence and enjoy an unmitigated and uninterrupted state of inner surrender, tranquility, and peace.

Like a diver preparing for a backward somersault, I slowly turned around so that my back faced the endless depth of space itself. Now my heels touched the infinite nothingness behind me.

"What are you doing?" asked the ego. "Giving up? Just going to walk away, huh?"

"Not hardly!" I answered.

"Oh, really?"

I could tell the ego was perplexed. I suppose he assumed that, by turning around, I gave in to my fear. The truth is that I was tired of his constant badgering. What he did not know would surprise him.

"Better ask for a sign," he insisted. "Don't you want proof God will actually be there? You can't be too certain, you know?"

"Shut up," I demanded.

For the first time, the ego got quiet. I turned and looked in his direction. What I saw was no snake, however. Instead, I looked at a full-length image of myself. What I saw was me.

"I'm done with you . . . uh . . . ." It was awkward this time talking to myself, although I had done it, just as you have done it, for decades.

"Never again," I said to me, "will you run my life or mess with my mind." Today, you will die and I'll be free of you forever. I'm going to let go and fall and ask for nothing. What happens to me doesn't matter anymore."

With those words, I closed my eyes, laid my hands over my chest like a corpse in a casket, and fell backwards into the infinite Nothingness behind me. I had no clue what would happen. As far as I can recall, nothing did. I only remember that, in the instant I turned loose and released myself into

Universal Uncertainty itself, I was at peace. Fear disappeared. Worry and anxiety vanished. A burden as heavy as an ox seemed to roll off my shoulders. In that moment, I knew that while it might be some time before I'd be completely free of it, the tyrannical monster, the serpent himself, the human ego, would never again drive me. Since that day, it hasn't.

What happened next, I do not know. What I do know is some time passed, and soon I opened my eyes. When I did, I realized I was more awake, more conscious and aware of God's presence, than I had been ever before. What began on that earlier Sunday afternoon was now at a deeper and more meaningful level. Since that day, I have been virtually free of the fear and panic that has characterized much of my life.

Is everything perfect? No. Is it infinitely better and more peaceful? Absolutely. I am enjoying the sacred art of living. I am walking with God.

I started the car, pulled away from the abandoned station, merged onto the highway, and made the short journey to my speaking engagement. Given my state of mind only an hour or so earlier, I was dreading the speaking engagement and seriously contemplated not showing up at all. Now, however, I was in a state of peace unlike I had known before. This is that about which Jesus spoke, when he said, "Peace I leave with you, my peace I give unto you: not as the world giveth, give I unto you" (John 14:26-27, KJV).

The speaking gig, by the way, was fabulous—if I do say so myself!

The Ego's Biggest Question: Will I Make a Mistake?

For years, I could rarely make a decision without fearing I'd make the wrong one. As I noted earlier, I depended on Dad and others to make decisions for me. When they could not, or would not, I turned to a common method practiced by many Christians today. It originated with a man named Gideon. His story is found in the Old Testament book of Judges, chapter 6.

Gideon laid out a fleece before God. I did, too, and frequently. That is, I often sought a sign before making a decision. The sign was like a peg on which I might hang my hopes or, more accurately, my fears. Like most Christians, I confused the two. What I called my hopes were actually my fears dressed in religious clothing. The sign gave me the temporary but illusory confidence I needed to go forward. Fearing failure, I used my religion to cajole God into behaving like a magician.

Gideon asked God for a sign. Christians have almost universally misunderstood this as an act of faith on his part.[1] The truth is that it was anything but faith. It was a gesture motivated by fear. Read Gideon's story, and you will discover many things, not the least of which is that Gideon, though a believer in God, neither knew God nor walked with him. When the Divine approached him, he didn't even recognize him (Jdg 6:11-13). When you know God, you see God everywhere and in everyone. When you know this, you talk less—and listen more.

Look closely into the mind of Gideon, or better yet, take a journey inside your own mind, and you'll likely see a scared Gideon (ego self) inside yourself. He talks and sounds as if he is a religious man. You find him in many churches today. Yet, he pleads for proof of God's presence, power, and protection precisely because he knows none of these.

> I am a little pencil in the hand of a writing God who is sending a love letter to the world.
>
> —MOTHER TERESA

When God answers him and grants his request, he isn't satisfied. Even the miraculous isn't convincing when you live in fear. He begs God to repeat the magic, much as I did when, as a child, I observed a magician pull a rabbit out of his hat. Astonished by the magic I saw but doubtful of its efficacy, I asked for a repeat performance.

"Do it again!" I shouted. The magician did. He pulled a second rabbit out of his hat, then a third, and even a fourth rabbit.

Did it make a believer of me? Nope. It made me suspicious of all magicians. To this day, I don't know how the magicians do it. What I do know is that I feel tricked, and I don't trust them.

That's the problem with seeking signs. Instead of building faith, it undermines it. Instead of helping you know God, it does the opposite. It feeds your ego but drives a wedge of suspicion deeper toward yourself, the ego in you, and between you and God.

To seek a sign, some form of proof that what you're preparing to do is not going to screw up your future, is to live from a place of fear. It's to be the coward that the ego is. When you live from a place of faith, however, you learn to trust yourself—your intuitions, your inner voice, your higher self. You come to know yourself beyond ego. If there's anyone in this world you can trust, it's *you*. You cannot trust ego, so your spiritual practice must be to know the difference.

In union with God, your thoughts are his thoughts. Your actions are his actions. You trust this. It doesn't mean you're perfect, you never make a mistake, or you always make the right decision. It means you pay attention to your heart, accepting the fact that you will sometimes misunderstand your heart and, at other times, you may not hear your heart at all. Either error is okay.

Why? Because you no longer engage in the insanity of self-recrimination. You're done with such ego stuff. You are learning instead to live beyond ego, to live by faith and step into the unknown knowing God is there. In other words, you accept yourself, you forgive yourself, and, when you make a mistake, you learn from it and move on. You don't have time for self-judgment, self-loathing, and pity.

Today, Christians are often fooled by the big egos of many media ministers who say things like, "God will provide all your needs if you have enough faith to plant a faith seed in our ministry!" That's a lot of phony God talk for "Give me the money!"

TV ministers often use faith the way magicians use hats. While the latter reach into hats for rabbits, the former reach into your pocket for riches. Magicians and TV ministers have a lot in common. Both are mysterious. Both wear makeup that makes them look all the more mysterious. Both are masters of illusion. Both are manipulative. Both are out to make money. I don't have it in for magicians, but I don't mind saying I've had my fill of television ministers. Magicians use sleight of hand to fool their audiences. Television preachers use signs and miracles to fool theirs.

Television ministers say, "Just believe!" Then they convince gullible people that, as a "sign" of their faith—as a sign that they truly believe—they should send a contribution to the ministry. They call it "planting a seed." Then they're told to trust God to return the seed to them in an abundant harvest, to meet their own needs.

But consider this: if television preachers really knew the God they pretend to know and believed themselves what they preach to others, here's a perspective I'd like to challenge them to embrace.

"If you really believe, Reverend TV Preacher, that God will provide for those who plant seeds, then instead of asking your viewers to send you their monetary seeds, why don't you send them yours? You trust God, like you tell them to do, to return the harvest to you and meet your needs. That would be a convincing miracle! Pull one off like that, and I'll send you some money, too!" Talk about a sign with substance, one with convincing power! You can imagine the headlines tomorrow: "National Television Minister Empties His Own Coffer Sending Millions to Needy Families Everywhere! Says He Believes God Will Return the Harvest to Him!"

Parenthetically, I wouldn't wait up, if I were you, expecting something as miraculous as this perspective ever being embraced by a television minister. You will, in fact, *never* see it happen. Why? It is not God who motivates these ministerial monsters of the media. It is their ego. Some television preachers know God about as well as psychics know the future. If psychics were as psychic as they pretend to be, then instead of asking you to call them, wouldn't they *know* you had a problem and call you?

Religious people are always looking for proof of Presence. If they knew this Presence, they would need no proof. When you *go within*, therefore, you will meet your own Gideon. By observing it, not judging it, your Gideon will morph into God. This transformation will produce real change—lasting change. As you come to know this God, as well as to know yourself, you will no longer need signs. You'll not need to test God to know that you can *trust* God to walk with you.

The Ego's Greatest Delusion: Controlling the Future

One of the clever ways ego confuses you is by getting you to succumb to the illusion of controlling your future. I can think of no example more current than that of the recent worldwide financial collapse—what history will remember as *the Great Recession* that took place late in the first decade of the twenty-first century. In an instant, nearly half the financial fortunes of millions of people disappeared. While some lost everything, most people just witnessed in horror the unimaginable devaluing of their retirement savings.

Once the initial shock wore off, panic filled the streets. Not only were people perplexed by the financial failure and worried about it, but in a matter of days, a paradigm shift occurred in the psyche of the collective ego. Many who lived lavishly on credit for years resolved not only to change their spending habits but to be more prudent and thrifty in how they saved for the future. I saw much of this same shift take place within me. Today, I regard the Great Recession not as an evil that should never have happened, but as a kind of redeemer itself, a wake-up call, to the financial insanity that has characterized our culture for multiple decades.

There's a perspective you may not have considered. Behind the widespread paradigm shift in how people spend and plan for the future, if you look closely, you'll see a frightened ego cowering in the face of what it perceives as threatening. The ego will likely create an identity for itself around the experience of this financial collapse. If you'll listen, for example, you'll hear some little egos developing a victim identity as they bemoan the situation this event put them in, and they will express their offense at the banking industry and Wall Street executives.

Listen further, and you'll see and hear other little egos flexing their muscles, becoming all the more determined to prevent another episode like this in the future. They will be energized by the failure, fixate on their finances, and decide to make their future more financially secure than it was prior to the meltdown.

My recommendation is that, if you're going to develop an ego-identity around the financial collapse, the latter of these two extremes would probably be the better choice. There is likely, however, a better response than either of these. Behind these responses hides an ego guilty of two delusional errors. For one thing, all of us bear some blame in the recent financial failure. The egos on Wall Street hold no patent on greed. Ordinary egos have lived for decades on credit they've neither earned nor could afford. Driven by the desire to have more, however, and to feed their idolatrous egos, "they have," in the words of Will Rogers, "borrowed money they don't have to buy things they don't need to keep up with people they don't like."

The other error is this: the future can be neither predicted nor made secure—no matter what we do. It holds no promise for anyone except, of course, the promise of death. Death is the only thing about the future that we can accurately predict. Our bodies will die. The rest of what happens in our lives is our guess and, more often than not, the ego will guess, or predict, the wrong future. A fortune today might be a misfortune tomorrow.

This thought is morbid and depressing only to an ego! Such a thought is never offensive to *you* because *you* know the body is going to die, just as everything material will disappear, and *you* are not the least bit concerned about it. Furthermore, *you* also know that whatever else the future may hold doesn't matter much, except in some relative sense.

We are born. We will die. Since that's true, then what matters is what transpires between these two irrefutable realities. What transpires between these two realities is your life. Tell me, what could be more important than your life being merged with Life itself? When you can answer that question, not in some esoteric fashion but from the core of your essential being, you will have found the Mystery to life. You will have awakened.

The Great Recession

I recently eavesdropped on a conversation between two men, both of whom were catching a ride, as I was, on a shuttle bus from the rental car lot to the airport at Chicago O'Hare. They were well-groomed businesspersons and deeply into their conversation when I began listening.

One man said to the other, "Well, it won't happen to me again!"

"What's that?" asked the other, who then answered his own question. "Oh, you mean your 401k?"

"Yep," his friend said. "I don't trust my accountant anymore. Hell, the damn thing caught him by surprise, too. I've paid him good money, as have other clients, to watch the markets for me . . . to protect our investments. But it won't happen again. I've made sure of that!"

"Oh, really?" the other man reacted, glancing first at his boarding pass and then at his watch. "How can you be so sure it'll never happen again?"

"Well, for one thing," boasted the first man, "I got my entire portfolio, all of my financial accounts, set up on my cell phone alerts."

"What are you talking about?"

"On my cell phone!" he tried to explain as he reached for his phone strapped in a holster like a six-shooter. "It's an application I've added so that, whenever there are any changes in the markets, and specifically in my accounts, I get a message on my cell phone. This way, I'll be ready next time!"

He sounded confident enough, certain that his clever plan would help him avoid any future financial setbacks. But he never answered his friend's question—"How can you be so sure?" Why? Because he lived from ego and preferred the temporary illusion of security the ego loves to generate.

> "My wealth is health and perfect ease,
>   My conscience clear my choice defense;
> I neither seek by bribes to please,
>   Nor by deceit to breed offence.
> Thus do I live; thus will I die;
> Would all did so well as I!"
>
> —FROM "MY MIND TO ME A KINGDOM IS" BY SIR EDWARD DYER

Contrary to this, an awakened person will learn the lessons this meltdown was designed to teach. Nor will he or she succumb to the illusion of controlling the future. No one does. No one can even predict it accurately.

Furthermore, whatever happens in the future will only ever happen in the present. You cannot prepare for the present. Your only choice is to either *be* in the present or be absent from the present. The latter aptly describes my life prior to the awakening. I lived mostly in memory (the past) and anticipation (the future). Gratefully, however, I can now say that I spend the greater part of my life living in and enjoying the present and, with it, Presence.

The Rich Fool

Do you recall the story of the Rich Fool, one of Jesus' many potent tales (Luke 12:16-21)? Once, there was a wealthy man whose financial portfolio had doubled and tripled in value. He had done well for himself and felt pride about his accomplishments.

Wondering what his next financial move should be, he sought the advice of his financial counselor. Rather than selling his stocks, which at first he was inclined to do, and giving Uncle Sam an inordinate share of the windfall in capital gains, his advisor suggested a greater diversification of his portfolio. Not only would that be a more sound financial strategy, but it would make his future more secure than his present. He would spend his retirement years reclining on luxurious cruise lines, drinking piña coladas by day and dining on the likes of caviar and Dom Pérignon at night.

Again, there is no security in the future. Obsessed as the Rich Fool was to prepare for it, however, he failed to prepare for the one thing for which he *could* prepare—the present moment.

If peace and security is what you want, then give your attention to your thoughts. Better yet, stop thinking altogether. Since most of us are taught to think all the time, this will take practice, which is why *going within* is important to staying awake. One of the primary objectives of meditation is to stop the mind, to hit the pause button on the ceaseless stream of thinking. It is the only way I know to tame self (the mind) and touch Source (God).

> The space between the notes makes the music.
>
> —CLAUDE DEBUSSY

Do you know the meaning of the Jewish word *Sabbath*? It comes from the Hebrew root word *Shabbat* meaning "to cease," "to pause," and, therefore, "to rest." In idiomatic usage, one could say the word literally means "to shut up."

Originally, the goal of Sabbath was to stop both the body and the mind. It was tied to the creative act of God, who fashioned the universe in six days and rested on the seventh. As religion is prone to do, however, it wasn't long before the collective religious ego developed a cadre of conditions about this Grace, replete with rules and regulations as long as the contrails behind a jet-liner. By the time of Jesus, its purpose was so widely distorted and compromised that Jesus frequently and intentionally broke the rules to give himself an opportunity to speak against its myriad distortions. On at least one occasion, for example, Jesus said, "The Sabbath was made to serve us; we weren't made to serve the Sabbath" (Mark 2:28).

How might the Sabbath serve you? When you *go within*, or practice meditation, you not only rest your body, but you also relax the mind. As I noted earlier, when I use a mantra like "Be still and know that I am God," I focus my attention for a few seconds on the word "be" and then on the word "still." Slowly, I turn my mental attention to the space between these two words. It's just empty space, but it is there that my mind temporarily stops and all thinking ceases. This is actually similar to the ancient method of meditation known as *Japa*.

Sometimes the mind stops for several seconds and at other times only a second or two. But in those brief seconds of silence and stillness, I touch Source in inexplicable ways. Achille-Claude Debussy, the French composer of the nineteenth century, purportedly said, "The space between the notes makes the music." The grandest melody your soul will sing waits for your regular visitation to the space between your thoughts.

Equally important, you will honor the intention of the Jewish Sabbath not because you refuse to shop, eat out, or mow the lawn on Sunday—prac-tices that, when I was a child, no Christian would be caught doing. Christians mistakenly believed they fulfilled the intention of the Sabbath because they had their checklist of things they didn't do on God's day. The only problem was this: they were not doing what God wanted, either. They lived then, just as people live now, at a killer pace and in a mind-obsessed state. Instead, you *go within*, and there in the sacred stillness of the inner kingdom you observe self and overcome it, touch Source and are trans-formed by it. You emerge refreshed, rejuvenated, and genuinely regenerated as a sentient being.

This is what it means to walk with God.

The Ego's Greatest Fear: Death Itself

Saint Paul called death "the last enemy" (1 Cor 15:26, KJV). Death is an enemy indeed, but it is only an enemy to the ego. Death is never *your* enemy.

You were born to die. In between birth and death is your life, which is Life itself. Either you awaken to this realization and enjoy your eternal nature, or you live your life in fear of death. Only the little ego in you denies death. Where it cannot deny death, ego will defy it.

Nowhere is this more evident than in the way people in the West preserve the body at death and place the body in the ground when it dies. I think this is an absurd practice, not to speak of a waste of valuable land space all for nothing. It is little more than the ego's last hurrah. Ego does everything it can to pretend it does not die. Since it knows it will, it has over the years led us to dress up death so that it looks like life.

The funeral home business, for example, is a billion-dollar industry that has capitalized on the fear of death for its own financial gain. My perspective here is not to fault funeral homes but to point out that death is not frightening to you. Just as ego is not eternal, neither is death. One day, death itself will die, as Saint John the Apostle predicted in the book of Revelation (Rev 20:14; 21:4). Again, *you* will never die. It is only your form that decays, dissolves, and eventually disappears. The sooner you recognize you are neither your ego nor your physical body, the sooner you'll be free of both. The ultimate goal of your spiritual practice is to dis-identify with ego and with the ego's attachments—roles, functions, titles, accomplishments, beliefs, opinions, and especially ego's greatest attachment, the human body.

Since most people think they *are* the ego, their thoughts, and so forth, they cannot separate who they are from their functions, roles, titles, beliefs, or human form. This explains their dismay and anxiety whenever they look in the mirror and see that their form, rather than staying young and vibrant, withers and ages instead. They do not realize they showed up only to disappear quickly. Again, only the ego finds such a thought bothersome. You, when you know who you truly are, could not be bothered by such a thought.

Whenever you feel frightened by death, and what human has not, know that this is the ego in you. Do not lose heart, thinking, *Will I ever rid myself of ego—once and for all?* With practice, you will. Remember that recognition is the key. God has made the path to spiritual awareness simple. It is true that Jesus said, "The way to life—to God—is vigorous and requires total attention" (Matt 7:13, The Message), but that's because the ego in you knows that if you make it your spiritual practice to *go within*, the ego must get out. If you are vigilant in mastering the art of *going within*, and I feel sure you will make spiritual progress.

In the inner Garden of God, what the book of Genesis describes as Eden and what Jesus called the kingdom of God (Luke 17:21), you will enjoy union with God. You will live a Christ-conscious life that bears a Buddha-like nature. *Going within* will be to your awakened state of consciousness what water is to a desert wayfarer, what food is to a starving man. In time, it will not be the struggle it may be now. In fact, it will become as important to you as eating, sleeping, working, or playing. In fact, it will be more important to you than all of these combined, which is precisely why Jesus said, "Man cannot live by bread alone" (Matt 4:4). When you know this, you will have taken your rightful seat at a banquet table called Presence. God is the host; the luxurious table spread before you is the Eternal Presence; and you, my friend, are Life's treasured guest.

> "Do not dwell on the past; do not dream of the future; concentrate the mind on the present moment."
>
> —BUDDHA

Note

1. Consider stopping now and reading the story of Gideon found in Judges 6:11-40. In three different instances, Gideon sought a sign to reassure him of God's presence and victory over his perceived enemies. This is not faith but fear. It is the ego. No one who is learning to live beyond ego and to walk in the joy of God's presence and provision would fear abandonment by that Presence. You only fear what you do not know—in this case, the God you do not know.

Conclusion

When I think back to the unanticipated conversion on a couch during the PBS special and the many other moments of awakening, like in the car at Winston-Salem, I still laugh in sheer disbelief. To imagine that an experience of the Divine could take place in such an ordinary fashion is downright laughable. Yet I have learned that this is often the behavior of Grace—that Mystery too mysterious to explain yet too personal to ignore.

Lao Tzu said, "The Tao [God] does nothing but leaves nothing undone." Divine grace isn't significant because it's stunning or sensational. God chooses the ordinary to reveal the extraordinary, the simple to confound the wise, even "the nobodies," as Saint Paul put it, "to expose the hollow pretentions of the 'somebodies'" (1 Cor 1:27).

I suppose that's why I have always found such affinity in the blind man Jesus healed. His simple response to the religious bigots of his day was blessed indeed: "I don't know how to explain what has happened to me. All I know is that once I was blind, but now I see" (see John 9:1-35). If you think about it, his was a type of couch conversion, too, an ineffable encounter with that "Pretty Amazing Grace," about which Neil Diamond sang.

> You overcame my loss of hope and faith
> Gave me a truth I could believe in
> You led me to a higher place
> Showed Your amazing grace
> When grace was what I needed
>
> Look in a mirror I see Your reflection
> Open a book You live on every page
> I fall and You're there to lift me
> Share every road I climb
> And with amazing grace You case my mind
>
> Pretty amazing
> Pretty amazing grace.[1]

Grace is not a gift you get for professing the right beliefs. It isn't a reward for having the "right" religion, either. Grace knows no creed, no class, no color, and no religion. It is the miracle of God consciousness, and it can happen to anyone anywhere at any time. It is as unpredictable as it is profound.

> **When you look for God within, you see God without.**
>
> —AUTHOR UNKNOWN

When God awakens within you—as you stand on a mountaintop, drive to work, sit at the bedside of a dying family member or friend, observe nature, pray in a temple, or do nothing at all but recline on a couch, everything, as well as everyone, will instantaneously become sacred to you. In a sense, the universe and everything in it will be to you as the sacred body of God.

When you awaken, your religion may or may not remain important to you. If it does, as mine has, it will take on a different, purer nature. It won't be the burden it used to be but the blessing it's supposed to be. Since the rules, the doctrines, the beliefs, and other insane stuff of the ego will no longer occupy your energy, your attention will go to the nurturing of your relationship to the Eternal. That will feed your soul forever.

My Christian faith has become more meaningful to me than at any other time in my life, but it isn't a club I use to coerce others to convert to my way of thinking and believing. It is instead a path I follow to Christ consciousness and a more compassionate way of living. I'm free of believing Christianity is the only way to know God. It's my way, and it is rich with meaning, but had I grown up in a Jewish or Muslim family, I might have just as effortlessly awakened to God on some dusty road in Palestine or in the mountains of Afghanistan. Who knows?

I love the story I read of a Frenchman who approached the Dalai Lama after hearing his lecture in a city in France. He said, "Your Holiness, I loved your words and I've decided I want to convert to Buddhism."

> **The most beautiful thing we can experience is the mysterious.**
>
> —ALBERT EINSTEIN

In great wisdom, however, the Dalai Lama answered, "Why Buddhism? Why would you wish to convert to this religious tradition? You are in France. In France, you have Christianity. There's nothing wrong with Christianity!"[2]

There isn't, is there? No more so than there's anything wrong with the numerous other paths one might follow toward the evolution of Divine consciousness. It is time that humanity stops the insanity of thinking, "We're right, and you're wrong!" "We're in, and you're out!" "We're the chosen ones, and you're not!"

Just like everyone, you were born to walk with God, so why would you walk alone?

Notes

1. Neil Diamond, "Pretty Amazing Grace," *Home before Dark*, Sony, 2008.

2. André Comte-Sponville, *The Little Book of Atheistic Spirituality*, trans. Nancy Huston (New York: Penguin Books, 2007) 39–40.

Bibliography

Armstrong, Karen. *The Great Transformation*. New York: Anchor Books, 2006.

———. *A History of God*. New York: Ballentine Books, 1993.

———. *A Spiral Staircase*. New York: Anchor Books, 2004.

Beckwith, Michael Bernard. *The Life Visioning Process* Boulder CO: Sounds True Audio, 2008.

Borg, Marcus J. *The God We Never Knew: Beyond Dogmatic Religion to a More Authentic Contemporary Faith*. San Francisco: HarperSanFrancisco, 1997.

Bourgeault, Cynthia. *Encountering the Wisdom Jesus: Quickening the Kingdom of Heaven Within*. Boulder CO: Sounds True Audio, 2005.

———. *The Wisdom Jesus: Transforming Heart and Mind*. Boston: Shambhala Publications, 2008.

Brother Lawrence of the Resurrection. *The Practice of the Presence of God*. John Delaney, Henri J. M. Nouwen. Garden City NY: Image Books, 1996.

Chödrön, Pema. *Start Where You Are: A Guide to Compassionate Living*. Boston: Shambhala Publications, 2001.

———. *When Things Fall Apart*. Boston: Shambhala Publications, 1997.

Chopra, Deepak. *How to Know God: The Soul's Journey into the Mystery of Mysteries*. New York: Random House, 2001.

———. *The Spontaneous Fulfillment of Desire*. New York: Three Rivers Press, 2003.

———. *The Seven Spiritual Laws of Success*. Novato CA: New World Library, 1994.

———. *The Third Jesus*. New York: Random House Audio, 2008.

———. *Why Is God Laughing? The Path to Spiritual Joy and Optimism.* New York: Random House Audio, 2008.

Coelho, Paulo. *By the River Piedra I Sat Down and Wept.* Translated by Alan R. Clarke. New York: HarperCollins, 1996.

Das, Lama Surya. *Awakening the Buddha Within: Eight Steps to Enlightenment.* New York: Doubleday Dell Publishing Group, Inc., 1997.

———. *Awakening to the Sacred: Creating a Personal Spiritual Life.* New York: Broadway Books, 1999.

———. *The Big Questions: How to Find Your Own Answers to Life's Essential Mysteries.* New York: Rodale, 2007.

Dawkins, Richard. *The God Delusion.* Boston: Houghton, Mifflin, Harquart, 2006.

De Mello, Anthony. *Awareness.* New York: Doubleday, 1992.

Dyer, Wayne W. *Change Your Thoughts—Change Your Life: Living the Wisdom of the Tao.* Carlsbad CA: Hay House, Inc., 2007.

———. *Getting in the Gap: Making Conscious Contact with God through Meditation.* Carlsbad CA: Hay House, Inc., 2003.

———. *The Power of Intention: Learning to Co-Create Your World Your Way.* Carlsbad CA: Hay House, Inc., 2004.

Ehrman, Bart D. *Misquoting Jesus: The Story Behind Who Changed the Bible and Why.* New York: HarperCollins Publishers, 2005.

Francis, John. *Planet Walker.* Washington DC: National Geographic Books, 2008.

Idliby, Ranya, Suzanne Oliver, and Priscilla Warner. *The Faith Club: A Muslim, A Christian, A Jew—Three Women Search for Understanding.* New York: Free Press, 2007.

Izzo, John. *The Five Secrets You Must Discover Before You Die.* BBC Audiobooks, 2008.

James, William. *The Varieties of Religious Experience.* New York: Collier Books, 1961.

Jung, Carl. "The Difference Between Eastern and Western Thinking." *The Portable Jung.* Edited by Joseph Campbell. New York: Penguin, 1976.

Kelsey, Morton T., Sr. *The Other Side of Silence: Meditation for the Twenty-first Century.* Mahway NJ: Paulist Press, 1976.

Lama, Dalai. *Becoming Enlightened.* New York: Simon & Schuster Audio, 2009.

Hanh, Thich Nhat. *Living Buddha, Living Christ.* New York: Riverhead Books, 1995.

Meyers, Robin R. *Saving Jesus from the Church.* New York: HarperCollins, 2009.

Packer, J. I. *Knowing God.* Downers Grove: InterVarsity Press, 1993.

Pausch, Randy. *The Last Lecture.* New York: Hyperion Books, 2008.

Reece, Erik. *An American Gospel: On Family, History, and the Kingdom of God.* New York: Riverhead Books, 2009.

Sanders, Scott Russell. *A Private History of Awe.* New York: North Point Press, 2006.

Schucman, Helen, and William Thetford. *A Course in Miracles.* Mill Valley CA: Foundation for Inner Peace, 2007.

Smith, Huston. *The World's Religions.* San Francisco: HarperCollins, 1991.

Starr, Mirabai, translator. Saint John of the Cross. *Dark Night of the Soul.* New York: Riverhead Books, 2002.

Tolle, Eckhart. *A New Earth: Awakening to Your Life's Purpose.* New York: Plume, 2005.

———. *Finding Your Life's Purpose.* Vancouver: Eckhart Teachings, Inc., 2008.

———. *The Power of Now.* Novato CA: New World Library, 1997.

Tolstoy, Leo. *The Death of Ivan Ilyich*. Translated by Lynn Solotaroff. New York: Random House, 1981.

———. *The Kingdom of God Is Within You*. Translated by Constance Garnett. Lincoln: University of Nebraska Press, 1984.

Walsch, Neale Donald. *Conversations with God*. New York: G. P. Putnam's Sons, 1996.

Young, Wm. Paul. *The Shack*. Newbury Park CA: Windblown Media, 2007.

Zukav, Gary. *The Seat of the Soul*. New York: Simon & Schuster, 1989.